SHUT UP AND WIN

Strategies to SELL Smarter, LEAD Better, and LIVE with Purpose

JED ETTERS

Published by:

Sandpiper Inc

SAN MARCOS, CA

Copyright © 2025 Jed Etters

ISBNs: 979-8-9985065-0-5 (softcover)
979-8-9985065-1-2 (hardcover)
979-8-9985065-2-9 (ebook)

Cover and interior design by Gary A. Rosenberg
www.thebookcouple.com

Printed in the United States of America

To the hustlers, the dreamers, and the doers—
This book is for those who refuse to settle,
Who wake up every day ready to chase their goals,
And who understand that dreams remain dreams
until action turns them into reality.

To my family and friends,
Your unwavering support has been my foundation.
And to the mentors, colleagues, and clients
who've shaped my journey,
Thank you for your lessons, your challenges,
and your inspiration.
This is for everyone who knows that with grit,
determination, and the right tools,
Winning is always within reach.
Let's make it happen.

Contents

Introduction

IN TODAY'S WORLD, WE ARE CONSTANTLY BOMBARDED with voices—opinions, advice, and promises that claim to have all the answers. It can be overwhelming, and sometimes it feels impossible to separate the noise from the truth. I've been there. Like many of you, I was searching for sales strategies and techniques that didn't just sound good but actually worked—tools that could help me thrive and, more importantly, help others like you do the same.

That search led me to write this book. But my journey didn't start here—it began when I was just fourteen years old. My first sales job was a training ground where I was given little to no direction. I had no idea what to say or do, but I quickly realized that figuring it out was up to me.

From there, I transitioned into real estate, where I honed my ability to connect with people and close deals. Eventually, I founded a tech company. I ended up managing thousands of sales transactions and learning through trial and error what worked and what didn't. I was never afraid to try a different approach. These experiences, spanning more than thirty years, helped me develop the tools, strategies, and insights that I now share in this book.

Shut Up and Win isn't about reinventing the wheel; it's about cutting through the noise to deliver an actionable and authentic perspective on a timeless topic: sales.

Some of the greatest lessons I've learned come from influential authors like Dale Carnegie in *How to Win Friends and Influence People*, Zig Ziglar in *Secrets of Closing the Sale*, and Oren Klaff in *Pitch Anything*. These books have shaped my thinking and inspired me to build upon their foundations with my own experiences.

What you'll find in this book isn't theory or fluff. It's packed with real-life examples and strategies that I've tested in the trenches.

If you're tired of losing and ready to start winning, then keep reading. This book is for anyone who's ready to stop and focus on what really matters: results.

So let's get to it. The strategies in these pages are here to equip you, challenge you, and help you transform your approach to sales—and life.

Now, it's time to shut up, lean in, and win.

1. Navigating the Sales Landscape

Discusses common mistakes salespeople make, including selling oneself instead of the solution, attempting to beat clients into submission, telling people what to think, and making assumptions. This chapter also explores the dangers of showing up without value and outlines the importance of patience and preparation in sales.

IF YOU'RE READING THIS, YOU PROBABLY WANT to be a high-performing individual. To be high-performing, you need to be fully functioning. If you've shut off pieces of yourself because feeling them is just too difficult, I would rate that as not fully functioning.

Part of the process of being successful is figuring out what is holding you back from success. Some people have put it to me this way: Imagine you're going on a backpacking trip, and you've filled that backpack with all the stuff you want to bring. Imagine climbing that hill with a giant, three-hundred-pound backpack. You can pretend like nothing's in the backpack, but it's still a really heavy backpack. Or you can go through the backpack and figure out what you need to leave behind and carry a light backpack that has just a couple of things you'll need along the way.

The backpack represents all the hardships and difficult things you've had to go through. The trip is going to end in your success. You're going to climb the mountain. How you get there and what you carry in your backpack to help you get there is what this book is about.

Imagine the world of sales as a never-ending mountain range filled with opportunity. It's big, it's tough, and, let's be honest, it can be extremely scary, especially if you're new or trying to go in a direction you didn't plan for. If you don't want to get lost, you've got to become a master navigator.

The Master Navigator

You've probably heard the saying about eating an elephant, "one bite at a time," right? This means you have to face big problems a little bit at a time. For example, there was an old man who had made a lot of money and had a very successful life. A much younger man came to him and asked, "How did you decide what steps to take and what you wanted, to have reached so much success in your life?" The much older man looked at the young man who was just starting his career and said, "Son, when I figure out what I want to do in life, you will be the first one to know." The much younger man looked confused and went home. The young man asked himself, "How could this older man become successful without knowing what he wanted in life?"

He realized he would need to remain flexible while searching for wisdom from others who had gone before him.

Life doesn't always go as planned even for the most successful people. Perhaps the best way forward is to gather as much wisdom and remain flexible? The truth is most of us have an idea we want to try or a general direction we want to go but little firsthand knowledge about how to reach those goals. In other words, we need to figure it out along the way.

For most of us, life is not a preplanned trip without surprises. In fact, it is quite the opposite. Life is more of a crazy story that takes twists and turns that you could have never anticipated or planned for. You never know what a day may bring. One day could be the biggest disaster or the best triumph of your life. But one thing is for sure: You never know what you will get by the end of the day.

So how do we make the best decisions to help us achieve success? How can we win? There must be a way. What we need is the experience and wisdom of those before us. As the young man in the story realized after talking to the older man, he would need to create his best future by searching for wisdom. What he found was people all around him have wisdom that can be gleaned if he looks and listens.

Most of the time, you will need to look and listen to things the average person will miss. Find hidden gems of knowledge wherever you go. Write them down and commit them to memory. You get one chance at life, don't waste it. Get every last bit out of it; don't live your life wondering what could have happened if only you had given it everything you had.

This book is a scavenger hunt. Try to find the little gems that apply to you and use them. If you do, you will be much more prepared even if you don't know what's coming next. Now shut up and win!

Leave People Wanting More

When you meet another professional, you will often look them up online to get a better idea of their experience. As I go through and read these bios online, I'm met with every single detail of a person's life. I get to find out where they lived, where they grew up, what college they went to, their family details, and likely any kind of accomplishments or award they've received. When you read someone's bio, you're probably reading it for a specific idea or a snapshot of a person's life as you try to figure out who the person is in general. When people overshare about everything and you have to read paragraph after paragraph about someone's life, it can be too much. Bios need to be distilled down to the most relevant parts of a career to keep them interesting.

The same applies when advertising something. If I list every single detail, I'm not leaving room for the consumer to have any kind of imagination. What do I mean by that? If I'm too detailed, and I overshare every last aspect, I may introduce a detail that people didn't even realize could be a problem. Here are some examples:

+ "Oh, it comes in red? I don't like red, and in fact, I don't buy anything that comes in red."

+ "It's only a two-day marketing campaign? I don't think I'm interested now; I wanted a seven-day campaign."

+ "The other party said they wouldn't be willing to have everything professionally detailed beforehand. I'm out."

This is where leaving certain things to someone's imagination can be helpful. I'm not saying to hide anything. I'm saying not to overshare. If I go over every single detail and tell them everything I know about a product, they may not even want to see it for themselves, and then they may miss out on something completely perfect for them, maybe exactly what they were looking for. What if I'm actually ruining the opportunity for someone to experience something for themselves by adding every last little detail in an attempt to be extra helpful? What if I cut myself off from speaking three-quarters of the way into my description instead? What if I just listed a couple of things that are most relevant and then let the other person discover the rest on their own? Could that create more opportunity?

Based on my experience, I think it does. Everyone has their own filter, their own way of viewing things. If I'm previewing a piece of real estate, I may think this room is too small, but somebody else might say that same room is too big. But if they don't get to filter or judge the room size for themselves because I told them it's too small, they picture a room too small for them. Because I shared how I saw the room size, they relied on my filter and lost out on a great opportunity. I see it time and time again. People give way too much information and overload the people around them instead of letting someone experience something on their own.

We live in a time of information overload. It's almost refreshing when you just get the details that are most relevant and then you get to discover something on your own. It almost takes the pressure off you, too. You have less to analyze at that moment. Then guess what else happens? When the time is right, you're open to experiencing and analyzing it yourself. Someone left you wanting more. The key here is wanting; you were left curious. When there's no curiosity, boredom strikes. And who wants to be bored?

I'll leave you with a possibility. What if you didn't know how something ended? What if you didn't have every last little detail? What if there could be something great at the other end. Would you want to know about it? Give just enough to get someone interested and then leave people wanting more.

Don't Give Up Without a Plan

When you don't have a plan, it's super easy to give up because you aren't working toward anything. What do you do when an obstacle or some sort of roadblock gets in your way? Did you plan for it? A good plan is a road map for handling the obstacles that may come up. It's your compass, your guiding light showing you the way. When you get shaken up, you have something to reference as a reminder of the direction you are headed so you can get to your final destination.

Convincer Numbers

Did you know people have a convincer number? What's a convincer number? How many times do people need to hear something to be convinced it's true?

Some people are one-time convincers. They believe everything people tell them the first time they hear it. This is someone who, if told one time in passing they were going to get the opportunity to work with you, they would believe you and be ready to go. There are also no-time convincers. These are a unique bunch of people who won't believe you no matter how many times you tell them something. The way to work with no-time convincers is to let them know the only way they actually have options is to make a decision and then more options will become available to them. Stress to them that they're at the end of their road until they make a decision and that a decision will open up a whole new world for them.

But what about the majority of the population? Most people are three-time convincers. That's why broadcast television, radio, and podcast commercials make an offer three times: "If you buy now, we'll throw in a free one-week stay, but make sure to call in now," followed closely by a version of "But wait! This is your last opportunity to call in now." The pitch is repeated in three different ways to reach the average convincing number of three times.

I often ask people, "If you were to call someone and they did not return your call, would you try to call them again? If you were to call them a second time and they didn't call you back, would you call again?" Most people will say, "Yeah, I would. Maybe they're busy or forgot that I called." Then I ask them, "What if, after the third time you call, they still didn't call back?" More often than not, they say they wouldn't call again. I ask them why they stop after three times? Why not try five times? Why don't they give up after one try? The answer is most of us have a convincer number of three times before we give ourselves permission to give up.

I refuse to give up; I try three, four, five times. Because I'm Irish, I jokingly repeat the line from Martin Scorcese's film *The Departed* that Sigmund Freud said the Irish are "the only people who are impervious to psychoanalysis."[1] I take this statement to mean you cannot analyze or reason with certain people.

I realize timing and opportunity can change. I also realize you never know when those might happen. Most things in life are a numbers game. If you play a game long enough, you're bound to win. Sometimes I feel like Jim Carrey in the movie *Dumb and Dumber*. His character asks a woman if there's any way she'll go out with him, and she says his chances are "one out of a million." After pausing to process her response, he replies, "So you're telling me there's a chance."[2]

---

1 Pallasch, A. (June/July 2007). The last word: Freud, the Irish & *The Departed*. *Irish American Magazine*. https://www.irishamerica.com/2007/06/the-last-word -freud-the-irish-the-departed/

2 IMDB. (n.d.). *Dumb and Dumber* quotes. IMDB. https://www.imdb.com/title/ tt0109686/quotes/ accessed 03.19.24

A broken clock is right twice a day. I guess I look at it this way because I am not a lucky person. I could buy a hundred lottery tickets and win, like, $5.00. Someone else could buy one lottery ticket and win a million dollars. I just know that's not me. I find the greatest blessings in my life when I incorporate hard work. I guess you could say the harder I work, the luckier I get. In most cases, giving up is not an option for me.

Be Willing to Change Your Plans

I want to highlight a few points. One is you need a plan, and the second is that changing your plan is not the same as giving up. If you realize you're doing something and it's not working, but you still want to accomplish the goal, changing your approach is important, maybe even vital, to your success. There's a famous saying that the definition of insanity is doing the same thing over and over and expecting a different result. I'm encouraging you to stick with it and continue doing things over and over—just not in the same way if it's not working. Change your method and you will get a different result. Plus, you probably won't go insane, which is a nice bonus.

Don't be afraid to adjust or completely change your plan. That's not the same as giving up. You need to understand that things can take time, and some may come to fruition after your time. That does not mean your plan is a waste of your time. It depends on what your ultimate goal is. To reach these goals, we need to understand the convincer number of others. When we understand how many times we will try something without success before we give up, we can plan ways to overcome future obstacles. If we don't understand this, we may give up prematurely and miss out on a lot of success.

How can the convincer number of others open my eyes and create more possibilities? Knowing most people need to hear things three times before they're convinced was a huge eye-opener for me. It changed the way I communicated. It changed the way I planned for things. Ultimately, it helped me communicate in such a way that I didn't have to give up at the first no. I had a plan, and hopefully, you, too, now have a plan you can work toward. Now get out there with that plan, and don't forget most people's convincer number is three. If you reach that third no, remember to change your approach. Now go out and reach your goal.

Sell the Solution, Not Yourself

A salesperson walks into a meeting, looks around the room, smiles at everyone, and makes small talk. They are formally introduced, then they start their pitch. They think to themselves, "This is my opportunity to really show them what I can do and win some business."

Then they get bombarded with questions, some easy, some tough. The questions asked by the clients usually center around how good a job the salesperson will do for them because the client wants to find the best person for the job. Most salespeople oversell themselves and their abilities in this situation; when asked about their ability or the quality of their work, their go-to is to sell their ability to dominate the world, saying how perfect everything will go and how much experience they have.

The problem with this is it's the same approach every other salesperson is going to take. What the client cares about is winning. They don't care about how many years you've been in the business, how many specialty items you've sold, or how quickly you respond. They want to be sold on the fact that you will do the absolute best job helping them achieve *their* goals. So how do you approach this?

You answer the questions the client should have asked, not what they may have asked. For example, a client might ask, "How many years have you been in this business?" The average salesperson then explains how many years they have been in the business and how successful and amazing they are. Let's pretend the client got right to the heart of what they really want to know instead. This would probably sound more like, "Prove to me how you can help me reach my goal and how you are better than everyone else." The answer they most often want is how you can get them to their goal, and how you can make them feel confident. You could maybe hit on the fact that you'd be happy to go over your long history of success but probably what will matter most to them is how you can help them be successful today.

This is the difference between coaching and convincing. A coach will tell their student they need to accomplish their goal so they are confident about what needs to be done. When asked questions, a coach doesn't defend the situation; they help mold the situation. The second you try to convince somebody you are the best choice, you appear desperate. When you're trying to convince someone of something, it says you are trying to sell, that you are not confident. Let me give you another example. If you talk to the top salesperson in the world about whatever product they're selling, they often communicate in a slow, steady, and confident way about what is needed to be successful. The people who have to sell themselves are scattered, searching quickly and frantically, trying to do everything they can to just catch that one sale.

Do not sell yourself; lead people toward success by offering what they say they need, and let them realize how working with you will help them achieve their goals.

Don't Beat People into Submission

Why does anyone do anything? That's a really good question: The answer is people do things because they decide to do them. How many times have you repeated yourself, over and over and over, to kids? I've told my kids what they need to do and somehow they forget. So what do I do? I repeat it again and again. I have this feeling that my kids will all suddenly wake up one day, realize I've been telling them to do something; then they will miraculously follow all my instructions and become an example of perfection. If you think this is a far-fetched possibility, oh, you are 100 percent correct.

How does this apply to sales? The old way of selling was to repeat yourself over and over and over. Beat people into absolute submission using your words. This is the sleazy salesperson mentality. You sit down at a car dealership, you ask for a price, they write a number down, they come back to you. They move a little bit, then they come back with another number, which goes on for hours. They know that with each passing hour, you're going to get hungrier and more tired, and they will ultimately wear you down.

The problem with this style of selling is the customer seldom leaves fully satisfied. They often feel like they were beaten into submission and the salesperson was against them; they were two opposing forces. Today, with the internet, people can look up pricing, cutting through a ton of the hassle of negotiating. This can cause people to get right to the point. Most people won't even take the time to meet at your office anymore, just because they don't want to be beaten into submission.

I'm going to say it one more time: Telling people what to think over and over is not a good way to do business. It's completely disingenuous and self-serving, and there's something about it that feels dirty. People who use this method fail to realize that, if their customers leave happy, their friends and family will take note and may even become future clients.

Leadership Versus Hard Selling

I often tell people I try never to give advice; I try to share my experience. Everyone's situation is different, and there may be many dynamics about which we have no idea. So, if you don't tell people what to think, then what do you do?

Lead people toward their goals. Ask questions to take people on a simple journey so they picture getting to their end goal. And I don't mean lame questions. I mean good questions that get to the heart of what they're looking for. And through that questioning, most people discover exactly what they want. And guess what, if they already want it, you don't have to convince them of anything.

You don't want to be known as a drill sergeant who lines people up, yells in their faces, and doesn't give them even an ounce of decision-making power. The goal is not to "break" the client;

our role is one of service. It can be tempting to take an approach of "This is what you need and want." Resist this urge and instead, ask more questions to understand what the client wants. This approach can give you great insight into a much more compelling offering where you don't need to beat them into submission.

Most people want to do what's best. We will assume for a second that they do feel empowered to take the next steps, you've cleared the way, you've helped them bring clarity to the situation, and they see very clearly that they need to take these steps. Guess what happens after those steps are taken? They feel 100 percent responsible for the decision they made. You didn't make it for them. This means if something bad happens because of their decision, they can't blame you. You gave them options; you didn't tell them exactly what they needed to do.

How relieving and refreshing is that for you? You didn't tell the person what they needed to do, so you have a clear conscience. You asked them questions that helped them find what they needed and wanted. You removed the obstacles so they could make it possible. And then they reached their goal, and if they changed their mind about their goal or didn't like where they were headed, it was their choice. That's what I call great leadership as opposed to hard sales.

Remember to ask questions and empower clients to reach their goals. You are here to serve, and when you do this well, you win.

The Gatekeeper and the Gate

In business, most of the high performers have gatekeepers. This is their trusted right-hand person. This could be the person who greets you at the front desk when you walk in; it could be somebody in a completely different department; it could be their spouse; or it could be a bunch of different people. But regardless, you need to figure out who the gatekeeper is and take steps to be kind, befriend, and show respect to that gatekeeper. Even if you make it through the gate once, if they don't like you, you will probably be stuck at that gate a lot and may never get in again.

I've seen this play out many times in offices when someone comes in to interview. They're rude or flippant to the person who greets them. What's the first question the interviewer asks the greeter? "Did they seem nice?" Go over and above to be kind and respectful to everyone. That way, the gatekeeper will say they really like this person and will let you right in. Even if they don't let you right in, they'll still have something nice to say about you. Be on the lookout; you never know who might have the keys to the kingdom. Being kind truly can't hurt you or your chances of winning a great opportunity.

Plenty of Room at the Top, No Room at the Bottom

People will often ask me if they should get into a certain business. I ask them what's holding them back, and more often than not, one of the reasons is that there are numerous people in that business. This is when I ask, "Do you plan to be in the top 20 percent or the bottom 80 percent?"

If you plan to be in the top 20 percent, and you do the things it takes to be in the top 20 percent, you most likely will survive and thrive. What you don't want to do is get into a business hoping you're going to survive just because you're in the business. The goal is never to just survive at something—at least not for me and the people I coach. The idea is to dominate and thrive.

I live in Southern California, where Mexican food restaurants are a dime a dozen. When I first moved here, I wondered how in the world there could be so many Mexican food restaurants that make enough money to stay open. In other areas, it might be pizza places or burger shops. How do these places stay open? Well, the answer is not all of them do. There are a couple of places that seem to survive—you know, the cash only, run-down places with excellent food. Those are the places I gravitate to. I figure if they're cash only and they don't spend any money on their restaurant building, their food must be amazing; otherwise, there would not be a line. Sometimes there is a really nice, new-looking restaurant across the street, but when you look closer, there's no line.

This leads me to my point. When salespeople come in and ask if, based on the success of several friends who sell the same thing, I think there would be an opportunity for them to be successful, I simply say, "There's plenty of room at the top. There's just no room at the bottom. If you think you can be one of the best and actually make good on that, there's a good chance you'll be successful. If you're not willing to put the time and effort into becoming the best, there are plenty of people behind you who have already failed. In fact, that's commonplace here." People often sign up for a new job thinking it's going to be much easier than their last job, only to find out that anything worth doing in life is going to cost them.

More often than not, it's not difficult to figure out what it's going to take to thrive. Look around at the people who are thriving and winning. You'll be able to tell what they're doing to make that happen. Take note and start implementing the things they're doing so you can do them, too. Don't go into something thinking you're going to be successful because you're awesome. That might be the case, and someone might make a Hallmark Channel made-for-TV movie about you, but for the rest of us, it takes hard work and dedication. Usually nothing in life that is worth anything comes easily. That's because if it is worth something, people have to pay a price for it.

Yes, it might cost you actual money, and in the whole scheme of things, that's a reality for whatever you do. But the cost I'm talking about is your time, talents, and energy. If you're not willing to be the first person to work and the last one to leave, you run a major risk of being at the bottom.

I'm not someone who likes to be last. If I don't think I can be exceptional, I need to find something else to do. I also understand success doesn't come overnight. There's the ten-thousand-hour rule that says if you practice a skill for ten thousand or more hours, you will become an expert.[3] Most people who start something think they're going to crush it. If they didn't think they

---

3 Gladstone, M. (2008). *Outliers: The story of success.* Little, Brown and Company.

would be able to crush it, they wouldn't do it in most cases. The issue is the in-between. When you get past the starting process, all the enthusiasm wears off, and then what's left? What's left is you against yourself. Do you have the will to make it through the in-between? There's a lot of time between hour one and hour ten thousand. Can you temper the ups and downs so you can stay emotionally level and motivated?

Before you get started with any kind of new sales job or opportunity, take a look around, see what the successful people are doing, and truly ask yourself, "Can I do this better? Am I willing to pay the price it will cost in my time and talents to be at the top?" If the answer is no, then that's okay. There should be something you feel so passionate about that you're willing to pay a hefty price. And when you find it, remember, there's plenty of room at the top.

All the Time in the World, or on Time

Have you ever been on an elevator, and it seems to stop at every floor? You stand in the back and try to patiently wait. Time is ticking away, and you need to get to your destination. Why are you waiting? Because you're polite. After you've watched all the floors go by, you realize you missed your floor, and there's nothing you can do about it now. You must continue waiting patiently until you can get to your final destination.

This is a great way to highlight what it's like when you ask someone to complete a task for you without a specific time frame. You wait patiently, hoping they'll get to it, but you don't get any feedback. They finally complete what they said they would do in the first place, but by the time this happens, you're full of stress, usually irritated, and flat-out frustrated because you relied on them to do what they said they would do in the time frame they said they would do it. Now why didn't you ask or follow up?

Most people would say it's because they didn't want to seem pushy, or they didn't want to offend anyone by checking up on them. I like the old Russian proverb that says, "Trust, but verify."

There is absolutely nothing wrong with checking in on people to make sure everything's on track to be done in the time frame that was committed to. In fact, if you don't do that, you're going to be standing at the back of the elevator, waiting for other people to get off before finally realizing you missed your floor.

Building Relationships

A lot of the time, it's not the message; it's the delivery of the message. "Trust, but verify," says, "I totally trust you to do what you say you're going to do, and I want to make sure you know how important it is that we hit this deadline." Another way to approach the situation and deliver a similar message is through acting curious. For example, I might say, "Hey, I've been waiting for this, and I'm just curious where it is on your list. If it's not next, when do you think you'll be able to get to it?" Once I have a response, I'll express my gratitude: "I want to say thank you so much for making my task a priority. I think you know how important it is." Then I'll finish off with a nice heap of praise: "You are awesome. I know I can always count on you to get things done when you say you're going to do them."

Remember the old maxim: You catch a lot more bees with honey than you do with vinegar. Most people take a less finessed approach: "Get it done because you promised you would. Now you lied. You didn't get it done like you said you would." This is not a relationship-building technique, and if you ever need something in the future, you can pretty much guarantee you're going to be at the bottom of that person's list, if not physically, then at least mentally. (Many studies have looked at the effects of positive and negative reinforcement, and they show positive rein- forcement works more effectively than negative reinforcement or consequences.[4]) If you want to build long-term success, you need

---

4 Cameron, J., & Pierce, W. D. (1994). Reinforcement, reward, and intrinsic motivation: A meta-analysis. *Review of Educational Research*. https://doi. org/10.3102/00346543064003363

to be relationship-building rather than relationship-killing. Part of the process I recommend is verifying expectations and that work is completed. If you ask for something to get done and then expect somebody will do it without giving a timeline, without checking in, and without making sure the person understands your expectations, you can pretty much guarantee you're going to be standing on that metaphorical elevator for a lot of floors. But when you master the art, results accelerate and things get completed. You're going to get right to your floor almost every time. Then, when you look around that elevator, you're going to ask yourself why someone didn't push that button for their floor.

A final thought: You don't have to do this with everyone. Some people show they're trustworthy, and they're going to get things done, come hell or high water. Those aren't the people you have to worry about. For others, always ask when something's going to be done so everyone is on the same page. This way, you can get off the elevator at just the right time.

Don't Major in the Minors

I've heard time and time again that we are most creative at the beginning of the day. The mind is rested and most creative when it is full of energy. If I know this, then that means I need to do the most difficult tasks or the things that require the most brainpower first thing in the day. I really like Mark Twain's quote, "If it's your job to eat a frog, it's best to do it first thing in the morning. And if it's your job to eat two frogs, it's best to eat the biggest one first." Eating the frog means doing the hardest, nastiest thing first, which will make everything after that seem like a cakewalk.

One thing I notice with work is that people like the simple tasks much more than they like the difficult tasks. I think people don't tackle the bigger tasks first because they fear failure or rejection. But knowing what we know now, if you are directing another person, look over the tasks and instruct them to take care of all the larger tasks and then finish the day with those small, insignificant tasks.

While you might tell someone else to do that, chances are you do the absolute opposite when it comes to directing yourself.

Let's say you need to reach out to some clients. The easy task would be to get on social media and like a couple of their posts. The harder task would be to pick up the phone and have a meaningful conversation. Or maybe it would be responding to all the quick emails, other than the time-consuming one that you need to research.

When we major in the minor things, we may find some small comfort in the fact that we feel like we're doing something and accomplishing something, but in reality, we're keeping ourselves from being productive at a high level. We're allowing ourselves to fail by not addressing the very things needing our attention, things that will actually move our success forward.

You may not even know cognitively what those big tasks you are avoiding are until you write them out. I try to write out the five-to-ten most important tasks for the day, every day, and once they're written out, I can clearly determine which are minors and which are majors. If you're making a list of things you need to accomplish, I highly suggest you make that distinction. Start mapping out your day for what's important and what's less important, and then start tackling them. It feels really good to look over the last few days' lists and see that you accomplished everything on it, large and small.

Challenge yourself for the next three days. List everything in three categories: most important, important, and least important. Do all of the most important items first, and stop majoring in the minors. You'll be light-years ahead of your competitors and will start to see the progress you've been wanting all along.

2. Mastering Your Emotions

Addresses topics such as fear, anger, and frustration in the context of sales. This chapter discusses the importance of managing your emotions, maintaining a positive outlook, and not allowing personal feelings to hinder your sales abilities.

IF YOU WANT TO BE SUCCESSFUL in business and life, you have to be able to direct your emotions. You cannot be constantly led by your emotions but must lead them in the direction that will be most beneficial for you.

Tame the Wild Emotions

People who are constantly all over the map, not knowing what to feel or do, are those we call a hot mess. They come in hot with their emotions and hope for the best but end up with a mess. Another example of letting emotions get the best of you is when you have a short fuse. You get irritated and snappy with people, sometimes cutting them off midsentence.

People will often read your facial expressions, so make sure you fix your face. It takes a lot more strength to control our emotions than it does to let them out of the cage. Handling our emotions reminds me of a circus. When everyone is seated around the circle in the center of the arena, random acts are performed in the center for everyone to see and judge.

Are you making a spectacle of yourself every time you let your emotions get the best of you? I would guess that whatever is happening, whenever you let your emotions get the best of you, people are watching. Others are forming opinions about you based on your actions. If you seem erratic, people will have their guard up, but if you are considered dependable, people will let their guard down.

It's pretty simple. People base their opinions about you on the emotions you let out and show to others. If people can't depend on you to be a steady and calm person, they won't know what they'll get from you. For them, it will be like going to the circus for the first time: They don't know what will show up next in the middle of that circle. If this is the case, you're going to have a difficult time trying to build trust necessary to move your career forward.

Your place of business is not the right place to let your emotions go wild. It takes a very long time to build trust and only seconds to break it. Think before you act and speak. Every word and action you take are steps in a direction that can either build up your career or tear it down. The last thing you want is for the circus to break loose while everyone is watching. It'll put you in a spiral of constantly apologizing. Instead, take the steps to build yourself up and gain the respect and adoration of those around you.

Have you ever lost control of your emotions? There's a time and a place for everything. There are companies that have created a successful business by renting out rage rooms. What's this? A safe place where you can go and let out all the aggression you have been holding on to. You put on some protective gear, and then you go wild in a soundproof room. Sounds to me like a great way to deal with your emotions in a way that won't hurt you or your business.

We all have emotions to tame; it's nothing to be ashamed of. I'll give you some things to think about in the following chapters, along with some strategies that will help you guide your emotions. Learning how to handle your emotions is all part of building a successful life.

Jumping to Conclusions and Dealing with Fear

Someone mentioned the TV show *Columbo* to me the other day. This is a detective show in which the title character looks at the clues to a crime and deciphers the smallest pieces of evidence that lead him to the truth. Another great show many people will probably recognize is *Sherlock Holmes*, about a person who looks deeper at the clues to find out what is happening or has happened.

What if there was a show in which all the detectives kept getting it very wrong? What if you were watching the show and saw some obvious clues that the characters completely overlooked? If they jumped to a wrong conclusion, you would be screaming, "How did you miss the clue?," at the TV screen if you're anything like most people.

Unfortunately, this is how misinterpretations happen most of the time. You're in your office or at some kind of networking function, somebody says something, and you completely jump to the wrong conclusion. Why do we do this? I would say, most of the time, because of F.E.A.R.: false evidence appearing real.[5] We are convinced that what we're scared of will get us once and for all, but a study shows that 85 percent of what we worry about happening never actually happens.[6]

In sales, when salespeople jump to conclusions, usually it's because they fear the other party is not interested in the service they're offering. People often jump to a no answer when the answer is not actually no. Don't get me wrong, no can mean no. But often it means you haven't shown enough value for me to say yes. When people say no to something that I think may be good for them or that they have stated they are interested in, I often take another approach to present the information in a way that may make the product or service appear more valuable to them.

---

5 The acronym is frequently quoted by motivational speakers, but its original source is unknown.

6 Pawlowski, A. (May 10, 2017). How to worry better. NBC News. https://www.nbcnews.com/better/pop-culture/praise-worry-why-fretting-can-be-good-you-ncna757016

Let's talk about fear a little bit more, though. Fear can paralyze you. It can keep you from saying and doing what you need to do to succeed. You don't need to be Colombo or Sherlock Holmes to realize what actual clues are in front of you. Stop jumping to conclusions because of fear. When people are scared or fearful, they act frantically, talk quickly, and ask questions repeatedly. Grounded and confident people talk slowly, carefully select their words, and speak with authority. Rather than being fearful, why not be faith-full: full of faith that something good will happen from the situation? Don't buy into a reaction; search for the root of what people are looking for and think to yourself, *Could I add additional value to help the person see this from a different angle?* If I'm going to be full of faith, I'm not going to give up on the first roadblock. I'm going to dig deeper and look for a real clue.

All this talk about watching for clues makes me want to watch some *Colombo*. Maybe you should, too.

With Experience Comes Pessimism

I remember when I was first starting my career. My world was full of possibilities. I truly believed anything could happen. And because of that strong belief, a lot of things that probably shouldn't have happened did.

I would talk to everyone around me. People would say, "That's not possible. I don't think it will happen. It could happen, but it's not likely." Because of my inquisitive mind, I would always take note of different people's responses. One thing I noticed was that the older people were, the more pessimistic their outlook typically was. I remember thinking to myself, "I will never get pessimistic. I think no matter what I put my mind to, it will happen. There's always a bright side."

Here I am later in life. I'm probably only at the midpoint, but life has beaten the crap out of me time and time again. And as I get older, I completely understand why so many folks get pessimistic. When the things that happen to you create a less-than-positive experience, you don't want to revisit the unpleasant situation or experience. So you start labeling things. You tell yourself, "These people probably are trying to manipulate me. From my experience, this situation probably won't end well. That's not worth my time because it probably won't happen. I'll probably be let down if I try too much."

Here's what I found. Whether you think you're right or you think you're wrong, you're probably right. There is absolutely nothing wrong with being so ridiculously optimistic that something unlikely could happen. I think it's more of a situation where, as you get older, you have less energy to put into things. You start learning the cost of making certain things happen.

As Jesus told his disciples, you can move a mountain with the faith of a mustard seed (Matt. 17:20 NIV). Imagine if you have faith and action while working toward what some people would say was an unlikely goal. Heroic things can happen. When I would broach an idea, my farther-along-in-life counterparts would be naysayers. Then I would think that maybe this thing couldn't be done. However, I would quickly realize that those people were being pessimistic. I also have always had a knack for doing things the hard way. If I thought it was possible, I would go for it, and if it didn't happen, I would try to learn from my failure.

I still remember an older inventor who told me, "What your heart can believe and your mind can conceive, you can achieve."[7] In the end, don't be surprised if a lot of older people lean toward pessimism. Because they've been in positions longer, they learn their patterns of what's doable and what's not. The thing to keep in mind is that what other people can achieve isn't necessarily what you can achieve. Each one of us is unique in our abilities. Are you Roger Bannister, the first person to break the four-minute mile? Everyone said it couldn't be done, but low and behold, Roger did it. And guess what happened after that? More people did it again and again and again. Where there's a will, there's a way. Don't be distracted by other people's limits. You get to

---

7 Hill, N. (1937). *Think and grow rich*. The Ralston Society.

write the story of your future. That story is going to be unique to you. Make it exciting, make it challenging, and let it be a story of someone who overcame all odds. Make the naysayers eat their words. You can do it!

Overcoming Anger and Handling Frustration

Have you ever been to a restaurant where they have the little kid activity papers with mazes or matching games and maybe tic-tac-toe or connect the dots? If you're a parent, you know those kids will go straight to the maze. The first few times, they struggle their way through; they'll try to scribble out where they went in the wrong direction, and eventually and painfully, they make it to the end. As humans, we adapt quickly; two or three years later, that same kid will completely change their strategy. What do they do? They start at the finish line of the maze. This is genius because they run into almost no roadblocks at all. They flawlessly execute this maze that's designed to be difficult.

Let me get to the point about what this has to do with your life. We talked about having a plan and a strong purpose. When you're looking at a business dealing, when you have a challenge in front of you, what do you want the result to be? All too often, people get stuck looking at the tree in front of them rather than the forest behind it all. If you can look past what's in front of you and see the bigger picture, you begin to start drawing the maze from the finish line. Let me give you an example.

Someone talks behind your back and says something rude. When you hear about it, you immediately tell them how rude you think this was and that you cannot stand them now. The same person is responsible for giving input on one of your projects. That short-term, feel-good, tell them what's up? You just added hours and hours of red tape to your project because you didn't think ahead.

When someone is scorned, often they go "scorched earth." But not openly; they do this behind the scenes, making your life as difficult as possible because they want revenge. Now, I'm not saying this happens every time. Occasionally, you run into someone who's wise and takes feedback well, and as long as the delivery was good, you didn't damage the relationship to the point of complete annihilation. But you do risk making your life more difficult when you're not strategic with your thoughts and plans. The saying I love to use is "Be careful about the toes you step on today because they're attached to the butt you will be kissing tomorrow."

So, before you lose your cool and make a move, take a deep breath, look around, and decide what result you hope for from this situation and what actions can contribute to your long-term success. Then, walk your way backward through the maze to figure out how you can make all of that happen. Sometimes it's very, very simple, and other times it will be a difficult journey. You may need to hold your tongue and hold your actions, but know that, by doing this, you are setting yourself up for success.

Strike While the Iron Is Cold

Have you ever had a situation where someone in business says something or does something that completely sets you off? I'm not talking about someone saying they like ham sandwiches and you like turkey. I'm talking about them saying something that reaches down into your soul and up springs a whirlwind of anger. There's always a fork in the road if something like that happens. You can choose either the high road or the road that feels good at the time. The high road is to control yourself and temper your response; the feel-good road is to let them have it, rip them up one side and down the other, chew them up, and spit them out.

Over my career, I've realized that while taking action can feel good in the moment, most of the time, we are left with a big mess to clean up. If we temper our response, sometimes we end up feeling like we should have stood up more for ourselves. Maybe we feel our response was weak. While all these feelings are normal, we have to look at one thing. What will have the best result and get us furthest in this situation and the others to follow?

I'll give you a piece of wisdom I've learned through years of making many mistakes: Strike when the iron is cold. This means I will not respond to the thing that has upset me while I'm emotionally charged. Once I'm calm and of sound mind, I plot my course.

I wish I had used this theory my entire career because it would have saved me a lot of hassle. While you are still angry, go ahead and write that email; just don't send it. Write out all your feelings about what you would say . . . but don't say them aloud. Go ahead and write that text . . . but don't send it. My rule has always been to sleep on my response overnight. If I wake up and I'm still super angry, I give myself permission to address the situation more directly. However, I wake up 95 percent of the time realizing that whatever I was so angry about the day before was not a big deal. This allows me to be strategic about how I want future interactions to go with that person. I can systematically work toward the goal I have in mind. This is one great way to ensure you get future opportunities and keep doors open for progress.

Anger Is a Big Cloud

Anger is one of those things that completely clouds judgment. You can't see clearly until you are out of the situation. If anger is a big cloud, and you're the pilot flying yourself all around the world, it's best to avoid the cloud: Avoid anger. The second best way is to get out of the cloud as soon as possible. Do not try to land the plane in a big cloud. Visibility is low, and chances are very high that you will do something that will get you hurt.

One thing you learn in pilot training is to stay calm if you fly into a cloud. In fact, many plane wrecks happen because a pilot is not used to flying in the clouds, becomes disoriented, thinking that the ground is up, and then flies right into the water or the ground. Basically, they lose control of the airplane and crash because they can't tell what is going on outside the plane.

I know there have been many times when I thought, "I'm good, I'm angry, but I know what I need to do." This is when things can get hairy. You want the best chance for success, and that is not when you're in the middle of a cloud. If you can take a break, excuse yourself, or pause the situation until a later time, your chances of landing the plane or the situation ending well are much, much higher. Some people struggle with the fact that when they're angry, they want to say things that make them feel better in the moment. As we discussed earlier, insulting someone or telling them what's on your mind might feel good in that second, but most likely, it will cause you a lot more pain later. You have to be strategic to reach your goal and to succeed in general. Remember, once words are spoken, you can't take them back. Speak your words wisely.

Keep Your Cool and Maintain Control

As pilots gain experience, they learn to fly using instruments instead of ground sight and are called IFR pilots. They are specially trained to fly in the clouds. This is true for every airline pilot you will ever ride on a plane with. They know how to use the instruments to make sure that even if it gets cloudy, they can use all the signals and lights and land that plane almost blindly. When I say blind, I mean they can't see anything out the window. All they have are the gauges that they must trust to stay in line with the runway that will take them and all their passengers safely to their destination.

So what does that have to do with us and anger? Metaphorically speaking, we can learn to read the gauges and instruments in our environment when we're angry. I think other people can be those instruments. Mentors, experts—how do they handle similar situations successfully? What tools did they use to stay calm?

I remember one training where the speaker did something hilarious that actually stuck with me. We were all in a room, seated in rows behind him, like most seminars. At one point, he picked someone from the audience to help demonstrate a technique—and that's when things got interesting. As the person began to speak, the speaker stood facing us and started quietly chiming in with a single vowel sound every time there was a pause. "A." The person kept talking. Another pause—"E." Then "I," "O,"

"U," and yep—"sometimes Y." It had the whole room cracking up. It felt kind of ridiculous, but there was something clever about it. He was using the vowels as a unique way to show he was still listening and engaged, without interrupting or stealing the focus. Unconventional? Absolutely. But it worked—and I never forgot it. He knew that to get through some situations, you can't look out the window. He used this method to take the focus off how he was feeling in the moment. He had some fun with it instead, which gave him space to keep his emotions from being clouded. You have to rely on proven techniques and use the gauges around you to land that plane.

So, if you find yourself getting angry, get your head out of the cloudy space. Get to your destination. Don't focus on what feels good in the moment; focus on the bigger goal, which is what happens later on. Once the sun comes out and your mind is clear, you can take a good look around and take the absolute best next step.

Don't get me wrong; I'm not saying this is easy. It takes a lot of self-control, and many people lack the ability to control themselves in the midst of anger. I do know that nobody ever says, "You know, I really like that super angry person. They are amazing. They thought so clearly and did everything perfectly, yet they were irate, out-of-their-mind angry." Be strategic and keep your head out of the cloud.

Don't Get In the Last Word

The other day, I was at home and needed to boil some water. I turned on my stove, put the tea kettle on, and waited. I was waiting for the water to reach exactly 212 degrees Fahrenheit. You don't know exactly when it will reach that temperature, but when it does, little bubbles start to form. They'll get a little bit faster at 211 degrees Fahrenheit, and then bam! You're at a full boil. Isn't this how it happens during conversations? Somebody says something that starts a little bit of bubbling, and you start getting upset. You tell yourself, "I'm okay. Don't get upset." The conversation continues, and you start feeling more and more bubbles. Now you're fully upset, but you're not showing it on the outside yet. And then the other person says something to cross the line. You think to yourself, "Oh no, you didn't." And your full anger comes out. You start bubbling over, telling the other person exactly what you think. You are full-blown mad. You could be completely justified, and it could be okay that you're mad. That's not the question. No matter what the reason is, don't let one person determine who you become. We are at our best when we maintain control over our emotions.

If you need to, take the pot off the stove; remove yourself from the situation. Give yourself a chance to cool off; this means don't finalize your conversation by making a closing statement that ends the conversation. Pause, and then put yourself back on the stove, back into the situation. Remember everything has a start and an end. Most of the time, winning is not about being better in the argument. Winning can be about just outlasting the other person through persistence and continuing the conversation without being fazed.

Another example is a specific situation where a young gentleman was being recruited. This particular individual was being downright pompous, and the recruiter's patience was wearing thin. No question the young man had talent, and the company was interested in acquiring that talent. The recruiter's frustration ran high during that conversation and began to boil. Then the recruiter blurted out, "Why in the world do you have to be so difficult?" If we could put that situation in slow motion, you would see everything completely turn. The young gentlemen immediately shut down and completely turned off. Needless to say, that recruit didn't get landed.

When your frustration rises, remember to be like water. Flow with the situation. When situations or conversations get heated, remember that you need to outlast the individual on the other side of the conversation by not making a final statement. In the struggle between a rock and water, which one is stronger? The rock is unmovable and known for its strength. And yet water is so powerful that it can flow around anything. Water is stronger than rock because even a waterdrop repeatedly falling in the same place on the rock will eventually break through the hardest of rocks. Don't get swept up in the emotion of the moment.

The secret ingredient? Add kindness to that persistence. Now you have a lethal mix. Most people aren't going to stay mad or keep arguing with a kind person who is persistent. This doesn't mean they're going to like it or you. But this will be your best chance of making the absolute best out of that situation. Don't be like some and boil over and say something you regret. Think bigger! Think about how the person who's saying the things on the other side does not have control over your emotions—you do—and that you will not let them reach their goal. This is not an easy task, and it takes practice. But if you can keep your cool and maintain control, you will exhibit true strength, maturity, and the ability to overcome situations you never before thought possible.

Every True Warrior Walks with a Limp

Have you ever met someone who talks a big game but backs off when it comes down to it? I've seen this happen, and you probably have, too. But you've also seen movies in which the little wimpy kid gets pushed around by bullies, and one day he snaps. He's a complete whirlwind of anger and destroys everything in his path.

Remember these two things: Strength can come from places you least expect, and kindness does not equal weakness. I would argue that being kind takes more strength in a lot of situations we deal with in life. So why do I say every true warrior walks with a limp? When I was dealing with something difficult in my younger years and didn't think I'd be able to make it through, I spoke to my mother about it and told her I didn't think that I could handle the situation. That's when she told me, "Every true warrior walks with a limp." She added, "Everyone can train for battle and be as ready as they think they can be. It's easy to be strong when you don't need to be, especially when things are easy. But it's very difficult to be strong in the face of difficult times. And if you're a true warrior, you're going to deal with real battles, and in real battles, warriors get wounded. They have the scars, the bruises, and the limp to prove it."

The one thing a warrior has is experience. You see, you can withstand difficult situations when you've made it through tough situations in the past. I often find a lot of wisdom when talking to someone who's already been through whatever I'm dealing with. They have sage wisdom that I often don't want to take. Why? Because I have this personal need to figure things out the hard way. And not every time, but most of the time, I find that the person who walks with the limp is right. Don't be afraid when you need to go to battle; don't be afraid of the scars or the limp. Know that to become a true warrior, you have to go through the battles.

A Reason, a Season, or a Lifetime

A friend once told me, "Everything happens for a reason, a season, or a lifetime." I thought about this recently when I met someone who was going through a very difficult situation. His was one of those heart-wrenching situations where you don't understand why it happened to him. He's a super good guy, has a great family, and is hardworking; if anyone deserves a gold star, it would be him. He didn't deserve this situation; at least, that's what I thought. Was this happening for some sort of reason?

Another friend of mine was stuck in the in-between. The in-between is the hard spot, right? Everybody's jazzed when they start and super happy when they're done. But what about the in-between? How many people love that in-between spot, the one that just won't seem to end?

Life has a way of throwing you surprises from every direction. How do you make sense of it? I see bad things happening to good people, or somebody stuck in a trial for way too long, and then others I don't think deserve a break have it easy. Why?

If something happens for a reason, you get to move on once you figure out what the reason is. If it's for a season, you can rest in the fact that it's a season, and it will end; once the season is over, you move on.

Some things are for a lifetime. When you get married, your goal is a lifetime. Maybe you get a negative health diagnosis, and you're going to be carrying that for the rest of your life.

To paraphrase Brian A. "Drew" Chalker's poem, things come into your life for a reason, a season, or a lifetime. "When you figure out which it is, you know exactly what to do."[8] Just knowing that whatever you're going through fits into one of these boxes can help you adjust your perspective to match the situation. No matter what it is that's going on in your life, always remember, it's happening for a reason, a season, or a lifetime.

You're Only Defeated Once You Give Up

Growing up with several siblings means you typically have a lot of disagreements. I was the middle child, so I had to fight at the top and the bottom. I was always trying to figure out my angle. Often, I would pick on my younger brother. Notice I don't say little brother because he's about twice my size. But regardless, since I was the older sibling, I could dominate my younger brother. We would get into some kind of scuffle, and I would try to pick on him. I'd give him a couple of jabs, he would lie on the ground, and I'd think to myself, "Okay, he's not going to mess with me anymore. He's definitely had enough, and I've won." As I would walk away, my younger brother, in the tiniest, screechiest voice, would say, "Jerk." I would turn around and rough him up some more, and once I thought I had roughed him up enough, I would start to walk away. And I would again hear the tiny, screechy voice say, "Jerk." I could not win because, no matter what I did, when I began to walk away, he would simply blurt out, "Jerk."

I think this highlights how you're only defeated once you give up. No matter what I did, my brother knew one simple thing: If he said, "Jerk," as I walked away, I didn't win. I wonder how many

---

8 Chalker, B. A. (2000). Why do people come into our lives? Motivate Us. https://motivateus.com/stories/reason-season-lifetime.htm

times you could have overcome a challenge if you had refused to give up and instead uttered "Jerk" at the problem trying to take hold in your life?

Changing Course Is Not Giving Up

You see, there's a difference between giving up and changing course. Many people get confused between the two. We have a brain for a reason, and sometimes it takes that brain longer for us to realize things—like a certain direction was a bad idea. So we use our brain by rubbing those little brain cells together and decide aloud, "Huh, maybe I should try a different way." To me, giving up says I don't believe I can make it; I don't have what it takes; this is a waste of my time. Yet all the while, I know in my heart of hearts that I need to accomplish that goal.

I don't ever want to live in a world of "what if." This means I don't ever want to walk away from a situation and wonder what would have happened if I had given it my all. I want to walk away and know I gave it my everything; I put it all out there, and there was nothing left in any way, shape, or form for me to give.

You decide when you give up, which means you decide when you're defeated. Don't let one person dictate who you become. You determine who you become. Don't look back at a bunch of regrets, wondering what could have been.

Easy on the Person, Hard on the Issue

A friend of mine was a very high-stakes paid negotiator. Hedge funds would often hire him to come in and reduce costs. As I'm sure you can imagine, he was not the most liked person walking through the door. But how could he be so successful at such a high level? Why would hedge funds with billions of dollars hire him to come in and reduce costs?

Well, that was the question I had in my mind. I asked him to come in and do a negotiation training at my office. He came in and was very unassuming and relaxed. If you were at a coffee shop looking around, he was the kind of guy you might see reading a newspaper in the corner. Not intimidating at all, almost a bit disarming. So let's get back to what he knew that others didn't.

As he began to go through his training, one thing stood out more than anything else. As strong negotiators, we should focus our energy on being hard on the issue and easy on the person. My friend went over issue after issue and demonstrated how he attacked each head-on but did not attack the person on the other end. An example went something like this: "Johnny, unfortunately, we can't continue to do business at this price. Now, I like you, and I'm hoping we can work something out because I think we both have the best interests of the companies in mind. I know if it were up to you, this would be simple. I don't want to come across as harsh because it's not you, but this price is not sustainable." This would be followed by a series of negotiations, but the biggest takeaway was that if you attack the person, you will get nowhere. You can make magic happen if you attack the issue and not the person. Everyone wants to win, but when someone's ego gets in the way or, even worse, if their feelings get hurt, that progress will just be flushed down the toilet.

Respect

By now, you should be seeing a theme in this book. People have feelings; they need to feel valued, and most of them need to be treated decently. If you disagree, it doesn't mean you have to treat the other person differently than if you did agree. I hear you on the other end, saying, "You have no clue. My situation is much more intricate than that. If I'm kind, they will walk all over me. They won't respect me."

Respect is not gained from fear or intimidation. However, respect can be gained from trust. You will see that I'm not telling you to avoid saying things that need to be said. You don't need to avoid saying hard things in a direct way. You just don't have to say them in a way that insults the other person. You don't need to act like your life depends on this. You can be cool, calm, collected, and say some very pointed and harsh things. The fact that you were cool and confident and did not feel the need to protect yourself often gains respect. When we do this, we will see major results.

The second you raise your voice and tempers flare, you lose. Remaining calm takes more strength than flying off the handle and spouting out everything on your mind in an unfiltered way. So take a deep breath, remain calm, and be easy on the person but relentless about the issue.

Life Weaves a String

Can you compartmentalize challenges so you're not affected by something bad going on in your life if you have something good going on somewhere else?

Let me give you an example. Your spouse leaves you, and that same day, you get the work promotion you've been waiting ten years for. Are you jumping up and down for joy, or are you down in the dumps after being left? Let's assume you actually still love your spouse. I could hear too many people saying, "Hey, I'd be really happy with both things." But the reality is you wouldn't be happy if the love of your life just walked out the door. But you have these two conflicting emotions that are very strong happening at the same time. Is this possible? And what do you do about this?

You've probably heard people say, "Fake it till you make it." Does that mean you should fake like you're not heartbroken and dying inside so everyone else can see the happiness you feel about the new job promotion? Let's say you do that (and I'm not even going to judge whether or not that's a good decision). Who are you faking all this joy for? Are you doing it for yourself? Or are you doing it, so you don't alienate other people?

What if I told you that to get past something, you must go through it? Different things going on at the same time often mount up and affect us. The only way to alleviate this is to work through each issue.

But if all the issues accumulate into one situation where you boil over and lose all control, you're going to lose. My point here is that life does weave a string. No matter what's going on in your life, even if you tell yourself it won't affect the other parts of your life, emotions have a way of weaving through everywhere. You can't run from something that's woven through you. And even if you think it's not affecting you today because you put it on a "pay no attention" shelf in your mind, that thing you put on the shelf may fall off later. The only way I've found to take care of that shelf is to acknowledge the issue for what it is. Feel whatever you need to feel, and then give yourself permission to let it go. Some psychologists will even tell you, "You have to feel it to heal it."

How Do You Talk to Yourself?

It's important that we acknowledge how other people feel and treat them kindly, and we must also treat ourselves kindly. If someone else were in your situation, would you speak kindly to them or harshly? I find myself speaking very harshly to myself a lot. "Hey, you should be able to do that." "Why didn't you do this better?" "You're going to fail if you take that kind of approach again." Are these things I would say to someone else? No. I have a lot more empathy toward someone else.

A very wise person told me that to have empathy for others, you must first have empathy for yourself. I never liked hearing that, but I found it to be true. It's a lot easier to be kind to others when we are being kind to ourselves.

So keep in mind that life weaves a string. It can also be woven through a lot of great things, and if there's something in that string you need to deal with, do it. Don't put it on the "it doesn't matter" shelf. Addressing your issues will help you succeed at a much higher level and make success sustainable.

Victim or Victor

Everyone runs this race called life, and not everyone wins. Part of what will set you apart is your attitude.

Here's an unpopular idea: The world doesn't owe you anything. Wow. You mean I don't get a first-place trophy? What?! If I don't get a first-place trophy, I'm going to complain to everyone because I'm owed the first-place trophy.

Do you have an attitude of gratitude? Even if something bad happens to you, do you have the attitude that you're an overcomer? Or do you sink down anytime something bad happens and feel like the victim? We all know these people. Everything bad always happens to them, and the one string that follows through all their stories is that they are the victim. They're driving down the street and someone cuts them off—they're the victim. They didn't get the raise they wanted at work because they were mistreated—victim. Their significant other left them for no real reason—victim.

Here's what a victor would say: "I'm going to own my life. I'm going to take responsibility for everything that happens around me. Because there's one common denominator, and that's me." Life is not what happens to you, it's what you do with what happens to you. Psychiatrist and Holocaust survivor Viktor Frankl wrote, "Everything can be taken from a man but one thing: the last of human freedoms—to choose one's attitude in any given set of circumstances, to choose one's own way." Frankl tells the story of how he survived the Holocaust by finding personal meaning in the experience, which gave him the will to live through it.[9]

I think a lot of people today are held captive by the bad things happening around them. Rather than acknowledging them and moving on, people hold onto them, thinking in some weird way that it will make them feel better. Can I tell you a little secret? Holding onto bad things does not make you feel better. Holding onto bad things leaves you feeling bad. And when you feel bad, guess what? You give a taste of what you're feeling to everyone around you.

When you're a victor, you run toward trouble and quickly subdue it. It doesn't matter if you win or not; what matters is

---

9 Frankl, V. (1946). *Man's search for meaning*. Beacon Press.

your intention and ability to take on whatever's coming at you. And here's the thing: Several different issues could hit you in one day. You have to look each thing in the eyes and say, "Not today. I'm not your victim today. I'm an overcomer, and I'm going to overcome you. I'm going to subdue you. You are mine." This fire inside you strikes fear into your problems, and when your problems are afraid, you are the victor.

What's something in your life that you've been running from or afraid of? It is time to turn the tables. Look at yourself in the mirror—do you see a victim or a victor? Because if you see a victim, you may never reach your full potential. Victors are the winners. This doesn't mean victors don't experience pain, don't experience hardship, don't experience difficult things in life. It just means that when they do, they overcome it. You have the ability to be an overcomer.

Look again in the mirror; what do you see? No matter what comes your way, you can overcome it. Sometimes, difficult things happen to us because life is preparing us for something even harder. And without first going through that thing we deem difficult, we may not be able to survive the next thing that happens. But with each passing challenge, we level up . . . or we level down.

But I see in you a fire; I see in you someone who's leveling up with each step. Start thinking of yourself as an overcomer. You do not need to have a spirit of fear. Fear does not help you. You are an overcomer. Let the victims be victims, and when you're at the top of the mountain and declared the victor, hold your hands up high. You are meant for greatness, and you have that ability—you simply need to take hold of it. If someone wants to be a victim, let them because we all run the race, and not everyone's going to run in such a way that they will win. But you will—because you now are a victor!

3. Harnessing the Power of Language

Highlights the importance of choosing words wisely, avoiding definitive statements, taking "I" and "me" out of the conversation, and refraining from feeding into negative conversations. Also discusses the concept of asking better questions and how to communicate effectively.

● ●

IF YOU WANT TO BECOME A MASTER of the art of sales, you must be able to speak in a way that people will hear and understand you clearly. This singular ability will change the direction of your conversations and dramatically increase positive results. Clear communication will also save you and your clients a tremendous amount of time and frustration.

Powerful Communication

Imagine you travel to a foreign country, and everywhere you go, you try to speak to the locals, but lo and behold, they can't understand anything you say. You try to order food at the local restaurant and end up with something much different from what you thought you were getting. You go to the hotel, which you were unable to call in advance, only to find out they have no rooms available, leaving you out in the cold. You feel no one understands you and that it may be useless even to try to communicate. Your internal frustration grows to where you feel completely misunderstood and helpless.

Unfortunately, this is how many people feel when they are unable to communicate in a way that is clear, concise, and easily understood by others. Once we can communicate in such a way, we can go to the next level and start to help others with their communication and help them identify their needs and desires.

Clients sometimes haven't taken the time to explore or understand what they are looking for. If this is the case, the client has no idea what they want and how to get it. As you go through this next section, you will learn from some hard-earned experience that will help you craft your language to navigate the sales landscape. You will learn to master the art of sales communication.

This is a skill that is learned over time. It may come naturally for some, but like learning a foreign language, you may become rusty and less effective if you don't practice regularly. Practice the concepts that follow at every opportunity, and perfect your language. Once you have honed your skills and learned to use the correct language, the results will be evident, and conversations that used to be stressful will now take place with ease. Remember, the more you practice, the luckier you will get!

Take "But" out of the Conversation

But, but, please tell me why people say "but" so much. In English, the word "but" cancels out everything said before it. "I want to give you a million dollars, but let's first talk about how that could happen." "You're the most convincing, energetic, thoughtful salesperson in the entire world, but you probably need to talk less." What happened here? Most people don't even realize they're saying the word, *but* they are.

Is there another word I use instead? How about "and"? "You're the most convincing, energetic, thoughtful salesperson, and you need to talk less." Don't get me wrong; telling someone they need to talk less may not be a good thing to do after such a nice compliment. But at least you're not canceling what you just said; instead, you're saying it as a continuation of the compliment.

When we collaborate with others, it's important they don't feel like we are disregarding their opinions. Using the word "and" feels collaborative rather than dismissive and invalidating. "Thank you for all your hard work on this project, but we will need to go in a different direction" could make anyone who put a lot of work into something feel defeated. They would probably feel devalued. What if you simply took out the "but" and instead said "and"? "Thank you for all your hard work on this project, and after reviewing it, we may need to go in a different direction." The difference is subtle and gives credit to the person for their thought or action without invalidating them.

The most common use of "but" is when we are in a conversation with another person. Examples include "I agree, but have you thought of this?" or "But I would not do that, I would do this instead." We are actually saying we disagree, and the other person needs to hear what we have to say. People can get quite defensive when we use this language in conversations.

I can't stress enough the value of replacing "but" with "and." Try it now. Next time you want to say something powerful, give a compliment, or respond in a conversation, replace "but" with "and." You'll soon realize what a powerful tool this is. Just replacing one word means you're no longer invalidating everything you said before it. Though there may be times when you need to say "but," stick with "and" as often as you can and give a little bit more love.

Know the Right Time to Speak

Have you ever said something at the wrong moment? And right after you said it, you knew you shouldn't have? This happens in personal relationships; this happens in business meetings; this happens everywhere. This also happens when you least expect it. A man was standing in line one day waiting for coffee when a gentleman behind him started talking with his companion about another person, someone he had interviewed. He said a few things about how much this woman made and how he didn't understand why she was doing what she was doing. The companion listened and didn't offer his opinion. Guess who was standing in line in front of them.

It was the husband of the woman being discussed, listening to every single word. Even though one of the gentlemen didn't say anything about her, he was guilty by association. Her husband went home and gave his interpretation of what had happened, and she ended up not going to work for the man in the conversation. Honestly, even though he didn't say anything harmful, I totally understand why. Even if you're not the one saying something, if you fail to stop the conversation that shouldn't be happening, you're a participant and guilty.

Think about it in reverse. What if someone was saying something about you, and one of the people listening was your confidant who said nothing to stop the conversation from continuing? Were they allowing and participating in an inappropriate conversation? Maybe your feelings would change toward that so-called confidant. We need to know when to stop conversations and when to keep them going.

I participate in a lot of meetings. There's one person in particular who, once given the opportunity to speak, does not know when to stop. All the other participants like this person, but when the speaking starts, they all know it probably won't end for quite a while. This causes most of them to tune out. That person is way less effective because they speak too often and are not concise when they do. So what do we do with this?

Before we rush to interject our idea or comment about something being said, we should ask ourselves three questions. Number one: Does something need to be said? Number two: Does something need to be said by me? Am I an influential party in this situation? If you're the professor in a science class and a student says something that's not scientifically accurate, everyone in the class will look to that science professor for the correct information. If you're the authority on the subject, you may need to speak up.

And number three: Does something need to be said by me right now? There are many times when addressing that particular situation after the matter is more effective. Maybe you would embarrass the person, which would be counterproductive if you spoke up. Often, a well-placed one-on-one conversation (or many) is far more effective than addressing things immediately and causing animosity in the moment. You have to determine what your best move may be.

Someone advised me to ask these three questions before saying something, and it has served me well, especially in business meetings. Too often, people don't ask themselves these questions. Then it goes both ways: People who should have said something don't, and people ramble on and talk about irrelevant things. Which are you, and how can asking yourself these questions help your business?

If you can master knowing when to speak by asking yourself these questions and begin to accurately predict when speaking will have a meaningful impact (versus when you are wasting your breath), you will find your words are more effective, which is a much more productive approach toward successful business relations.

Less Is More

Have you ever met a chronic oversharer? Maybe you haven't heard this term before, but I believe you should be familiar with it. Someone who overshares tells you every last little detail, so much so that it's painful. You can't walk away from these people because they just talk your ear off. Another example of oversharing is when a work meeting that should have ended quickly goes on and on. As you leave the room, you turn to your neighbor and say, "I think we could have gotten all that information in a two-minute email." Less would have been so much more in this case.

When dealing with clients, sometimes we want to give them so much value that we beat their attention to death. Perhaps all they need is a small portion of what we can share, but we want to give so much value that we end up oversharing or overdoing. Don't mistake this for going above and beyond out of kindness.

What I'm specifically talking about is oversharing information. How often have you been in a situation where halfway through sharing the information, you go, "Oh no. I shared too much, and now I can't go back." When I think of oversharing, I think of it as the little ghosts in a Pac-Man game. I am Pac-Man trying to eat the little pellets, and every time I overshare, I release a ghost. My goal is to get through the conversation by eating all the pellets and not getting killed by the ghosts, my oversharing. Some of those ghosts might be things like bringing up something that wasn't a concern or even a potential concern. But now that you've brought it up . . . the other party says they hadn't thought of that. You were almost finished, and that Pac-Man ghost got you because of your oversharing. Now you have to pick up extra pellets before you can level up and move on to the next deal.

I'm not saying you shouldn't disclose important, relevant information but *only* disclose the relevant information. If I'm selling some delicious food, I don't start talking to people about how salmonella outbreaks have been killing people around the world. What do you think would happen if I did that? The person wasn't worried about salmonella, but now they're looking at your tasty food like it's a salmonella-infested swimming pool. This is an example of ill-timed oversharing. Now, if you're worried that salmonella could have contaminated your food, then sure, talk about it. But otherwise, that's not a relevant topic. No one will think you're super smart because you read something about a salmonella outbreak. This is where less is more.

How do you stop yourself from oversharing? Plan ahead, be ready with your relevant topics, and stick to those. When talking about business, there's little room for error or oversharing if you want to be successful. Sometimes, people will trick you into oversharing. People usually do this by asking an open-ended question like, "Tell me more about that." Focus on the goal, and remember that just because someone asks you a question does not mean you need to answer. If you find yourself being cornered with your back against the ropes, they're probably trying to get you to overshare.

You can respond in one of several ways. First, push back gently: "I think I've shared pretty much everything I have or have available on the topic." Second, put it back on them: "What part don't you understand?" You can do this in a friendly manner and make it more inquisitive. You don't have to draw a line in the sand. You can make it cordial: "I appreciate your curiosity; let me think on that some more."

But why would someone want to trick me into oversharing? Because knowledge is power. The more they know about anything, the more options they have to address the situation. Small details you might think are irrelevant can suddenly be flipped on their head and become the most relevant portion of a conversation. Don't release the ghosts. They may not pop up during the conversation you're in the middle of today, but something you said a week ago, two weeks ago, could come back to haunt you.

This is such a difficult balance. You want to be friendly, relaxed, and conversational, but you don't want to overshare information that will come back to bite you later. I admit this can be challenging. I find if I stick to the one relevant topic and don't wander off the path toward all sorts of other wonderful things, I'm able to keep from oversharing. You often know when you're about to say something you shouldn't. You get the feeling in your gut that they're asking you for information you probably shouldn't share. If you have that feeling, it's for a reason. Listen to it. It's much easier not to say something when it's questionable than to say and regret it, sometimes for the rest of your life.

When You Are the Recipient of Oversharing

Oversharing can sometimes benefit you when you're the recipient. When others overshare with you, keep this in mind: These are little nuggets of information you wouldn't have otherwise. You may want to keep track of some of these things because they may help you later. You need to be strategic, not evil. Try never to put people in a bad situation by getting them to overshare and then using it against them later. When you have the knowledge to protect yourself against something, you realize how vulnerable other people are. This is when being a good human being comes into play. Use words and information as a shield. Don't use them as a sword. This means if something of value comes up, note it, but don't go after somebody with it. If the information is relevant and could save you from what I'll call ill-fated situations, use it as a defense.

I realized that when people do have ill intentions, karma follows them. I don't have to be the one to make sure they learn their lesson. Does this speak to you? You've probably already identified a few times when you overshared. Anytime you're about ready to overshare, go back to the main point of the conversation and stick with that. Don't release the ghosts.

Logic Gets You the Appointment, Emotion Gets You the Sale

I think it's important to understand the difference between logic and emotion and the part that each piece plays in the sales process.

Logic is how you get people to take notice of things. An example would be telling someone, "You really need to eat your vegetables because you don't want to be unhealthy." This logic will probably get the person to stop and take notice that they probably need to eat more vegetables and that they also would like to stay healthier. The problem with logic is that it doesn't usually inspire action. Do you feel inspired to grow vegetables or stop by the grocery store, buy a bunch of vegetables, and cook them up tonight by hearing that? I didn't; it sounds like work.

We've established that logic can get you to take notice, but it doesn't usually inspire you to action. So how do you inspire people to action? First, it truly should be something that is good for the person. They have to feel motivated and inspired to take action. Something that might spark emotion in someone is talking specifically about their situation. Using the earlier food example, you might say, "Did you know that if you cut out soda, you could lose ten pounds a year on average? Just by simply cutting that out, you can make a huge difference in the look and feel of your body. Can you imagine what you would feel like if you were ten pounds lighter and could run longer distances? That could be amazing for you, couldn't it?"

Now, I'm speaking about something they want, something they may be striving for. Part of the inspiration process is showing someone they can achieve the goal. That it's right there, and all they have to do is reach out and grab it.

In business, we do a lot of talking logically, and we should help people realize their goals by inspiring them as well. Most people are afraid of failure and need someone to lead them on the successful path they believe they can complete. Are you that person? Try using logic and inspiration today. Get people to take notice of something by speaking logically with them. If you know they desire to achieve something tied to the topic you are discussing, encourage them and inspire emotion in them so they can achieve their goal.

It's funny: When you inspire others, you, too, become inspired. If you inspire people toward things that are truly good for them, you will have an ongoing, life-changing experience. So go out and inspire people and never look back again.

Getting the Buy-In

Have you ever noticed that when you're talking to someone and they are not interested in what you're saying, their eyes wander, or they keep checking their phone? Or maybe you ask them a question, and they ask you to repeat it because you didn't have their attention? They're completely detached from the conversation. It's because you don't have their buy-in. You can easily tell when you have someone's buy-in because they're 100 percent attentive and interested in what you're saying. It's almost like you have them eating out of your hand. You ask them a question, and they're like, "Where do I sign up?" They clearly see the value of what you're offering. They buy into the outcome. They want what you have to offer.

You cannot assume that just because you are interested in something, someone else will be as well. Nine times out of ten when you're talking about something that's interesting to you, the other people become lost. You miss the mark. You can always identify if someone buys in by the amount of information they offer. You ask for a name and phone number, and they give it to you immediately and ask if you need anything else. That's the sign of a 100 percent buy-in. The willingness to participate is apparent.

So how do you deal with someone who is obviously not interested? You win them over. You need to solicit their buy-in. But how do you do that when they're brushing you off and are clearly not interested? Just ask. Over and over, I've found that if you ask people what's interesting to them, they will actually tell you exactly what they want to hear. They'll let you know what they value and what they want. All you have to do is simply ask. How could it be this easy? From my experience, it really is. Pose the question and just wait and watch. They'll tell you everything.

Occasionally, you run into somebody who takes a bit more time to open up. If you follow up and say, "I just really want to know," indicating your genuine interest, then bingo bango, here comes the answer. It's like you're playing a video game and hit a bonus round that gives you all the secrets. Once they tell you everything they're interested in hearing about, tailor your whole conversation to exactly what they told you to talk about. Now you have the exact road map to their 100 percent buy-in. You're talking about what they want to hear about. How do you know? Because they told you.

Now we can get into how to keep people's attention once you have it. This is the creative part. Somebody tells you they want to hear about puppies and how cute they are. Or about plants and how to grow them successfully. I don't care what it is; you need to come up with an interesting story that captivates them yet answers the questions they have and shows them value. If you can do this for something that is interesting to them, you will earn the buy-in.

Where many people go wrong is that they don't create any kind of story or ask any questions to lead the person to a successful outcome. Getting people to buy in is simple if you know what they want. If you're looking for a red car, and someone asks you what you're looking for, and you say a red car, suddenly, they are talking about red cars, and you're interested. You're invested in the outcome because you have a need. It's not rocket science; you ask what people need, and then you repackage it in a way they can easily understand. That's how they can see the value or a successful outcome.

Storytelling is a vital part of the discovery process. Two people could be pitching the same thing, but one has no story at all, and the other has a captivating story. Hands down, the person with the captivating story wins almost every time. Stories are a way we can identify with different situations. If we can imagine ourselves as the characters and identify with how they feel, we are emotionally invested. Logical information doesn't inspire most people, but emotion can move mountains. Each situation is so different, but one thing is the same: If you know what people are looking for and show them that you have it available, they will be all ears. Now get that buy-in and watch people listen to you.

Take Out "I" and "Me"

One thing that's very important for every conversation is to take "I" and "me" out of the conversation. People typically do not care about you when trying to make any decision that can shape their future success, from small decisions to the critical ones that will potentially affect the rest of their lives. It's crucial to solicit what is important to them, and the whole situation gets derailed when we start using "I" and "me" in the conversation. Let me give you an example. "I think this house would be good for you. If it were me, I would move forward in purchasing this." In both statements, the person you're talking to feels you value your opinion more than theirs.

Now let me give you an example of a salesperson saying the same thing without the words "I" and "me." First, you were attentive and took notes on what would be best for them before commenting. Then, you frame it like this: "Others have been pleased when purchasing a house like this. You need to find out if this is good for you." In the new scenario, you have successfully guided the person you're talking to.

Taking "I" and "me" out of conversations takes practice. Begin by practicing communicating without using I and me. Instead of saying I think, say things like "Others have said," or "Do you think," or "It seems to be a great option." Many people default to the standard communication method of giving unfiltered opinions about anything asked. In most cases, people want an idea of the best way to move forward but don't want to be told what to do, especially if someone is putting their own interest in front of the customer's.

This is where a lot of salespeople go wrong. When you serve someone, you need to ensure that they see you are servicing them and, foremost, make sure they understand that you are putting their needs above yours. Many people have heard the story about the sleazy used-car salesperson at the other end of the sale who's waiting to prey on somebody. Why do people have that idea about them? It's probably because that sleazy salesperson obviously doesn't care about the person they are selling to. The customer is just a means to an end. Make more progress by doing what's best for others; they will notice.

Ask Better Questions

One thing I have learned is that most people are creatures of habit. Most people are not deep thinkers who calculate their every move. It's more realistic to think people default to certain tendencies. If I like coffee, I drive to the local coffee shop and order the same coffee time after time. Seldom do I change because I know what I like. I think people are like this in conversations as well. They know what they like and feel is safe, and they don't change from that often.

We live in a time when many are trying to impose radical ideas and strange ways of thinking. So, how do you help people realize something is in their best interest without making them feel manipulated? You ask several yes questions leading up to the last question. Let me give you an example. You're in a store, and you are helping someone who told you they need a new shirt. They've given you a few details to work with, and you know which shirt they should buy. But you can't just tell them, "This is the shirt you need to buy." They need to realize it's the shirt they need to buy. "You said you wanted a form-fitting shirt, correct?" They respond yes. "You also said you wanted it to have buttons, correct?" They respond yes. "And blue is your favorite color?" They respond yes. "Well, it looks like this shirt has everything you're looking for. Do you feel like this is the right shirt?" What do you think the last answer is most likely to be?

People prefer to have things work easily. In this instance, the salesperson did all the heavy lifting by going through the criteria set by the customer before looking at shirts. They walked the customer back through their own criteria and showed them how the answer was right in front of them. This enabled the buyer of the shirt not to have to go through the process of elimination on their own. Most of their internal questions were addressed, and the easy answer was yes.

Now, take that same situation, but start asking a lot of random questions about whether the customer likes this shirt or that shirt or what have you. They probably would have been there looking at shirts for a long time. Most people know what they want, but they don't know how to identify it easily. By taking the several yes steps, you can help them determine what's in their best interest and offer a solution, so all they have to do is say yes. Suppose I asked a bunch of no questions, then asked if this was the right shirt. What do you think the result would be? It's the same shirt; it's still what they're looking for, so why would they have a hard time saying yes? It's because they're in the "no mode." Most of the time, if they are in the no mode, they will default to the easy solution, which is to push away the option and just say no. It's easier and safer, so most people default to no rather than yes. Help them find the yes by asking several yes questions before getting to the final question. Do you think this can help you?

Tell a Story

Let's talk about one of the most epic stories of all time. There was a girl whose father died, and he married this evil lady who treated the girl badly. One day, a prince was looking for someone to marry. The girl went to a ball after somebody helped her get all dressed up, and she lost a shoe. Later, the prince found her because her foot was the right size to fit the shoe. The End. Because I have three little girls, I know the story of Cinderella. This story inspired generations, yet did I do the story a disservice by the way I told it? I think so; do you feel inspired? Are you going to be thinking about this story all night? I doubt it.

The reason is that I rushed through the story and only gave a level of detail that was anything but inspiring. So what does Cinderella have to do with winning? Most people interpret the stories in their heads, and their conclusions don't always line up with your meaning. I can almost always guarantee that if they are left to interpret the story on their own because you did not elaborate or clearly communicate the story, it will not be the story you thought you told. As I've said before, logic gets you an appointment, and emotion gets people to move. If they miss the meaning of the story because you did not tell it clearly, you will most likely miss the opportunity to inspire them. One way to build emotion is to walk people through a story about what their success can look like. If I were to ask someone their goal and then walk them through the whole journey, what it will look like with a little taste of what it will feel like, so much so that they get excited about the end of their story, then they could see the result. They could walk through the story you offered about how everything will take place. It is a very simple way to inspire people into action if they believe it'll actually end with a win. Most people picture the opposite in their heads. They don't get past the evil stepmother ruining their life. It is your job to paint a winning picture in the form of a story.

Why don't most of us do this to begin with? There are several reasons. Most of the time, it is because we are too rushed. We think people inherently know they can win. Or we're just too lazy to take extra steps that will lay out a situation for success. If you don't take the time at the beginning of the situation to create a story that paints a successful path through the process, you will have to take extra time during or at the end of the process to clean up all of the mess and potentially lose the whole deal, all because you didn't tell a good story that the people understood, and as a result, your entire sale derailed. Either way, you're spending the time, so you can either set yourself up for success or set yourself up for failure.

Set yourself up for success by taking the extra time in the beginning, walking people through the entire process and inspiring them with a great story about how their story will lead to their success. You will end up with happier customers and less stress during the process.

4. The Art of Listening and Responding

Delves into the importance of listening to understand, answering the question that should have been asked, using the wraparound technique, and dealing with problems head-on.

●●●

"GREATER IS THE ONE WHO LISTENS BEFORE SPEAKING than the one who speaks, then listens." What if every time you said something, everyone stopped and listened, hung on every word, and refused to make even a peep until you had fully expressed yourself? How would you feel? I am willing to bet you would feel pretty important and understood.

When was the last time someone did this for you? A better question might be, when did you last do this for someone else?

We live in a time when everyone is trying to be heard, and very few listen to understand. In the news, we see people talking over one another, or perhaps we scroll through social media, and all we see are people trying to be heard. Think about all the commercials and ads trying to capture our attention so they can tell us something. What if there is a better way to navigate this noise?

Thankfully, I believe there is. The greatest chess players of all time look at their opponents' moves before deciding how they will position their pieces. Some would argue that to become a master chess player, one must be semi-intelligent. If we can agree this is true, then perhaps we should look at how they master the art of chess. They wait for their opponent to move, then they move accordingly. When the chess players are fatigued or impatient, they don't look at the chessboard as clearly and may miss moves they should have seen or anticipated. This results in losing pieces or the entire game.

Let's take this same strategy and utilize it in our conversations. While others we are in conversations with most likely won't be opponents, we should look at the situation with the same level of attention. When dealing with an opponent, we are on high alert, and we should utilize the same level of awareness in our important conversations. Let others speak; we listen intently, thinking about what they said and then giving the best response while anticipating where they are going with the conversation. While you may not be a master chess player, you can become a master of listening and responding. Take a few moves from the next sections of the book. You may learn something that will change the way you view your conversations.

Timing Can Be Everything

Imagine you're watching the biggest basketball game of the season. The clock's ticking, and it gets down to the final seconds. The star player looks around, steps back, and shoots, just as the clock counts down to end the game, he scores. Such amazing timing. Because he shot when he did, at the last second, he won the game for his team. What a great example of perfect timing.

Now, let's take that same basketball player, and instead of taking the final shot at the last second, he waits, and the timer expires just as he's trying to shoot. Not such great timing anymore, huh? He lost his opportunity.

Have you ever been in a conversation when somebody walks in and talks about the exact same thing? Another example of perfect timing. Have you been to a comedy show where the comedian is nailing it; his timing is perfect, and everything is just flowing, which sucks in the whole audience, and they're rolling with laughter. Those are all examples of perfect timing. But what about the other side of the coin?

There's a time and a place for everything. There's also the wrong time and the wrong place for everything. For example, if

I want a raise at work, I probably shouldn't ask when my boss is upset about the recent earnings report. The timing would be much better if I asked after having a phenomenal month of sales. Timing can be critical with everything. If you're watching a comedy show and the timing is off, all of a sudden, those great jokes are not funny anymore. It's not because the content isn't good but because the timing is off.

Many of our conversations are high stakes, meaning success or failure could follow. So how do we make sure our timing is correct? We do this by putting ourselves in other people's shoes and examining the situations around us. You can also do this by asking a couple of questions and getting a feel for the situation before acting. You want to do your best to make sure the person is receptive to whatever you're talking about. And if they are, the timing could be correct. If you're getting a lot of signs that they're distracted, they're in a rush, or otherwise not receptive, the timing may be off, and you may want to choose a different time to address the topic.

Driving the Conversation

There are times when people may not be receptive, and they are avoiding the conversation. Most of the time, this happens because they know the conversation you want to have. Sometimes you need to push the envelope a bit and create timing for that conversation. An example of this was a high producer who, for whatever reason, did not enjoy working with their office manager. Every time the manager tried to set a time to talk, that person was busy. Every time the manager saw they were available, the manager would try to sneak in to finally have a conversation, but it didn't matter what the manager did, the high-producing employee was not open to having any time for the manager. So one day, after the manager tried everything to be understanding, they decided to let the high producer know that the time was now, and they weren't going to be waiting any longer—the conversation was happening that day. This went over about as well as you can imagine, but the high producer made time to talk right then. This is an example of being a driver—watching for an opportunity, taking advantage of the timing, and making the conversation happen now.

This technique of forcing the timing of situations isn't always recommended. In fact, I suggest using this only as a last resort, but I use it to illustrate how some people will never make time, and the timing will never be right. In those situations, you have a decision to make. Will you force it or not? For the majority of people, opportunities randomly appear to make it the right moment.

There's a saying that a cheerful greeting too early in the morning will be considered a curse (Proverbs 27:14 NIV). If somebody's going through something difficult, you want to be understanding. If somebody's on top of the world, you don't want to rain on their parade. Part of timing is matching people where they are, and you can only do this by identifying where they are beforehand. Ask yourself these questions to make sure the timing is correct.

✦ Have I seen this situation before? What happened?

✦ If I ask the question or take action now, will it be off-putting?

✦ Will it create more opportunity for me to ask at a different time?

When you're able to identify the right timing and take advantage of it, you'll be hitting the game-winning goals and making strides like you've never made before. Things will be clicking perfectly. Part of this success comes just from practicing your timing. Most of us have no idea what the right timing is for things, but if we put our ears to the ground, open our eyes, and look for clues, we'll discover the right time. We benefit from using the correct timing because timing is everything.

Persistence

Have you ever been told no about something and found out later that someone else was able to get the yes? You think back to the situation and say to yourself, "I asked all the questions, I kept on getting dead ends, and no one would say yes. I don't know how other people have navigated the same situation and gotten through it with a yes." This has happened to me on many occasions. I kept running into roadblocks, and other people kept getting the green light to proceed.

So, I have a rule: Ask three times in three different ways before giving up. That way, you make sure no is really no.

Never Accept a No from Someone Who Can't Give You a Yes

But even before you ask the first time, remember that if the person telling you no doesn't have the authority to say yes, then you're talking to the wrong person. The person who could say yes may have instructed the people below them to just say no.

Here's another rule: Never take no for an answer from someone who can't tell you yes.

When I think about this particular rule, I'm reminded of a story. Someone who owned a real estate company before the real estate market crash in 2008 lost everything over the few years that followed, and they had to declare bankruptcy; we'll call him Bob. If you've ever talked to someone who has gone bankrupt, you realize that no one wants to give them credit right after bankruptcy. Bad credit was new territory for Bob; he had previously enjoyed some of the highest credit scores available. Bob had heard it said that banks would give you money when you didn't need it but then wouldn't give you money when you did, and he found that to be true in his situation.

Fast forward: After going bankrupt, Bob needed a credit card again. He had a good job and was making good money but needed a way to rebuild his credit. Apparently, Bob never chose to do things the easy way, so he asked the largest bank in the industry for a credit card.

Bob called the bank and spoke with a kind woman who told him, "We do not give credit cards to people who have gone bankrupt." Next, Bob asked, "Do you have the ability to say yes?" The woman finally admitted she did not. Bob then asked to speak to her supervisor, who was also a nice man. Bob explained the situation to him, how he had struggled as an owner through the real estate crash, now he had a good job, and he was looking to restore his credit rating. The man gave the same answer: the bank did not offer credit cards to people who had gone bankrupt.

Bob spoke to five different people, told each of them the same details, and received the same response from each one. Now, they were not mean, nasty, or short with him. They tried their best to be kind and thoughtful in the way they communicated. But what Bob learned was that none of the people from the bank actually had the authority to say yes. When he spoke with the sixth and final gentleman, Bob asked him, "Do you actually have the authority to say yes if it makes sense?," and the gentleman admitted he did.

Bob realized he was now talking to the right person. He described his situation in great detail, explaining how he had an impeccable repayment history except for the bankruptcy (which, by the way, is a pretty big blemish on your repayment history). Bob explained he would be happy to continue utilizing their bank and its services, but he needed a credit card.

After close to an hour of back-and-forth, the banker relented and said, "I'm going to give you a $500 credit card. I have to put my personal guarantee on it that you are going to repay. Do not screw this up." Bob promised he would take the utmost care, and guess what? He still has the same credit card today. (If you are wondering, his limit is much higher than $500 now.) But he wouldn't have been able to build his credit back without that simple credit card. And he wouldn't have been able to make any of it happen had he accepted no from someone who couldn't have given a yes. Even if he had asked any of the others more than three different ways, they would have still denied him the credit card. The point here is persistence.

If I know I am talking to someone who can't give me a yes to help me proceed, I'm talking to the wrong person. And as far as taking a no from someone that can't give you a yes—I'm willing to bet you have something right now that you got a no on and are rethinking how you can go back and speak to the right person or ask that person several different ways.

Ask for the Discount

This tactic used to embarrass my wife, but anytime we are at a store of any sort where I'm making a large purchase, I ask if there are any discounts. Then I ask if there are any coupons. Then I'll ask, "Are you sure there isn't anything going on right now that would reduce the price?" You will be surprised by how many times there is some kind of discount by the end of the third question; it pops out of nowhere. My wife didn't believe me on this at first, but now she does the same thing because she's seen it work so many times.

Now, if we're not limiting things to credit cards or department store purchases, what could you ask for in three different ways that might give you traction? Maybe it's asking someone to assist you with something? "Would you be able to help me with this sales presentation?" "Are you sure you can't help me present this weekend?" "I know they will be difficult, and with your experience, I think we can win. Would you be open to a least stopping by?" No matter what it is, ask in three different ways, and you will be amazed by the response.

Is this a surefire way to always win? No. But this is the best way to get you to a yes that I have found. Remember these three things: Always be relatable; people want to help people like them win. Always be kind; people usually want to help good people. And it doesn't hurt to have a good, reasonable story. This will back up the reason why they should tell you yes. With these newfound tools in your tool bag, get to work. You've got some yeses to get.

Not Why, but How

Have you ever asked someone why they did something? When you understand what drove people to make the decisions, you can figure out the best way to address the situation.

A couple of young men decided it would be a good idea to jump off the roof of their one-story house. When one of the men's girlfriends came home and found them jumping off their roof, she asked her boyfriend why. His response: "I don't know; I just thought it'd be fun." I'm pretty sure that wasn't the end of the conversation and can only imagine the conversations that came after it. The interesting thing was that the men probably hadn't put much thought into what they were doing. The question the girlfriend asked about why they were doing that enabled the man to give a nonanswer.

What if you could ask a better question that led to outlining all the thinking about why someone made the decision they did? I bet it would be helpful and would bring a lot more understanding to the table.

When you get a surface-level answer like "I don't know," "Because I just wanted to," or "I just did," you don't have an answer for how they ended up where they're at. While I don't suspect you'll come home and catch people jumping off your roof, I do think you will be confronted with situations where someone will do something bothersome or off-putting.

I will give you one of the most valuable tips someone taught me. Don't ask why; ask how they made the decision. If the young man's girlfriend had come home and diffused the situation, then asked how they decided to jump off the roof, she probably would have gotten some answers like "We were talking, and one of the guys said they could jump higher than the other without getting hurt, so we all decided that would be good to see. So we did a contest, and just about when someone was going to win the contest, you came home." I'm not saying this is the answer she would want. But look at all the extra information she got. She now understands how everything took place.

In business, if someone decides not to move forward with something, I would argue that you shouldn't ask why. A better question is "How did you decide this?" If you can figure out their thought process, you can unlock a lot more possibilities. Many times, when I ask this question, I uncover a big misunderstanding.

Perhaps they think they will need to pay for something additional. Maybe they think another person isn't on board with them moving forward. The list can go on and on and on. The point is when you ask how, the person can describe their thought process to you, giving you a lot more information to work with. This will allow you the opportunity to be strategic and correct any kind of misinformation. If this is someone you work with regularly, they'll explain exactly how they process through and make decisions. When you understand how people think, you're positioning yourself to help them arrive at their best goal.

Quality over Quantity

Some people look at customers as a numbers game. If someone says no, you take it, and you move on. I look at it as a quality game. Someone says no, you figure out how they decided, you interject into the situation and help that one reach their goal. Start practicing this today. Next time you want to ask why, ask how instead, and watch the magic happen.

Slow Is Fast, and Fast Is Slow

We live in a world of go, go, go. Don't tell me to be slow because then I'll lose. I assume most of you have heard Aesop's fable about the tortoise and the hare. It goes something like this: A tortoise and a hare are in a race. The hare starts superfast and runs and runs and runs and then decides he's so far ahead of the tortoise that he's going to take a nap. In the meantime, the tortoise keeps taking steps forward and slowly moves past the superfast hare, who is sound asleep. The tortoise wins the race—not because of speed, but because of a thoughtful process that was also consistent.

Here's how this affects us at a sales level. I've recently been working with a bunch of people on cold calling. First of all, if you haven't cold-called before, it can be very intimidating. When I started making some cold calls, I was scared about it. The only way to overcome that fear was consistent practice. In other words, by doing it. Let's get back to the point. Slow is fast, and fast is slow. When I'm making cold calls and the person on the other end does not know me, I have a much higher success rate when I slow down the conversation, listen for cues, and take the correct steps forward in the conversation. This is the opposite of quickly asking some questions and then hanging up if you get a no.

WORDS THAT IDENTIFY HOW THE OTHER PERSON IS FEELING

Here's a simple breakdown of common words associated with different emotions that are frequently used in everyday conversations.

Positive Emotions
Excited: happy, pumped, thrilled, glad
Happy: joyful, cheerful, content, pleased
Thrilled: delighted, excited, overjoyed
Great: awesome, fantastic, amazing, superb
Wonderful: amazing, fantastic, awesome, great

Neutral Emotions
Okay: fine, all right, good, acceptable
Fine: okay, good, all right, satisfactory
All right: okay, fine, good, satisfactory
So-so: okay, average, not bad, neutral
Normal: typical, regular, usual, average

Negative Emotions
Upset: sad, bothered, troubled, unhappy
Frustrated: annoyed, irritated, upset, bothered
Annoyed: irritated, bothered, upset, frustrated

When I coached someone recently, we discussed this very topic. I explained, "You're going to take extra time at the beginning (meaning slowing it down) or extra time at the end (making a ton more calls). We can have a much more successful close rate if we take a little extra time at the beginning to consider what's needed in that conversation rather than looking for a super easy conversation. If we get better at the conversations we are having,

Angry: mad, upset, furious, enraged
Disappointed: let down, sad, unhappy, upset
Stressed: anxious, worried, tense, pressured
Concerned: worried, troubled, anxious, bothered

Anxious or Uncertain
Worried: concerned, nervous, uneasy
Nervous: worried, uneasy, afraid, scared
Unsure: doubtful, uncertain, hesitant, apprehensive
Anxious: worried, nervous, concerned, uneasy
Confused: mixed up, puzzled, unsure, baffled
Doubtful: unsure, hesitant, skeptical, uncertain

Enthusiasm or Interest
Curious: interested, curious, eager to know
Interested: curious, intrigued, eager, fascinated
Eager: excited, enthusiastic, keen, eager
Intrigued: interested, curious, fascinated
Keen: excited, interested, eager, enthusiastic
Enthusiastic: excited, eager, passionate, thrilled

These simple words can help express or identify emotions in everyday conversations without needing a more complex vocabulary.

we can have half of them because we're going to be so successful at closing the conversations we do have."

The old way of doing things was to make enough calls that someone finally said yes. It's a numbers game, and it's probably correct. But what if 90 percent of the people you talk to could be a yes, but you simply didn't take the proper steps by slowing down and asking the right questions to find out what someone wants and needs? I say slowing down and having quality conversations is a much faster way to success than having bulk conversations. Here's a bonus tip: Most people stay in their heads when they're having bulk conversations. They have a specific script; they're not paying attention to any kind of social cues, emotions, or hints from the other party. When you are present and not just using your head but also your heart, you can hear the frustration in the other person's voice and ask them, "Has this been a stressful situation for you? Would you like some help with it?" It's amazing how, when people feel the sincerity and care on the other end, the whole process of connection speeds up.

Dealing with Problems Head-On

I know this is hard to believe, but in most situations, there will be disagreement. The more intricate the sale, the more opportunity there is for this disagreement. Someone once asked a billionaire how he dealt with problems. He said, "Focus on the biggest problem first. Solve it. Then move on to the next one. Keep going, step by step, until every challenge is handled. When you handle your problems like this, nothing is too big to overcome."

This was a valuable piece of information because I try to be strategically minded. In the past, when faced with a disagreement, I thought maybe I would need to talk to this person in a certain way and then wait a day or so and then talk to another person. But, in fact, someone who's made a billion dollars has a simple approach of hitting problems head-on and not letting them fester.

How can we apply this as a strategy to help us shut up and win? When there are disagreements, people often don't stick to the actual issue. They go off into la-la land and hope to convolute everything so much that they will win on some front. The reason they do this is because their actual position is not strong. So how do you combat this tactic? When you're speaking with someone, bring the conversation back to the point of contention. If I have a disagreement with someone's comments and, when I bring it up, they say something about something I did a week ago, I bring the discussion right back to the point of contention that we were initially discussing. I say something like, "We can talk about what I did last week, but what I'm talking about right now and what we're dealing with right now is what we need to deal with first." People will still try to squirm out of dealing with the issue at hand if they're not in a strong position. You may need to bring it back to the same point three, four, or five times.

Ultimately, if we keep bringing the conversation back to that specific issue, we will remain focused, and the issue will not be derailed but dealt with instead. I say, be relentless about bringing it back to the point. Don't let others lead the conversation or the direction of the discussion. Take the lead, and bring the conversation right back to the main point of contention until it's dealt with or acknowledged. Then, when you are ready, let it go.

Use the Wraparound Technique

One day, a couple of friends were jogging along a beach in California, where some people exercise or run alongside a beach wall. The friends met there regularly to do workouts by running up and down the long walkway and giant stairs. As they ran along one day, they noticed another man practicing his fighting moves. Being familiar with mixed martial arts (MMA), one of the men asked what he trained in. He responded, "I trained in it all." They again asked if he'd trained in anything specific. He said, "I do the wraparound." Puzzled by what that meant, one friend asked him to explain. The man said, "Whatever you throw at me, I'll wrap it around and kick your ass." The friends giggled a little, talked to the man for a few minutes longer, and then went on their way.

What they didn't know was that the simple phrase would inspire a lot of action. You see people come at you with all sorts of words or actions, and if you can wrap it around and use it back on them, it kicks their butt. Most people can't handle what they give out.

How I've used this: When someone becomes irate and starts yelling on the phone, I'll use their own words against them to help paint them into a corner. Most people will use the best argument they can come up with against you. Maybe you make a sales call, and the person says your products are horrible, and they would never buy such a product. This is the attack. This is where you can wrap it around on them. "So you would never use a product like this that could help you improve your business?" you respond. "Have you seen how your competitors are doing 20 percent more sales by using this successfully?" They are suddenly at a loss for words. Why? Because you wrapped it around on them. Even if it's their best argument, if you use it back against them, people crumble most of the time. If they don't crumble, they struggle to find a new best argument. Most of the time, though, they just get upset and become completely ineffective. Take what someone uses against you, wrap it around, and kick their proverbial ass with it.

The man on the beach was a trained MMA fighter. The people you are most likely to encounter are not using their fists but are using their words instead. If you study MMA, you know it's really not barbaric. You have two people in the center of a cage trying to anticipate each other's next move; they counter that move, effectively protecting themselves against the flurry. This goes back and forth for three to five rounds. And then, when the right opportunity presents itself—bam—they lay their opponent out on the floor. They win the fight with one well-placed punch—the punches being well-placed words—and the knockout comes when the other person gives up on the conversation.

If you're a fly on the wall when two people are in the middle of an epic strategic argument, you will notice all these tactics come to life. The question becomes what your strategy is when it comes to disagreement. Most people don't have one. They're just the skinny kid in the middle of the cage waiting to get pummeled. Have a plan, and think about how you can wrap around anything that someone throws at you and use it back against them. If you can do this effectively, you will learn verbal skills no one will want to go against. And last but not least, remember, not everyone needs a wraparound; save it for the people who truly deserve it.

If You Can't Beat Them, Surround Them

I'm a sucker for action movies. Especially those where the action is one-on-one: two guys duke it out, and one prevails. *Rocky* is a great action movie. A boxer gets beat and beat and beat, and eventually, just at the very last minute, overcomes this huge obstacle and beats the opponent. When we're dealing with real issues in the workplace (or anywhere, for that matter), we hope we'll be like Rocky. We duke it out, duke it out, and duke it out, and eventually, in the end, we somehow pull it off with a win.

You often have to defend yourself from other salespeople who are trying to get the same clients, or worse, other people in the workplace who don't want you around as a competitor any longer. They're more like the boogeyman waiting for you to fall asleep so they can get you. The difference between these two adversaries is that one is very intentional and shows you they're your adversary, and the other one does not show you they're your adversary but instead does things at every opportunity to undermine you with your work colleagues. In situations where the other person is very cunning and knows how to pull strings, they are well-equipped to undermine you at every turn and are strategic in their approach.

This is a dangerous combo. I'll tell you what someone told me. If you can't beat them, surround them. What does this mean? When someone's out to get you, or at least out to undermine you (maybe they're trying to get your work position or trying to give you the opportunity to be successful somewhere else), the only way they can typically do this is by using the players (other coworkers or individuals) around them. So, if you strategically put the people you trust around them and your supporters surround them, at every turn, you've essentially neutralized the threat. It's even better if they don't realize you've surrounded them. But if they do realize this, they will probably try to squirm out of the situation by going above you.

Part of surrounding them is successfully anticipating what move they will make next. Simply put yourself in your opponent's shoes. Ask yourself what you would do strategically, and nine times out of ten, that's what their next step will be. If you know they could go above you, you can easily have a conversation with the person above you to alert them. That way, it's already been brought up. While the adversary may be bigger, faster, and stronger than you, when they are completely surrounded, the strength of your group should be enough to turn the tide in your favor. You will probably find that if the adversary can't get their way, they won't hang around.

This is an extreme tactic, and you should only use it when you've tried everything else to no avail. Now remember, if you're in the ring, don't just hope you'll be able to make it through with one lucky punch in the end. Be strategic and set yourself up for success by surrounding your opponent with the people in your corner.

Don't Feed the Dog

Sometimes we reward people for bad behavior by giving in and answering the question we shouldn't have. We don't say anything when somebody crosses the line and oversteps boundaries. We don't mention something that bothered us because we're afraid of what the reaction might be. All of this sets a bad example and feeds the behavior we don't want. Like animals in a zoo, the more you feed them, the more aggressive they become about getting that food.

People sometimes approach their supervisor and say, "I'm scared to respond to my coworker. If I say the wrong thing, they're going to unload on me in a way I'm not comfortable with." If you're that supervisor, perhaps you can tell them not to feed the proverbial dog. Dogs are the same way. Imagine a dog running down the street, and it smells some food on your front porch. It now knows there's food on the front porch, and it will return to look for food again. But if it realizes that food was a one-time thing and that it won't find more there, it keeps running down the street, looking for a place to eat.

When we say, "Don't feed the dog," we're saying not to add anything to the situation or conversation. If you can do that, the other person will realize there's nothing there for them. They may say things to try to get a rise out of you, just like a dog will bark to see if you'll bring more food. But if you don't respond—you don't bring out any food for the dog—they quickly realize there's nothing there for them. They will often go and look for a new victim. The important part about this is that the victim is not you. You have now made the dog go away and look for food somewhere else (or find its next victim) by simply not reacting, not feeding the dog.

Most people feed the dog just a little bit. They try to be nice to the dog. They think if they're nice to the dog, the dog won't attack them. I have news for you. If it's a dog, you will always have the threat of it acting like a dog. There are many ways to get out of a situation when a toxic person won't leave you alone. I haven't found a better way than cutting off the food source—meaning cutting off the communication. So the next time someone comes to you and asks what they should do about this person who just won't leave them alone, tell them to quit feeding the dog and the dog will find food somewhere else. Stop feeding into what someone is looking for, and they will most likely look elsewhere.

Be a Closer

Have you ever been to an incredibly boring movie where nothing happens? It's this long, drawn-out show with no climax. You watch the whole movie, bored out of your mind, waiting for that special moment that never comes. After it ends, you ask yourself, "Why did I even bother watching that?" I can think of several movies like this, but more importantly, I can think of several salespeople I've dealt with in very similar situations.

Sales don't happen by accident; selling takes intentionality. Some people's sales tactic is just to befriend people and talk with them and hope that, at some point, they ask the question. What question is that? The closing question: "Hey, can I buy this? What's it going to take for me to leave with this? Can you please help me complete this purchase?"

I can think of many salespeople I've met who I thought would be spectacular. They had the right personality, and they warmed up to people. I thought there was no way these salespeople could fail. I was right that people liked them, but the one thing they lacked was the ability to close the deal or, in other words, ask for the business.

Now on the completely opposite side, I can think of an example where I thought a person had the personality of a doorknob, and yet, even without any personality at all, they were able to ask for the business and closed a lot of sales. This highlighted for me that being a closer is a lot more important than being a schmoozer. People can like you, you can have a good laugh, and you can build lots of rapport, but if you don't ask for the business, none of it matters.

When you mention closing, many people reference the 1992 movie *Glengarry, Glen Ross*. In this movie, the characters come up with the saying "A.B.C.," meaning "Always be closing."[10] Some of my colleagues and I sometimes joke about this acronym, but it does remind us that we need to close the deal or at least ask for the business. Why do most people not ask for the business? I truly don't know; there's a whole variety of reasons. Maybe it's the fear of being pushy. Maybe it's the fear of rejection. Maybe they're just afraid to ask and don't even know why. I do know most of the deals in business don't happen without intentionally asking people and walking them through the process of what it will take to get the deal done.

Most people haven't been through whatever process you're walking them through; some are not sure they want to go through

---

10 Foley, J. (Director). (1992). *Glengarry, Glen Ross* [Film]. Zupnick Productions.

that process with you. Both situations are okay because, ultimately, they're sitting there with you. People don't typically go to a flooring store just to hang out; they go because they need flooring. People don't go to the grocery store just to hang out; they go there because they need groceries. Whatever your business is, there is a high likelihood the person is sitting there because they want or need the services you provide. Most of the time, salespeople make it harder to do business with them than they need to because they don't realize the people already want or need their services. They ask a lot of questions to qualify potential customers, almost trying to convince them when potential customers don't need convincing. By nature, most salespeople ask a lot of questions and make it difficult for people to make an easy decision.

What they need is a clear path forward to the next step and closer to their goal.

Here's a wild idea: What if you made it easier for someone to do business with you than not to? How can you do that? Imagine going to a restaurant with two hundred things on the menu. How long will it take you to decide which item is best for you? Now imagine going to In-N-Out Burger, where there are three main items on the menu. You can choose between the three menu items pretty quickly. They make it easy. So easy that they have lines going out the doors and around the block. Not to mention, they are masters at quality control and customer service. Plus, they have delicious burgers. Make sure your products are top-notch, like theirs. They've streamlined the process. If you know that the people are there for the items or the services you are selling, why not assume they are going to do business with you?

What does this look like in practice? If I'm selling T-shirts, I don't tell the people to look at other T-shirt shops and let me know if they're still interested. After hearing what they're looking for, I tell them why we've got a great T-shirt, ask them if it's the right color and fit, and then let them know we will ring it up out front and ask if there's anything else they need. Instead, too many salespeople will ask, "What color T-shirt do you want? Do you like the feel of the fabric? Does the fit seem right? I don't want you to get something that isn't perfect." When the salesperson asks all these questions, the customer starts to second-guess themselves.

Assume the sale; it's better to assume it and be wrong than not assume and be wrong for sure. People will tell you when they don't want something, and if you are a good closer, you can lead them toward their successful outcome by making it easy. Take steps toward helping people reach the goal they state without second-guessing yourself.

Being efficient is not pushy. Most people overthink things way too much. I'm not telling you to sell people garbage. My hope is that you sell a quality product. And assuming that's the case, why wouldn't people want to buy your product or service?

Look at your sales process right now. Are you asking too many questions and steering people away from your product? Are you asking questions that make the customers feel less confident about what you're offering? If you are, streamline your process, and make it easier for people to proceed than to stop and talk to ten other companies that offer something similar. Believe in your product so much that it's easy for you to assume the sale.

The next thing on my list for you to do is to try it out. When somebody comes in looking for your products or services, give them a few options to make sure you offer what they're looking for, and then assume the sale and ask them how they want to pay for it. How? Find a unique way to do this by asking your customers questions that assume they will be doing business with you. If you are selling houses, maybe ask what kind of home they are looking for and offer to show them some right away. If you are selling ad space, ask what their goal is, have a few options pre-designed, and ask them which one they like best. My guess is you will be amazed by the results when you find new ways to close or help your customers finish their transactions. I like using humor because it can take the heat off the situation and make things run smoother. Remember that you may need to try several things before finding the right mix. The quickest way to find the right way is by doing it wrong in various ways. Go out there, find your mix, be engaging, and simplify things so you can be a closer.

5. Presenting and Negotiating with Confidence

Covers topics like dressing the part, using statistics in sales pitches, understanding motivations, and knowing when to speak. Discusses strategies like the "push and release" technique, leaving a simple out, and creating a compelling power statement.

CONFIDENCE IS A KEY INGREDIENT FOR SUCCESS. When building your career, the goal is to gain people's trust so they follow your leadership. If you lack confidence, people struggle to follow you. The sections that follow will show you how to create and project confidence rather than fake it.

Some people think that to be confident, you must know all the answers to all the questions. While this would be helpful, most of us do not have all the answers, so this may be too high a standard. Being confident enough to know where to go or who to turn to if you need assistance is a real confidence booster.

We can't be too proud to ask for help when we need it. We all can use a good mentor in our lives. A lack of confidence is usually a lack of preparation or experience or both. If I am not prepared for a presentation and have never presented before, I am nervous and may even be downright afraid because I am not ready for what is ahead. Having no confidence is like eating salad without any dressing; the dressing is your plan and presentation. Salad and dressing are just ingredients, but the combo is legendary. Following are some ingredients that will help you create your own legendary combo. You will be able to build confidence, know how to handle situations, and ultimately learn the tools to become a more confident and effective leader. Now grab a peanut butter and jelly sandwich and get reading.

Pacing with Your People

Have you ever been grocery shopping with someone else when you notice something on the shelf and start talking about it? You even point it out. Then you turn around, and either the person is gone or somebody else is standing next to you. And then you think, "How long was I talking while no one was listening?"

Unfortunately, this is how conversations work sometimes. We get really focused on something that's important to us, and we don't realize the person with whom we are talking has gotten distracted and mentally walked away. You can often see it on their face. You think, "No, please, please stay with me." They look around the room; they look at their phone; you completely lose them. They probably don't hear anything you say.

Keeping people's attention when you're talking is an important skill I call *pacing with your people*. If you were on a walk, you would make sure you walked right next to your friend the whole time. To make that happen, you must constantly pay attention to how fast they're walking so you can match their speed. Pacing with people in a conversation is the same. How can you make sure you don't lose someone you're talking to? It's not difficult. All you have to do is ask questions. If you ask questions that require the person to think about their answer, you can tell they're pacing with you when they answer.

In conversations, I'll often ask a question, and the response will be, "What?" I caught them when they weren't listening. I don't bring it to their attention; most people are embarrassed when they're caught not listening. Instead, I simply repeat what I was talking about and then ask their opinion again. Seldom do I find someone doesn't pay attention twice in one conversation. If it happens, it's blatant, and there's probably some other situation going on.

Let's focus on the majority of people. You're pacing with them; you ask a question; they don't know the answer because they are not listening. So you follow up, politely restating the question. At that moment, you have their attention. You can begin talking about the topic again.

If you watch high-level speakers, you'll see them snap their fingers or clap their hands at random times during a conversation or speech. Motivational speaker Tony Robbins constantly snaps his fingers while he's talking. Why? The snap kind of "snaps" you back into paying attention. It's the equivalent of grabbing somebody by the shoulders while you're talking to them and giving them a quick shake. When you hear that snap or clap, your brain says, "Hey, this is something you need to pay attention to." I also think it gives you a small shot of adrenaline. If done correctly, this is a great way to keep people engaged in longer conversations. No, I don't advise you to go around snapping and clapping the whole time you're in a conversation. But if there's an important detail, snap when first you bring it up. You'll be amazed by how well this works if done correctly. You may need to practice a few times; I did.

So what's the point here? If you are going to pace with your people, you need to make sure they're right beside you in the conversation the entire time. Don't talk over them or bore them to death; ask questions to make sure they're right there with you in the conversation. Don't be frantic; frantic people talk quickly and try to get everything out in one quick second. This often happens when they know a topic well but lack confidence. A confident person speaks at a good pace because they know their audience will listen. Whether speaking to one person, a group, or a crowd, they feel confident that their audience will stay right next to them. Ask relevant questions that keep people engaged, which will help you gauge their understanding of the topic so you get their opinion. If they completely disagree with what you're talking about, you've lost them because they've shut down.

Quite often, people misunderstand part of what you're saying and literally go off on a completely different path. Avoid that by ensuring the person is standing next to you during the conversation so you won't turn around and feel completely embarrassed when you discover you're talking to yourself. Pacing with your people will save you a lot of time and effort and help you make tons more progress in conversations.

Walk, Wait, and Walk Again

Have you ever been on a walk, or better yet, a run or jog with someone? You're headed in the same direction, both exerting energy, but one of you is clearly more fit than the other—at least, that's usually how it feels. When I meet up with one of my friends at the beach for a run, we'll run along the beach wall, and about halfway through that run, I am beat. I look over, and my friend has plenty of energy; in fact, he's picked up the pace. I'm like, "How? How can this possibly be?" Then comes the tough part: I'm so far behind that he'll say, "I'll meet you at the finish line." The finish line is our starting point. It's just one big loop.

Several questions go through my head during this process. First, why am I not as fit as I need to be? Second, how is this other person moving at such a fast pace? And third, when are we going to get to the end? When you've been left behind and are on your own, you realize you are falling far behind. Maybe your pride kicks in, and you give it extra effort. But what if someone matches your speed and ability? You jog a little, and maybe they're ahead by a bit, but they slow down and wait for you. I might actually enjoy that jog, that little bit of exercise, because someone paced with me throughout. Now, I'm willing to bet because the other person is a lot more fit than I am, this is not their preference for how they would like to enjoy their exercise. In fact, they probably would go full sprint the whole way and feel good about it if I wasn't on that journey with them. Heck, they might even take a few side roads to throw a little spice into their run. But here I am, the boat anchor keeping them from going full throttle. Hopefully, whoever I am on a jog with enjoys my company because we need to be shoulder to shoulder for me to enjoy it and feel good about the jog.

This is a great example of how conversations go. There's always one person leading the conversation. They have the bandwidth and understanding already. They're the physically fit one. And then there's the rest of us. We want to be right beside them the whole way, understanding everything they're talking about. But the leader can quickly lose us if they keep going without making sure we're on the same journey—meaning we understand what they're talking about.

Pacing with someone in conversation looks like this: You talk about the topic, then pause and ask a question or give the other person an opportunity to interject. And I don't mean asking a vague question or accepting a superficial "Yeah," "Sure," or "Uh-huh." I'm talking about something that needs brainpower for an answer. Sometimes there are awkward pauses, but in my experience, it only takes one awkward pause; people don't want you to think they're not listening.

Here's an example: If you were talking about the weather and about it raining, you might ask them what they think the next bit of weather will look like. This type of question requires them to think and engage in the conversation. You don't keep going without feedback. If you do, you've gone on the jog all by yourself.

A conversation is different from talking *at* someone. I don't know about you, but I haven't gotten very far when I'm talking at people. I get much further when I'm talking with people. I have to remember to wait for feedback and to pause in the middle of the conversation so the other participant is in the same place as I am. And until they're right beside me in the conversation, I can no longer proceed; I have to let them catch up.

We form our opinions and make decisions based on the information we have. The only way we can get information is if we're paying attention. If you've lost someone in a conversation, they're no longer using any of their brainpower. This is the equivalent of you running ahead two miles on the jog you were taking together. Then you get to the finish line and wonder where the heck they are. You lost them a long time ago, and they did not take in the information you thought you were getting across.

When you've mastered the ability to keep people in the conversation and know how to keep pace with people, your conversations will be much more productive. You won't have the same conversation two or three times because the quality of your conversations will have increased. So the next time you have a deep or important conversation, pause about a quarter of the way through it and ask a few questions, like "Do you have any thoughts on that?" "What did you think about the angle I took on that?" and "Would you do the same thing?" You get the idea, and I'm sure you can develop some engaging questions to make sure they're listening. From here on out, don't get to the finish line of your conversation without the other person standing right next to you.

Dress the Part

The small town of Ashland, Oregon, is the site of the Oregon Shakespeare Festival, and the town is decorated like something out of Shakespeare's time. The actors' costumes are award-winning. Every little sash and color is intricately put in place to reflect the character and scene of each play. The entire effect is one of immersion that creates a world-renowned experience.

Now let's put you in a place of business, wearing flip-flops and a T-shirt. If you work at a snorkel shop in Hawaii, congratulations, you are playing the part correctly. You probably missed the mark if you're working at a law firm. I have often heard people say, "This is who I am, and people need to accept me despite who I am." Guess what, people don't need to accept you. People don't have to be nice; they often are not.

Looking and acting the part someone is hiring us to play is important to win the opportunity for them to do business with us rather than with our competition. If you are a real estate salesperson going into a high-dollar home, take a few extra minutes to make yourself look presentable. Dress accordingly and make a great first impression. You never get a second shot at a first impression.

I once was told a story about an old lady who dressed to the hilt with lipstick and full makeup and her hair perfectly in place no matter where she went. One day, she walked into a store she regularly visited, and the lady at the front desk said to her, "You know you don't need to dress up like this every time you come in." She knew this was the only stop this lady would make all day. The older lady told the young woman, "Honey, I don't do this just for you. I do this for everyone who sees me. It's my way of showing everyone around me that I care enough to actually dress up so they see something beautiful today." This story spoke to me about the importance of respecting the people around you by spending a little extra time on your appearance. Remember, it's a gift to everyone who sees you.

Use Statistics when Possible

My favorite saying about statistics is this: There are lies, damn lies, and statistics.[11] You can manipulate numbers to pretty much say anything you want. So the question is, why do people believe statistics if that's true? The answer: They just do. Why? Because statistical data lends credibility to your research, educates about how things work, and often creates an emotional response in your audience.

Why do we believe so heavily in numbers? My personal opinion is because people see numbers all day, every day. However, they don't know how to process the information, so when you can put numbers in an easily digestible form—a statistic or a percentage—people can measure performance, analyze problems, and educate themselves on the issues. Telling a potential client, "A lot of these items have sold for a large amount," might be a true statement, but it isn't as powerful as saying, "Eighty-five percent of these items have sold for 102 percent of the asking price." All of a sudden, you've moved from a vague statement to a crystal-clear picture.

---

11 Origin unknown.

I am not saying to make up statistics. I think no matter what you do, you need to be credible. You should be able to back up all your statistics and numbers with facts. I often tell people to have a couple of statistics on hand. Number one, it shows you care enough to study the details. It shows you analyze things. Number two, most people will also hold on to those statistics and repeat them. When people repeat what you told them, you receive 100 percent free advertising.

In 2023, two blogs for salespeople found that 43 percent of sellers said buyer data was very important,[12] but only 23 percent of buyers agreed that sellers "always" put the buyer first.[13] Think of it this way. For most people, statistics are a way to bring clarity to a story. They add credibility to what you're saying and give people bullet points to hold on to from your conversation or presentation. Statistics are a powerful tool that should not be overlooked. I will often go online, find a percentage calculator, and calculate the percentage of change between the numbers I'm using. This has had a big impact and can quickly show people the possibilities for gain or loss.

Now, there's always that person who complicates something simple. Don't be that person. Remember that the most critical part of any presentation is the story that goes along with the statistics. People will often remember a story first and foremost. Weave your statistics into the story for a better result. (Remember K.I.S.S.: keep it simple, stupid.) Use statistics to create a powerful presentation. You just might find 80 percent higher satisfaction with a 75 percent better result. But whatever you do, make sure that at least two out of three people you meet leave your presentation as raving fans. My goal is 100 percent customer satisfaction; make it yours, too.

---

12 Storm, A. (December 20, 2023). 78 key sales statistics that'll help you sell smarter in 2024. *Hubspot.* https://blog.hubspot.com/sales/sales-statistics

13 Pipedrive. (n.d.). 74 essential sales statistics for 2024. *Pipedrive.* https://www.pipedrive.com/en/blog/sales-statistics

USING GRAPHS AND CHARTS

Percentage Difference Graph:
Compare the percentage difference between two values.
Example: Compare sales from Year 1 ($100,000) to Year 2 ($120,000).
Graph: Use a bar graph with bars for each year's sales.
Design: Make Year 2's bar 20% higher than Year 1's to represent the 20% increase.

Bar Graph:
Compare categorical data.
Example: Compare sales of three products (A, B, C)— $50,000, $70,000, $60,000.
Graph: Use a bar graph with bars for each product.
Design: Arrange bars vertically or horizontally based on sales amounts.

Line Graph:
Show trends over time.
Example: Display monthly website traffic (1000, 1200, 1500, . . ., 2000 visitors).
Graph: Use a line graph with months on the x-axis and visitors on the y-axis.
Design: Connect data points with lines to show the traffic trend.

Pie Chart:
Illustrate proportions of a whole.
Example: Show market share of three companies (A: 40%, B: 30%, C: 30%).
Graph: Use a pie chart divided into slices for each company.
Design: Label each slice with the company name and its percentage of market share.

These different visual aids simplify complex data for easier understanding during presentations.

These graph types should be easy to create using common presentation software like Microsoft PowerPoint, Google Slides, or Excel. Just input your data and choose the appropriate graph type and design options.

The First Person to Speak Loses

Have you ever seen one of those old Western movies where two cowboys line up for a quick-draw gunfight? It's usually set in an Old West town with wooden houses or saloons surrounding them; they face each other from opposite ends of the main street. The camera focuses on them standing in silence. There's usually a close-up of their eyes. They stare at each other, waiting to see who will draw first.

This scene highlights the way I feel in a high-stakes situation where words matter; I may say the wrong thing too quickly or too slowly. In real life, I say the first person to speak usually loses.

It's not that speaking first is a sign of weakness, but people who are cool, calm, and collected don't need to speak to fill space, and especially not first. Usually, the frantic people do all the talking, and the person in the driver's seat does a lot of listening and waiting for their opportunity for a verbal quick draw. A lot of people speak first because they get nervous with silence. I've had to learn to be comfortable with silence. You know that time in a conversation when nobody says anything and it feels awkward, and then somebody finally says something to break the awkward silence? I'm the guy who isn't fazed by the silence. I usually want to see what the other person's going to say.

People know what they're thinking and typically have a position in their minds about how they feel about something. When I talk too much, I don't know anything about what affects the other person's thinking. But when they're talking, I get to hear all about what they're thinking, and if I ask some leading questions, nine times out of ten, they'll tell me way more than I even need to know.

Someone who used to work for me was negotiating the sale of a family ranch, and I had explained to him that the first one to speak loses. This advice applies in a variety of situations, but in negotiations, it is usually something like "What price do you want?" I'd instructed this gentleman not to be the first one to offer a price. Fortunately for him, he listened. When he was negotiating the price for his ranch, the potential buyer asked him how much he wanted for the land and the ranch. He responded, "Give me a price; what do you think it's worth?" Now, he had a price in mind that he would sell the property for, but as fate would have it, the man offered even more than what he was looking for. So naturally, he stayed cool, calm, and collected when the man gave him this offer, and he said that price sounded like something they might be able to work with. Later, he told me, "You'll never believe what happened. You told me not to be the first one to offer the price. To explore what they were thinking, I did that and ended up with way more money than I ever would have been paid if I'd just named my price. Thank you for teaching me that lesson."

Of course, when I see people winning around me, it makes me happy. In this particular case, he did shut up, and he won. Most of us don't want to shut up because it can be uncomfortable. I've sat in the room, waiting for people to talk many times. Many of those people thought I would be the first to speak; they'd look at me, and then I'd look back at them. The problem with some of us is that we can be too stubborn, and when we make up our minds, we can be steadfast. Unless, of course, it has to do with my better half; we always work to be flexible there, right?

I'm not suggesting you walk up to people and say nothing and just listen. What I am saying is in negotiations, when you've had a natural conversation and have built some good rapport, hear what the other person has to say first. Don't be the first one to speak. If we know what the other person's thinking before we speak, we're in a much better position to win. Write your own Western story, one where you let the other cowboy draw first. Then ride off into the sunset with all the loot, but don't forget to stop by the saloon on the way out of town.

Be the Change

I'm reminded of a story about a hot dog vendor in New York City. This particular hot dog vendor was a Buddhist monk and, as such, had a very centered look on life. People would come from far and wide to visit this monk and buy a hot dog. Some said they were the tastiest hot dogs in all of New York City. One day, one of the monk's regulars came by. The hot dogs cost $5 each, but the man only had a $10 bill that day. He got the hot dog with everything on it and was so excited to eat it. He handed the hot dog vendor his $10 bill. The vendor took it and then started making someone else's dog. The man stood there and waited, looking at the vendor. After taking some time with no response from the vendor, the man finally asked, "Hey, what about my change?" The hot dog vendor looked at him and said, "Change? Change comes from within."

I don't know if there's really a hot dog vendor in New York City who says that, but I love the story. The truth is that change does come from within. When we're looking for change, though, what are we trying to change? Usually, we feel we lack something, so we strive to increase competence or acquire more of what we lack. I recently did an exercise with a group where I had them identify one person in their life who was a strong leader. Each person identified someone who had made a significant impact in their life, and they wrote down three attributes they felt made the person the strong leader they were. Then I asked the group to compare themselves to the person they identified as a strong leader. Did they also exhibit those traits?

It's much easier to hit a target when we know where the bullseye is. Just setting out to change but not having a specific example or goal is difficult, and we'll end up wandering aimlessly.

Remember not to judge yourself or your abilities unrealistically. Most likely, the person you would like to emulate had years to develop their skills. Expecting instant perfection would be like riding a skateboard for the first time and comparing yourself to Tony Hawk, a pro skateboarder. You may get there, but it will take a little time and effort, and it would be unfair to judge or compare your abilities to those of someone of that caliber.

Imagine you are the number one salesperson in the world. How would you act? How would you respond to people? What would your day look like? Something is different when we deal with someone of that caliber. They have an abundance, and they know where they're headed and where to spend time and energy.

What if you woke up today and knew you wouldn't fail no matter what you did because you were crowned the number one salesperson in the nation? What would your day look like? How would you respond to people? Rather than doing things out of desperation, worried about whether you'll be at the top of your game or if this might be your one deal, you treat your customer with confidence because you know several other people will be using your services soon. I'm not saying to become full of yourself and self-absorbed. I am saying to be the change by acting as if you are already there. And by already there, I mean you've already reached a level of success you can feel confident about. Don't get me wrong—without substance, this won't work long-term, but as you implement training and abilities, acting confident will have a lasting effect.

I usually see people holding onto failed mentalities and then wondering why they're not succeeding. Let go of past failure, learn from it, and accept your ability to be the change. Start by practicing something small. Imagine how you would treat your customers if you were in high demand. Would you still negotiate out of desperation? Probably not. Start with that, then make one more change. Keep a journal of all the changes you make; if one doesn't work, change it again. Pretty soon, you'll find you like being the change, and change can be good. Why? Because when we adapt and change for the better, we can create a winning formula.

Know Your Audience

Imagine you just walked into a room; you have your whole presentation set. It's on the exhilarating effects of fast cars and acrobatic airplanes. You have your presentation dialed in, including amazing pictures showing how these speeds affect the body. You'll share everything anyone would ever want to know about fast cars and airplanes. About halfway through the presentation, you notice no one is engaging. So you tell a few jokes, but no one laughs. You try to get serious and give more details to show your passion for the subject. Still no reaction. You're at a complete loss for words, and you have no idea why the audience is not engaged until you look around the room. That's when you notice the room is full of young mothers. None of them are looking for anything even remotely dangerous.

A famous saying from the movie *Jerry Maguire* is, "You had me at hello."[14] But this is the opposite situation: You lost them at hello. The reason why? You didn't know your audience.

Just as important as the topic is the audience and whether the topic is relevant to them. I recently witnessed a well-intentioned sales guy commenting on a social media group about a new truck he had for sale priced way above MSRP, hoping to cash in on a potential buyer who might be less than knowledgeable about pricing. Immediately, the comments poured in, and they were not kind. "You greedy dealership, why would I give you my money," one read. Another one simply commented, "Not in my lifetime. Keep your truck." This reminded me how, even when people are well-intentioned, when they don't know their audience, it's almost like lighting themselves on fire. They don't even have a chance.

How to Prepare for Your Audience

One way to be sure you know your audience is to ask. If you'll be speaking to a group, ask the organizers who they've enjoyed

14 Crowe, C. (Director). (1996). *Jerry Maguire* [Film]. Gracie Films. https://www.imdb.com/title/tt0116695/

hearing from in the past. Did you find out what their interests are? If it's a real estate investing group, please don't talk about botany. Unless, of course, it has to do with real estate investing.

Another great thing you can do before your actual presentation is show up thirty minutes early and talk to a few of the people you will be presenting to. Simply ask them if there are any topics that have been on their minds that seem most relevant. Just because someone says your topics are most relevant to them doesn't mean you have to speak specifically on those topics. But if you talk to three or four people beforehand, and there seems to be a common thread, you can guide your presentation in a way that engages your audience.

If you're meeting one-on-one, I hope you have an idea of what you're meeting about. Don't go far off-topic unless it's simply for rapport building. Stay the course and ask questions in an engaging way. And with each question, build on the last, getting your audience closer to their goal with what they're looking for. When someone wants more information on horses, and you bring pictures, information, and maybe even a couple of saddles for them to sit on, pretty soon, as long as you've done the work to make a great presentation, you will be riding into the sunset with an engaged audience. Simply put, find out what people want beforehand and get to know your audience.

"Push and Release"

You may find this surprising, but people are looking for a lot of guidance. I often tell people that others wouldn't hire you if they could do it themselves. Most people are just looking to make the wisest decision they can. They want to make sure they're not screwing up when making an investment. Who do they turn to? They turn to the expert—you, assuming you're an expert.

People often don't feel confident in their decisions, especially when risk is involved. Oddly, though, most people don't want to be told what to do. If you tell them what to do, they will probably do the opposite for the simple reason that you told them to do something. So how do you help people make a great decision? One thing I tell people over and over is that the best decision anyone can ever make is their own. I use what I call the *press and release* technique. You want to show people how they have a very good option in front of them, exactly what that option is, and that you would take that option if it were you; then you completely back off and tell them, "But it's your choice."

Let me give you an example. I worked with a couple considering a house above their budget. Now, keep in mind they'd been looking for homes for a year, and every house had a problem with it. But not the one we were looking at: It was perfect in every way except for the price. Of course. They were quite nervous and didn't know if buying it was the right decision. So I used the press and release technique. "Does this house have the lot size you want? You love the primary bedroom, right? It's in the neighborhood you said you wanted, and it's only two blocks from your kids' school. If it were me, I think I would move on it, knowing that it's an investment, and several years from now, you'll think, 'We are so glad we invested in the house we wanted.' But that's me; what would you like to do?"

I was showing them that this was their opportunity to get everything they wanted, and I brought them right to the decision point but not across the line. I'll bring someone 99 percent of the way and then completely back off and let them go that last little bit on their own.

Let's say they struggle a little more after you do this. It happens; after all, it's a big decision. You just go right back through that process, even at the risk of sounding like a broken record. "You have been looking for the last year and found nothing. Now, this house has everything you say you want," and you go through the list of things they asked for. "If it were me," you continue, "I would take action on this now, but that's a decision you have to make on your own."

Most people want to know they'll make a safe and informed decision, and you wouldn't recommend it if it weren't. When you have confidence, other people will have confidence along with you, and most of the time, they're just looking to be reassured that they're making a good decision. Remind them of the reasons they gave you, help them identify the solution that is in front of them, and then make the decision easy for them, but back off and do not push them. Let them make the final decision to proceed. If they want it, this will be their opportunity. I think you will find this technique to be very effective, especially when you use it to benefit your clients and put their best interests first.

Leave a Simple Out

Have you ever realized in the middle of an intense conversation that there was something you hadn't considered, and everything you said was a little misguided? Or perhaps you have an intense conversation and then change your mind. But this little thing called pride kept you from admitting anything to the contrary. These are regular occurrences; how do I know this? Because we're all human. None of us is perfect, and we're going to make mistakes. Knowing that, let's talk about how we handle other people making mistakes in conversations and how to give them a way to keep their pride intact.

When you're the one directing the conversation, and the other person digs in their heels and becomes completely unreasonable, you can do one of several things. You can rub their nose in the fact that they're wrong. This most likely will get you some satisfaction but no good results. You can give up on the conversation and give in. This is usually a bad example to set for future conversations if the person is wrong. Or you can stand your ground in a very polite way and leave the other person a simple way out of the conversation, a way for them to save their pride.

I've often used this technique in conversations when people become completely unreasonable. Think of this as though you are stuck in the ocean, and someone throws you a life preserver. You certainly don't have to take it, but it will make your life a lot easier and a lot better. An example would be if a customer gets heated and says some things that are pretty off-putting to you.

Before it gets out of hand, I'll say something like, "Perhaps there was a misunderstanding, and what you intended was something different from what I'm hearing, but it sounds like you're upset. Is that correct? If so, no big deal." I'll even self-blame sometimes. "I think I may have completely misunderstood you. Did you actually have good intentions here, and what you meant to say was this?" Another option could be, "Is this your goal? And if it is, you can just say so, and we can go that direction. I'm happy to accommodate." This can often happen when customers become afraid that things are not going as they think they should or as they had planned. They become agitated and upset. Rather than communicating in a healthy manner, they lash out.

The key here is that you're giving the other person the opportunity to save face. You're giving them an opportunity to leave the conversation with dignity. Not everyone will take you up on this opportunity. But you'll be surprised how the majority of people will. If you're in a fighter jet, and all the gauges and indicators show you're about to crash, and someone offers you an ejection seat, there's a good chance you'll take it. And if you didn't take what was offered to you, you were just too stubborn, and perhaps the crash is needed for you to learn a lesson.

There are always at least two people in a conversation: a leader and a follower. Who holds which position can swap several times during a conversation, but there is always a leader and a follower. If you're leading the conversation, and someone becomes unreasonable by saying things they will later regret, think about giving the other person an easy out. It will make things more productive and lead to better results in most cases. If you're the follower in the conversation, and someone gives you an opportunity for an easy out, save face and take it; they're doing you a solid. Do not dig into words you will later regret saying, and don't be the stubborn person who ends up hurting themself just because their pride got in the way.

I often think about a cornered dog. Its back is against the wall and things are closing in, and it's going to fight its way out. What if it was backed into the corner, and one person moved to the side so it could safely walk out rather than have to fight? Nine times out of ten, that dog will walk out the easy way. If you feel like you've got somebody cornered, step aside and let them walk out. You don't need to win every single conversation. Be strategic about your goal. Saving relationships with people can get you much further than winning one measly conversation.

If You Don't Believe, They Won't Believe

Do you know someone in your life who doesn't believe in their ability? Someone who isn't sure of themselves? How do you know? Did they tell you? People don't usually say, "You know, I've been thinking about things, and I really don't believe in myself." I may sense someone's lack of security in a situation, but I don't think I've ever heard someone come out and say that in a conversation. Even if they did, it would be embarrassing for them to admit that they don't.

Do you believe in your ability? Because if you don't, no one around you will, either.

Before you talk to someone about something important, you need to feel strongly that what you'll tell them is true, accurate, and in their best interest and that you fully believe in what you're about ready to say. If you doubt, there is a good chance they will doubt. If a general told his troops to follow him but admitted he thought the enemy would annihilate them, how ready would his soldiers be to follow him?

With this in mind, consider how you appear to a prospective client. If you don't believe in yourself, your product, or your ability to do a great job, how can you expect them to have confidence in you? At this point, you might be asking, "So, are you telling me I need to just fake it until I make it?" The problem with faking until you make it is you still don't believe. Self-talk is critical. Talk to yourself before you talk to others, and make sure you believe what you're going to say. Sometimes, I have a short conversation with myself. "Hey, what do you think about this? Well, you've been here before, and it was fine." Now, you can confidently say you've successfully navigated this situation before, and you believe you're going to be able to do it again. Or maybe you've never navigated something like this before, but you still feel strongly that this is the right direction, and you are the one who can make it happen for them. If you believe, others will have a much easier time believing as well.

Answer the Question They Should Have Asked

How long have you been in the business? Why should I choose you? What is your history in this business? What is your marketing plan? All these questions have one thing in common: The person asking these questions most likely doesn't care about the question they just asked. That's right, they don't care how long you've been in the business. They don't want to hear why you think they should choose you. They'll decimate your marketing plan no matter how good it is. So what is it they really want?

When someone asks a question, it is often not the question being poised. If we know what they really want, we can answer the question they really have. How do we know what they actually want? Spoiler alert: Everyone wants to win. No matter what the situation is, no matter what the goal is, they want to feel like they're going to win by working with you or having you on their team.

Let's take the question about how long you have been in the business. People ask this question to figure out whether you're new or experienced so they can lower their chances of losing. Most of the time, new means inexperienced. As we discussed, if you don't believe, they won't believe. So back to the question. When they're asking how long you have been in the business, you could say something like, "I'm brand-new. This is my second week." How do you think that's going to work for you? In their minds, they're going, "Red flag—run!" What if you said something like, "I'm newer to the industry, and I work harder and longer than anyone else. I make sure every one of my clients wins at every opportunity. If you want someone who's going to aggressively go after your goals, that's me." You want to paint a picture that makes it simple for them to see how they can win by working with you. Your picture will highlight how choosing you is the right decision. Do not answer the question they ask. Answer the question they should have asked. I would argue that by answering the questions at the beginning of this section, you will not only be doing yourself a disservice, but you'll also be doing them a disservice.

"When [Steve] Jobs took his original Macintosh team on its first retreat, one member asked whether they should do some market research to see what customers wanted. 'No,' Jobs replied, 'because customers don't know what they want until we've shown them.'"[15] People don't know what they don't know. Most of the time, they don't know the questions they should ask to get the results they want. Instead of asking, "How is giving me your whole background going to tell me how you're going to help me win?" they ask evaluation questions that I guess could help in a roundabout way, but in my opinion, it really misses the mark. Tons of extra information can be interpreted in a ton of different ways that could help or hurt you. Too much extra information gives people the opportunity to get off on the wrong track.

Concentrated information about the specific topic they want an answer for can be very helpful. Don't go off on tangents; that has an opportunity to hurt you. Focus on their needs and their goal. Answer the heart of the question. If you're having trouble figuring out what the heart of the question is, ask yourself (hopefully beforehand) why you would ask this question if the situation were reversed. Ninety-nine percent of the time, you can engage a couple of brain cells and come up with the answer. If you don't know or can't figure out the answer, ask a few more clarifying questions. Don't be afraid to ask tough questions. The tough questions give you the knowledge you need to give a great answer. One

15 Isaacson, W. (April 2012). The real leadership lessons of Steve Jobs. *Harvard Business Review*. https://hbr.org/2012/04/the-real-leadership-lessons-of -steve-jobs

of the biggest differences between experienced and inexperienced people in any industry is the ability to feel confident enough to ask tough questions.

Once you determine what someone is really asking, answer those questions. Show them how they win by choosing you.

The 30-Second Power Statement

What if I told you that you have the power to inspire people to the point of action on command almost every single time? What if you could say something so powerful that people would remember it throughout their entire day? What if you said something that motivated people to move in a direction they never thought possible?

What I'm talking about is the 30-second power statement. Have you ever heard Martin Luther King's "I Have a Dream" speech? How about Vince Lombardi's speech "Never Give Up"? These are just two examples of something so powerful that they've inspired people for years. Let's look at what you can do to inspire people to action. Let's create a power statement.

One of the first things required for a 30-second power statement is the belief that it's true. Have you ever heard someone make a statement and act like it is the answer, but you can tell they are nervous and probably aren't sure about what they said? Did it create doubt for you? If it didn't create doubt, I would say you're probably not human. Humans are wired to look at our surroundings and make good decisions for survival. If you see danger, you avoid it. If something seems suspicious, you use caution.

Not long ago, I was teaching a class about the 30-second power statement, and I told a story about an appliance salesperson. A guy went into an appliance store to buy a refrigerator. The salesperson explained to the man that he'd been missing out. The man's ears perked up. How had he been missing out by having the wrong fridge? The salesperson explained how, with an extra compressor, the temperature in the fridge could maintain the same level for a longer time, increasing the food shelf life by 20 percent.

He explained how the man was essentially throwing away 20 percent of all the money he spent on food all year long just by not having the right fridge. The salesperson had the man sold! How could he possibly throw away all that money?

Here are some key takeaways from this situation. Number one, the salesperson believed his statement wholeheartedly. Number two, he had a compelling story. Number three, he instilled confidence in the man that moving forward with the purchase was the right direction. And last but not least, the salesperson showed the customer how he could win.

Why You Need a 30-Second Power Statement

Though people typically don't ask directly why they should work with you, they often ask a variation of that question in their own way. Maybe they don't even realize they're asking why they should work with you, but your answer should inspire and give them a clear understanding. We actually do this all the time but by using a weak explanation. When someone is unprepared, they tend to give a flat and uninspiring answer, like "Because I am the best" or "You will like what I can do for you." These vague assertions usually do the opposite of what we hope they will do. Instead of instilling confidence by showing people how they will win, these weak statements create doubt, and potential customers lack the confidence they need to follow you.

Crafting a compelling 30-second power statement involves refining each step to be concise and impactful while conveying the essence of your business or offering. Practice will help you refine and polish your power statement further.

Only promise things you can make good on. You can discuss a bigger goal and a grander idea without getting specific. In my power statement, I tell customers how I'll help them win.

At the end of the chapter is a graph showing the parts you need for your 30-second power statement. Write it, practice it, and memorize it. You'll see many opportunities to insert your power statement and create opportunities that didn't exist previously.

5 STEPS TO BUILDING YOUR
30-SECOND POWER STATEMENT

Here are five simple steps to help construct a powerful 30-second elevator pitch.

1. **Identify Your Audience and Goal.** Understand who you're talking to and what you want to achieve. Tailor your pitch to resonate with the listener's needs or interests.

2. **Start with a Hook.** Begin with a compelling and concise opening that grabs attention. This could be a thought-provoking question, a startling statistic, or a scenario related to the problem you are offering to solve.

3. **Explain the Problem or Need.** Clearly articulate the problem or need your product or service addresses. Describe the pain point or challenge your target audience faces.

4. **Present Your Solution and Unique Value.** Introduce your solution and highlight its unique value proposition. Focus on how it solves the identified problem better or differently than existing alternatives.

5. **End with a Call to Action.** Conclude by prompting action. It could be inviting further conversation, scheduling a demo, or directing them to your website. Ensure it's clear what the next steps should be after hearing your pitch.

By the way, a closing statement and a power statement are two separate things. A closing statement is meant to ask for the business and set up a time to formalize your business relationship. A power statement is meant to powerfully inspire the person. Combining too much at one time can be less effective and may turn the person off. Let them be inspired, and once they're inspired, go in with the closing statement.

Your Weakness Is Your Greatest Strength

During the class I mentioned earlier, we discussed turning our weaknesses into our greatest strengths. Whatever your greatest weakness is, I guarantee you can turn it into a positive. If you address it right up front as a positive, it probably won't come back to haunt you.

Several of the class participants were brand-new in their business. They were concerned—and rightfully so—that people would realize this and be apprehensive about working with someone who had little or no experience. They asked how they could turn that into a positive. I suggested a version of the following: "You have a lot of choices to work with people, and because I'm brand-new, I can give you a fresh set of eyes and an opportunity to work with someone who is going to make sure you win at every turn. The level of dedication I'll have to you will be unsurpassed." They agreed this suggestion sure beat saying, "I'm new, and I can always bring someone in who can help me do the right thing." If you run from the fact that you're new (or whatever your issue is), you'll be worried it will come up later and that you'll lose the client anyway. Better to address it up front.

Depending on what you're talking about, your power statement will be different from everyone else's, and it will be in your voice, not mine. This means don't try to be someone you're not; just try to be the best you can be by instilling confidence that you'll see the customer through to the very end, and they'll win by working with you. Then execute.

Let's start crafting your power statement. Keep in mind you need to inspire people to have confidence in you and let them know they will win by working with you.

We usually start a power statement with something like this: "You have a lot of choices, and the right one could be difficult to identify, but one thing I know is no one will work harder than me toward helping you succeed. What's great for the people who have worked with me is they get up in the morning, grab their cup of coffee, and feel confident that they know everything's in good hands. Is that the kind of confidence you want? So you want to win? Then we need to talk."

THE 30-SECOND POWER STATEMENT

- The goal of your 30-second power statement is to inspire confidence and show you will help the customer win.

- Paint a picture of how working with you will help them win; give examples.

- Memorize your statement and exude confidence in your ability to lead them to victory.

- I recommend using your closing statement as a separate part.

- Creating a succinct and impactful elevator pitch involves highlighting key elements of your business offerings. Here's a graph outlining the components for a 30-second power statement:

- | Problem/Solution Identification |

- | |

- | Value Proposition |

- | |

- | Unique Selling Proposition |

- | |

- | Call to Action/Next Steps |

Problem/Solution Identification: Quickly identify a problem or need your business addresses. This sets the stage by drawing attention to a relevant issue.

Value Proposition: Explain the value and benefits your product or service brings to potential customers. Focus on what sets you apart and why it should matter to them.

Unique Selling Proposition (USP): Highlight what makes your offering unique. This could be a special feature, approach, or something else that differentiates you from competitors.

Call to Action/Next Steps: End with a call to action—what you want the listener to do next. It could be scheduling a meeting, visiting your website, or trying out a demo.

Remember, the goal of a power statement is to create interest and curiosity, prompting further conversation or action. Tailor these components to fit your specific business and audience.

6. Recognizing and Responding to the Customer's Needs

Discusses the importance of understanding the client's goals, anticipating their needs, and delivering valuable solutions. Also emphasizes the importance of not assuming anything and leaving room for any outcome.

DO YOU FEEL LIKE YOU KEEP GETTING a red light with your customers? You just keep getting the no. Wondering how to get the light to turn green? We all need good strategies to keep our customers engaged. You can learn valuable ways to solicit and execute your customers' needs. Without acting on and responding to the right signals from our customers, we are setting ourselves up for a fender bender. Let me give you an example. Have you ever said the wrong thing at the wrong time, causing your whole conversation to come to a screeching halt? Do conversations or interactions feel awkward because you don't know what to say or do? Whatever the situation, there is nothing like the feeling of an open road to get you to your destination quickly. Most of us want freedom from the roadblocks that hold us back. If you want to navigate customer relationships in a way that will give you a clear picture of how to move forward, buckle up. I've got some great stuff ahead. You may want to take notes.

Showing Up Without Value

People often show up without value to add, but they seem to be willing to take as much value as possible. We see this in a lot of places in life. A gentleman I used to work with had a relatable saying: "Are you showing up without a dish? It looks like you just have a fork and a spoon in your hand." I always found this pretty amusing, and it's a good analogy for being unprepared for an important client meeting. It was scheduled weeks ago; you knew exactly what you needed to go over, yet you never took the time to prepare the essential details so you could show up with real value. Instead, you came with the expectation that you would get the business anyway, so you didn't need to present any value. If you've done this before, you've shown up at a potluck with a fork and a spoon.

Now, what about the person who comes to the potluck with three main dishes? You're probably blown away. Look at all the time and money they invested to ready these dishes for us to enjoy. Your whole perception of them and what they bring to the table, no pun intended, is completely changed. That simple act of being prepared when presenting to the client demonstrated your dedication and care about their outcome. It showed you were invested in making sure they had the best results.

Where in your life are you showing up with a fork and a spoon and no dish? It's detrimental to miss the expectations and time frames you set. When people see you not doing the things that you have stated you will do, in the time frame that you said you would do them, they start to believe you are unreliable. The last thing you want in a sales scenario is for people to think you're unreliable. You should probably invest more of your time for a better outcome and show the people you work for how you are invested in their best interest. The simple act of giving our time and talent allows us to receive more than what we give. What if you showed up at that client meeting super prepared? Do you think they're going to tell everyone else that they need to use you because of the amazing job you did? When you under-promise and over-deliver, people notice. It's a simple thing to beat the expectations you set.

When something good happens, people tell six others on average, but when something bad happens, people tend to tell fifteen others on average.[16] So, for every bad thing you do or mishap you have with a client, two to three good things are needed to make up for that one bad thing. Next time you go to a potluck, tell people you're bringing one dish and then show up with two. Watch how people react. It may be subtle, but they'll likely be thankful you put a little extra on the table. Likewise, next time you have a meeting, come up with one extra bit of value, something you need to research. Watch how people react. They'll be so thankful you didn't show up with a fork and a spoon. And hey, when you put in the extra effort, there may just be a great reward in the end. Try it and find out.

Don't Make Definitive Statements

One thing that often makes me cringe is when people make strong, definitive statements about things with many variables, such as "The other party will definitely accept your offer; there's no way they wouldn't do what we ask." The first thing I think is that they must not be very experienced. A better statement would be, "We will make the best effort to get them to accept what we're asking for. I feel very good about it."

We know why people make definitive statements: They're worried the people they're talking to don't think they are firm in their conviction toward the outcome. We live in a world where anything can happen. We can have the best intention, but, if someone along the line who is not us falls short, and we make a statement that the thing we promised will happen and it doesn't, we pay the price.

---

16 Stattin, N. (December 1, 2023). 32 Customer experiences statistics you need to know for 2024. SuperOffice. https://www.superoffice.com/blog/customer-experience-statistics/

Most of the time, when we make definitive statements, they are out of fear that we might lose the sale or the confidence of the person we're serving. I would argue the opposite. People can ask me, "If you're so sure, why can't you promise me?" and a good option is to tell them I feel strongly that we're in a very good position, but until something happens, it's not a sure thing. I think people want to be led in such a way that they're confident that whatever you say is 100 percent the truth. I'll often start a conversation by saying something like, "You may not like what I say, but you'll know that whatever I said was the truth," to set the tone that I'm not saying things to impress them. I'm trying to lead the conversation in a truthful manner regardless of the cost. I might tell them, "You see, the truth will come out eventually—either during this conversation or later. If I wait to tell you, you'll likely be more upset with me for not being honest from the start. I'd much rather help you make the best decision based on all the actual information." We can talk later about being too brutally honest.

The point is that you don't have a crystal ball, so don't make statements like you do. Make statements that leave room for real-life scenarios to take place. There have been countless situations where everyone thought something was in the bag, but in some weird twist of fate, something occurs along the way that derails things. Even a small hiccup can make me look like I didn't know what I was talking about. Be a better guide for your people. Don't make definitive statements. Make statements that leave room for all the possibilities to take place but also give the other party assurance that they're in great hands with you.

Don't Assume Anything

Have you ever assumed that people have bad intentions? Have you ever assumed that people have good intentions, only to be corrected? You've heard the saying, "Assume makes an ass out of you and me." I guess we need to look at why we assume things.

Most of us assume things because of our past experiences. If we make this comment, we will get this response. We have those assumptions because whatever they are, they've held true for the majority of the time. Assuming things can be a kind of self-preservation method. We learn to assume things as a way to avoid pain. It's part of the learning process.[17] If I have a hammer in my hand and my thumb is too close to the nail, danger! If I don't trust myself, I assume I might hit my thumb. This is actually a reasonable assumption. It will probably save me from destroying my thumb or my hand.

Why can assuming things be a disadvantage, and what kinds of things are we assuming that we shouldn't? One thing I've learned is that we can't assume people's intentions. We also can't assume what people's ultimate goals are. How many times have you read a text or an email and completely taken it out of context? We assume we know what the sender means, but without all the information, voice inflections, facial expressions, and back-and-forth communication, we often misconstrue people's written intentions.

Assuming Makes an A$$ Out of You and Me

Imagine you're talking to someone you know, who doesn't like another person, so you go through all the reasons why they should like that person: They're really good with people; they're sweet and kind; they're good-looking; they're excellent businesspeople. You say, "I just don't understand why you don't like them," and their reply is, "I never said I didn't like them." How many times has this situation played out in different scenarios?

How do we avoid making assumptions even when we think we completely understand the other person's thinking? We ask several questions. You see, you don't know what direction to take a conversation or what action you need to take if you don't have complete clarity about what's going on in the situation. If someone's not ordering a certain kind of food, is it because they hate

---

17 Lumley, M. A., Cohen, J. L., Borszcz, G. S., Cano, A., Radcliffe, A. M., Porter, L. S., Schubiner, H., & Keefe, F. J. (2011). Pain and emotion: A biopsychosocial review of recent research. *Journal of clinical psychology*, 67(9), 942–968. https://doi.org/10.1002/jclp.20816

it? Is it because they don't like one of the ingredients? Is it because the colors are off or the smell is wrong? We don't know, even if we think we know. We have to be willing to dive deeper.

Why don't people dive deeper by asking more questions to gain a deeper understanding? They might be embarrassed to ask or are in a rush, or just flat-out too lazy to ask. One key thing to remember: You're going to spend the time on either the front or back side of the situation. If you spend time on the front side, you seem intelligent and thoughtful. If you spend time on the back side, you seem unprepared and inconsiderate. Either way, it's going to take up your time. Do yourself a favor and be strategic and proactive. Don't assume anything; ask the extra questions beforehand, put together your best strategy utilizing a deeper understanding, and then watch yourself win.

Communication

In work situations, people ask you to accomplish something. You gear up for it and start down a road toward completion, only to find out they meant or requested something completely different. You could have saved a lot of time by clarifying and not assuming. Has this ever happened to you?

Why don't we ask rather than assume? Some people are just straight-up embarrassed to ask questions because they don't want to look like they don't understand. When we become more confident in our abilities and ourselves, we're not afraid to clarify. As I said before, you can either have some pain up front, or you can have a lot more pain on the back end. Where do you want the pain to be? Asking clarifying questions up front may be uncomfortable or feel painful or embarrassing, but how much more painful will it be to do all the work only to find out that it's not what they wanted? I argue that the latter is way more painful because not only do you have to redo all the work but you also let the person down.

This happens a lot in negotiations. We assume we understand the goals of the person we're representing, so we do everything we can to accomplish those goals; great, but a good portion of the time, their goals and what they ask for differ. They say they want everything to happen by a specific date, so we work hard to make everything happen by that date. What we don't know is why they want it to happen by that date. If we had asked clarifying questions, we would have known the real intent and desire behind their request: They thought they might lose money if it did not happen by that date.

When we take time to understand the real problem and don't assume we know it, our whole process changes. So does the amount of satisfaction the person we're representing ends up with. When we assume things and work very hard, even with great intentions, we can still miss the mark with our people because they don't know what to ask for. And why should they? If you are a professional, you need to look at the whole landscape and understand what the client is trying to do. "If Henry Ford [had] canvassed people on whether or not he should build a motor car, they'd probably tell him what they really wanted was a faster horse."[18] Most people don't know what they want, and it's our job to explain how they can accomplish their goals. But we can't do that if we assume things. We have to dig deeper. We have to be willing to risk looking like we don't know everything so we can help people accomplish their goals. I'm writing this because assuming things is dangerous. And I think it's more dangerous to assume than take the risk of being humble and asking questions so you have complete clarity and the ability to help your people.

By the way, this is also a good practice in your personal relationships. Countless times, communication with those around me could have been better, and the people around me assumed something different from what I meant to communicate. So not only is it important to ask clarifying questions to understand others, but it's equally important to ask clarifying questions when you

---

18 Quoteresearch. (July 28, 2011). My customers would have asked for a faster horse. Quote Investigator. https://quoteinvestigator.com/2011/07/28/ford-faster -horse/

are trying to explain something to make sure everyone around you understands what you are communicating.

Try asking those questions: If you do it right, you'll do it once. Show maturity and wisdom; don't assume anything. This simple rule of thumb has the potential to increase your productivity tenfold because now you have clear direction wherever you go. Don't assume; instead, clarify.

The Stuffed Baker

Everyone has a different way of describing things, but if you can do so in a way that others can identify with, they will feel more comfortable and excited about whatever you're offering.

A young man, age fourteen, had an opportunity to get his first real job. It was a restaurant job at a place called Sizzler. He loved steak, and at the time, Sizzler also had all-you-can-eat deep-fried shrimp. The young man sat down with the manager, letting them know the schedule he was willing to work. I guess this shows how highly he thought of himself and the worth he could provide. After the interview, the manager did not call him back. He started thinking to himself, "I guess I probably should have been a little more humble and more willing to work." After all, he did need a job, and this would have been his first. He called the manager back and said, "Hey, just so you know, I'm willing to work pretty much any hours." The old tail-between-the-legs move. After some back-and-forth, the manager hired the young man to be a counter person. If you've ever been to a Sizzler, you know this role is to take orders and send them back to the kitchen and servers. The young man thought this was an excellent position for him. He got to talk to people and didn't have to stock the salad bar or bus tables. That's what he called a win.

After he'd worked at the job for a few months, the company decided to hold a contest to see which counter person could sell the most stuffed baked potatoes. They offered a prize of $350. Keep in mind the young man was making $4.25 an hour at the time, so $350 was a lot of money, and he was in it to win it. Three months later, he was declared the winner: He was the Stuffed Baker King. No one in his home state sold more stuffed bakers than he did.

How did he sell more stuffed baked potatoes than anyone else in the state? Many of his coworkers asked him this question, and here's what he told them. Someone would walk in to order dinner. He would talk to them for a second and assess them. If they were a fit individual and ordered all healthy food, he would offer them the Healthy Baker, "with 100 percent real cheese and all of the healthy toppings to really support your health journey." If someone came in who was super hungry, he would offer them the Hardy Baker, "with one of our extra-large potatoes and all the fixings, guaranteed to top that hunger right off." If somebody mentioned they were watching their diet, he would offer them a Light Baker, "all the flavor in a light little package." If they had kids, he'd offer them the Family Baker. He must have come up with close to fifty different ways to describe the stuffed baked potato. All he did was tailor the name of the baked potato to the person who might order it. He thought one size doesn't fit all, so why not name it something people could identify with and get excited about? At the end of the day, it was the exact same baked potato for everyone.

Some of his coworkers accused him of bending the rules. Then he asked them to describe their cars. After they described their cars, he offered to do the same and then described it in a completely different way. Then he asked them, "Is it the same car? Am I lying because I described your car differently?"

People use their own filters and ways to describe everything. Whoever came up with the original Stuffed Baker description used their filters. The Stuffed Baker experience is a great illustration for how you need to meet people wherever they are. If you're selling something, don't expect everyone to identify with your standard description. Find ways to be creative, and tailor things to your unique audience. You just might become the next Stuffed Baker King.

It's More Important to Be Respected Than Liked

One of my goals in life is to find the most successful people around and ask them how they became successful. If you're fortunate, they will tell you and share the wisdom they gained over their many years of experience. In a small town in Oregon, there was a basketball team coached by Danny Miles. Danny would recruit basketball players from around the globe to play at his Division II school. Because this wasn't a top-tier Division I school, he wasn't getting the seven-foot Yao Mings of the world. He got the players who might be good and had a lot of potential to grow. I called Danny Miles one day and asked him if he would have lunch with me. We made small talk for a bit, and then I asked him, "How did you become one of the winningest coaches in basketball history without being able to recruit the top talent?" He told me that to have a strong team, you don't need a star player. What you need is a bunch of players who are very good at their specific positions. He preferred not to have a prima donna he would need to cater to. He talked about his relationship with all the guys and how he would inspire them. And he said something that stuck with me for the rest of my life. He said, "You know, it's more important to be respected than liked. Being nice and not telling people what they need to hear doesn't get you respect. Being there saying the hard things and being the leader, even in tough times, making decisions that aren't necessarily liked but are needed—that earns you respect." I thanked him for his time, and we went our separate ways as I digested the words of wisdom he shared.

I thought about the many conversations I'd had with clients or employees when I worried about saying the things I needed to say because I wanted to be liked. I feared being rejected and thought about how much harder my job would be if people didn't like me. Then I thought, "Here's one of the winningest coaches in basketball history; he must know something."

I challenged myself not to worry about being liked as much as being respected. This does not mean saying things rudely or telling people everything they have to do. It simply means saying the things that need to be said and doing the things that need to be done, regardless of the popularity of it all. You see, Danny knew exactly where the team needed to go, and as the leader of that team, he knew exactly what needed to take place to make that happen. All the players knew only what was happening in their present situation because they didn't have the larger point of view.

Looking back twenty-five-plus years later, I still think about that conversation and how it molded me and my leadership style. Is it perfect? No. Have I made mistakes along the way? Yes. Lots of them. But had I not learned that respect is much more important than popularity, I would not have been as successful. I think most high-level leaders figure this out at some point. The sooner you figure it out and start implementing that idea, the sooner doors will open to a more focused, better future.

You see, to lead successfully, you have to know where you're going. And to know where you're going, you need a purpose. If you have purpose, you can make decisions that create respect rather than just trying to get people to like you. I realize this is not an easy task at times. Nobody wants to be the nerdy kid. But then again, I don't want to be the kid who needs all the help because I didn't make good decisions. Remember, it's great to be liked and respected, but it's way more important to be respected than liked.

No Doesn't Mean They Don't Want to Know

Learning how to say no is an important part of being an effective communicator. And learning how to understand what no means is also an important part of being an effective communicator. During coaching sessions with our team, we practice saying no. Most of the time, people default to no because it's the easiest answer. When someone comes up to us and offers us something and we're unsure about it, what do we say? "No, thank you." If we feel like somebody's trying to sell us something and we want the conversation to be over, what do we say? "No, thank you," or "I'm good."

I would argue that people sometimes default to saying no as a way of saying, "I don't have time for this; I don't think there's any value, so I want to do something else." It could also mean "I'm worried this isn't going in the direction I want it to."

In our culture, no means no. If we're talking about personal space or touch, this is absolutely true. But in the context I'm talking about, it does not mean that other people don't want to know the whole story. When people hear that dreaded word, they often throw their hands up and surrender. They don't take the conversation any further or ask any additional questions. I tell my people that when someone says no, it's because you haven't shown enough value. It's easy to say no unless you give people an offer they can't refuse.

Let me give you an example. "Would you like to come and meet a couple of my friends at a happy hour tonight?" No. "Would you like to come and meet a couple of my friends at a happy hour? Russell Wilson will be there." Yes. The difference between a yes and a no is often a little information or incentive.

What do you do when someone says no? I usually do what I call taking another run at it. I say, "Can I ask you one more quick question?" And then I describe the situation a little differently, perhaps adding something of additional value. The other thing I can do before I take a second run at it is ask the person a few more probing questions so I have a better understanding of what would be valuable to them. Once I know what's valuable, I can describe the situation in a way that fits their need for value. Don't get me wrong, this doesn't change every no to a yes. But it does change a lot of them.

When recruiting people, I joke that I don't really have a chance to recruit them until they've told me no at least three times. I keep taking runs at it until I'm able to add value in a way they understand and appreciate. One of my friends said if he had taken no for an answer, he wouldn't be married to his wife. We laugh about this, but it's true. If you take the first no for an answer and give up, you may miss out on something spectacular. Don't give up on the first no.

Bring People Back to Their Goal

Growing up, I had lots of friends and heard many stories about people getting lost in the wilderness. This is a scary thing. You think you're headed in a certain direction, and then all of a sudden, things don't look familiar anymore. Before you know it, you're too far from the main trail to find your way back. When you reach this point, you begin to panic. You go back and forth, frantically trying to retrace your steps, only to make things worse.

This is why it's essential to have some kind of guide. People use GPS, compasses, or actual people (guides) who know the area, and these all share the same ability: They get you to your final destination. If you freak out, they are there to help guide you. Lord knows that without assistance, I might still be wandering around in the wilderness.

Dealing with Your Customers' Emotions

Let's talk about your customers. They're going on a journey they've most likely never made before. You are their guide. Sometimes, they have friends who will also try to act as their compass or other people who may ultimately get in the way of your attempt to guide them correctly. When you ask around, it's amazing how many experts you will find on any given topic, yet very few of them actually know anything. The only thing they "know" is they have a strong opinion, and opinions are like armpits: all of us have them, and most of them stink.

Your people have hired you or are working with you because they believe you are the right person to get them to their destination. The problem is that when things don't go perfectly (and most often, they don't), people become emotionally charged. They can be stressed because things aren't going as planned; they can be mad because someone said the wrong thing; they can be elated and overlook things. No matter what the emotion is, your goal is to get them to their final destination. You have to bring them back to their goal.

People get tangled up arguing back and forth. They don't want to be seen as wrong, which might hurt their ego, so they don't relent in their position. They can be wrong about the issue and know they are wrong, but by golly, they think to themselves, "It's the principle. In order not to appear in the wrong, I will become completely unreasonable, will not admit fault, argue for an otherwise bad idea, and refuse to make good decisions. All in the name of not admitting fault or that I was wrong." I've been in many situations where this seemed to be the case. People want to be right at all costs.

Redirecting Emotions

I remind people they hired me to help them win. They often have to step away from their emotions so they can look at the bigger picture, which is their final destination. What you don't want to do is just cut them off from describing everything to you. You have to remember to be a safe place to discuss all the emotions and frustration, take it all in, and repeat it back to them so they know you completely understand. Once you know they feel completely understood, lay out the road map. Show them where they're going and where they need to go if they want to stay on course.

People's emotions are not easy to deal with, and I'm not going to pretend they are. But I found that most of the time, if I can remind them of their original goal, what they set out to do, and how following their feelings completely distracts them from that goal, people will hop right back on the right trail. If you don't guide your people correctly and bring them back to their goal because they got lost in the mix, who do you think they'll blame? You were the guide; did you guide them? You see, you either guide people or they guide you. You have to be strong enough to lead if you're going to guide them. Even if things get tough or emotions run high, you look through the entire situation and say, "This is the direction we're going." And when they ask why, you say, "Because you hired me to get you there."

People may not always like it at the moment. But they know what they hired you for, and they will appreciate you getting them to their final destination safe and sound. As a professional, you have to watch people and make sure they stay on track the entire time. The second you let down your guard, someone wanders into the wilderness and gets lost. Set regular check-ins with your people; always have a plan and have them watch for what's next. When people don't need to think much, they feel like everything went easily, making it harder for them to go off course than to stay on course. But if they have a personality anything like mine, they'll probably wander off here and there. Make sure to go after them and bring them right back on course. People know a good guide when they see one. People also brag about their fantastic guides. So be a leader, and don't let their ego or emotions take them—or you—off track. Bring them back to their goal; they'll thank you for it later.

7. Creating Mutually Beneficial Relationships

Outlines the importance of focusing on the client and their needs and building trust and rapport. Delves into the concepts of creating an irresistible offer, the value of networking events and how to get the most out of them, and the power of seeking advice over asking for money.

● ●

HAVE YOU EVER RUN INTO A SITUATION where someone doesn't want to take the time to explain what is going on in detail, so they just say, "Trust me"? How did this make you feel? I worry when someone I haven't built a trusting relationship with says something like this. They are basically saying you need to trust they will do the thing that is in your best interest without questioning them. . . . What? How do I know what they have in mind is in my best interest? They don't even know or understand me. My own mother never told me just to trust her. She would explain what she was planning and get my buy-in before moving forward.

Now, I'm not saying there aren't situations where you can trust people. I think many of us have people we can trust, but this trust has been built up over time; it wasn't instant trust, like some little packet you rip open, dump in a glass, and add water. I wish it were that easy. In my experience, trust is built over time.

How do we build these kinds of relationships, and what steps can we take to strengthen them or at least give them an opportunity to grow? We need to create mutually beneficial relationships if we want to earn others' trust and business. Simply put, the people who know, like, and trust you will do business with you. In the next section, I will give you some strategies so you can grow your network and build beneficial relationships, which can be the heart of your business.

Pick Up the Phone

Imagine you are walking down the street. Someone asks you to look around at the different people you pass and say precisely how they all feel. How would you determine their feelings? People often choose to email, text, or use another form of written communication when looking for clues about someone's state of mind, but I would start with all the nonverbal clues. Is the person holding their head high, or are they slouched over? If I greet them, do they respond slowly in a quiet tone or quickly in a cheerful tone?

You are being senseless if you're not using all of your senses. What do I mean? Most communication is nonverbal.

Answer with a Smile

My first job was working for a small company, and I still remember my boss, Jean, telling me, "When you answer the phone, answer it with a smile. People can hear a smile over the phone." I started trying out this theory because it was revolutionary to me, and by golly, people could hear the smile on my face over the phone. This means they can hear every other type of emotion over the phone if they genuinely care to listen.

When you're in a high-stakes situation because your livelihood depends on making a sale, your phone demeanor becomes even more important because most salespeople live sale to sale or paycheck to paycheck, and every deal counts. If you can't meet someone in person, the next best thing is to pick up the phone. In most cases, when you pick up the phone and call someone, you can detect immediately if there's any kind of issue. When you go automatically into problem-solving mode, you'll resolve the majority of those issues before you hang up. When you text people back, people can and often will take your response differently than intended. Here's an example: You text a one-word response, something like "Fine," but this could be taken a bunch of different ways— as off-putting, factual, kind, mean, or any other way someone wants to take it. Why would you risk having them take it the wrong way? The answer is to pick up the phone, listen to the person's tone, keep an ear out for verbal cues, and if they hesitate, ask them if there's anything else they're thinking about. None of these opportunities can be found in nonverbal communication. Give yourself the upper hand: Pick up the phone and start listening. You will be amazed by what you uncover with clear verbal communication.

Get Your Foot in the Door and Network

Everywhere I go, I see people connected to technology. And I'm not a hater of technology. In fact, at one point, I helped start a technology company. I believe I have a good understanding and a healthy balance of technology. Yet, technology does create a barrier between human interaction in general. We get good at the things we practice and rusty at the things we don't. More and more people are having issues connecting human to human (some call it face-to-face). If you look around in a restaurant, you will see married couples, families, older folks, and kids sitting next to one another while on phones, tablets, or even laptops instead of connecting with one another. This isn't a judgment on my part; it's a reality. Someone jokingly told me we'll need classes on human interaction and how to talk to people. I don't think that's too far-fetched. But I do want to encourage you to master networking, which we'll discuss in a moment.

In the nineties, many people only had pagers; cell phones and texting came much later. In those days, we had to cultivate human interaction to build business. I feel the same rules apply today. I also think that people who master human interaction will win over almost everyone else.

Don't Mistake a Contact for a Relationship

What do you try to accomplish with marketing? All the marketing in the world is simply trying to get you face-to-face or to have a meaningful interaction with a human. That's the end goal. Technology is useful when you're making initial contact with someone through social media or some type of digital channel.

As an experiment, I asked a large group, "How many people you've never met in person would be there for you and be your biggest cheerleader?" Most people couldn't think of one. My guess is you can't either. There's something powerful about being in a person's presence.

So let's talk about how to network by looking at two things: the why and the how. I'm a big believer in the saying, "It's not what you know, it's who you know." If you are one of three people for the same position or opportunity, and you have a good rapport with the hiring manager or the decision-maker, who do you think will win? If we can agree on that, then we know the why.

Now, let's talk about the how. When I moved to a big city (Seattle), I knew only my brother, his wife, and their two children. I had come from a smaller area where I knew almost everyone. This was a major culture shock. I lived among more than a million people and had no way of knowing all of them. I went from a big fish in a small pond to a giant ocean where I was the tiniest little fish. Fast-forward through the eight years I spent in Seattle, and by the end, I had a very strong network. How did I build the network? Here's what I did. I joined the local chamber of commerce, Rotary, and other service and referral groups. With several other people, I also created a networking group. I began making a full-time job out of networking. I would show up some nights to three different networking events.

The great thing about networking events is that everyone is there to meet people. Usually, they have one goal in mind: build their business. When you attend networking events, you can either go there asking for business or you can go there to give business. I love the saying that anything you want in life can be accomplished by helping others achieve what they want. It's amazing how much you can accomplish just by meeting people and being a connector. If you meet a great chiropractor, save their information. If you're talking to people at a later time and somebody says they're looking for a chiropractor, give them the number for the chiropractor you just met. Then follow up with the chiropractor to let them know you recommended them to so-and-so through an email or text or, better yet, a phone call. People will be grateful. And grateful people want to give. They will think of you when they have a recommendation. When you add value, most people want to add value back.

TIPS FOR SUCCESSFUL NETWORKING

- Before attending a networking event, learn who the event organizer is. They probably know everyone. Let them know you're interested in participating and ask if they would introduce you to people in the group who are connectors or who would be relevant to your business. Most people running networking events love connecting people. You simply need to ask.

- Remember to add some kind of value. Don't be a taker. Try to find some way to give.

- Don't show up at one event one time and expect people to know you, like you, and trust you. You have to be consistent. You need to show up to the same meeting at the same time on a regular basis if you want people to remember and recommend you.

- As your relationships build, so will the number of referrals you receive, as long as you add value.

Getting the Most from a Networking Event

I'll admit that I did not feel like going to many networking events. Yet when I forced myself to go, the experience was great most of the time. If you feel anxious about attending an event where you don't know anyone, make it simple. Walk up to people and say, "Hi, my name is _____." That's one of the best icebreakers/conversation starters. What next, you ask? I usually talk about FROG; it's a great acronym for family, recreation, occupation, and goals. Remembering to use this simple acronym can keep people talking for hours. But locking one person into a conversation is not your goal. You don't want to tie up someone's time for too long. Take their information and follow up with them the next day. Find out how you can connect and give to that person, help them accomplish their goal, and then introduce yourself to someone else.

A NETWORKING HACK

Rather than making a bunch of individual appointments with prospective clients, invite everyone to the same networking opportunity. Everyone is looking to connect. Everyone is trying to better their lives.

When you look around the room and see that everyone feels out of place, perhaps thinking how in the world they will talk to all these people, you suddenly become a superhero when you walk up and start a conversation. Stop being embarrassed and stressed about what people may or may not say. Go into every conversation hoping to add value, and people will appreciate you. Challenge yourself to attend three networking events in the next week where you know no one. I'm willing to bet you'll make some great connections, and things won't be half as bad as you make them out to be in your mind. One last thing: Practice makes perfect, or at least better. Keep talking to people. Chances are networking will play a part in the way you succeed.

I learned that if you wait too long to follow up with a new connection, they'll forget who you are. Recap with people while it's fresh and they remember your conversation from the night before. I also enter each new connection in my phone, including their name with a label for their occupation or business. That way, as I'm talking to people and need to search my phone for someone I previously met—for example, a chiropractor—I can simply type "chiropractor" in my phone, and they will all show up. Don't waste a connection. Stay connected somehow.

Create Your Own Networking Group

Starting your own networking group could be a powerful and advantageous opportunity. If you build a good value proposition around the networking group that you start, people will come to you. People will search you out, looking for connections. The advantage is you don't have to go to others; they will come to you.

I will warn you that creating a networking group is a lot of hard work that, if not done correctly, can yield little return. You have to be intentional to get the full value of your networking group. Regularly state what you offer and let people know how they can help you. It's easy for the event organizer to get lost in the mix, so stay in front of everyone with your value proposition.

Stay Connected

People attend networking events because they are looking for connections, but the one thing most of them don't have planned out is how to stay connected. Occasionally, you'll give someone your digital business card, text them your number, or hand them your physical business card, and they happen to need your service at that time. They remember you and call. But in my experience, leaving everything up to chance is not very valuable. The amount of return you get is severely diminished. If I meet ten people at a networking event and hand out ten business cards, maybe one of those people will keep my card and contact me. So here are a couple of things you can do to stay connected.

+ Ask for their information or their business card. This puts you in the driver's seat, so when you have their information, you can reach out to them. Once you have their information, you can give them your information, but it may be best to just reach out to them.

+ Follow up consistently. After doing two or three different networking events a night for about a year, I realized that if you don't get back to people within a day or two, they can forget who you are. So make sure to get back quickly and recap part of your conversation or follow up on a question they had.

+ Always have something you can invite people to. If you're attempting to build a lot of connections, it's hard to set up individual times to meet with each person. Let's say I met ten people at an event, and every single one of them set up a coffee with me to follow up on their business. Most of these appointments will last about an hour, and that's ten hours of my week. I simply don't have enough time to network with all these people and stay connected. What's the solution? Maybe it's another networking event? Maybe it's a group coffee at your local coffee shop on Wednesday mornings? I met one woman who enjoyed horseback riding and would invite people to come out to the ranch and ride. Initially, she didn't think many people would take her up on the offer, but she discovered a lot of people like to ride horses. Regardless of how you're connecting with people, you can create any kind of event you want. Keep it simple, and give people the ability to stop by and plug right in. Most likely, you'll find like-minded people whose interests are similar to yours. Some of the best business connections are people who share some of your interests.

+ Use a client relationship management (CRM) tool. If you're not using one already, you need to find one today. You can buy great products that will help you stay connected and remind you to follow up with people. Trying to do it yourself can be a nightmare. I have found that most good salespeople are not strong administratively and can miss many opportunities. So make sure to keep everything updated every night. After I returned home from networking, I would write notes on people's cards or text myself a note, then enter it into my CRM. Bonus points if you can do that from your phone on the spot, but most of the time I find it difficult to carry on a meaningful conversation while typing notes into my phone.

+ Be present. When talking with people, be engaged; don't scan the room while half answering people, and then slide off. It can be a real turnoff for the people you're talking to, and you can lose some opportunities. If you're new to a group, remember most of these people probably know one another, and word will spread fast if you're not considerate.

+ With every conversation, remember one thing: Always have a next step. The next step could be anything. "Let's set up a call this next week," or "Come join my networking coffee on Wednesday," or "I'd love to come by and see your business." Whatever the next step is, always have one.

+ Another way to stay connected is by inviting people to follow you on social media. You can give short little updates about what you're doing, and people will scroll through and remember who you are. The more people know you, the more they will like you, trust you, remember you, and do business with you.

+ A personal touch is extremely valuable in today's world. Think about handwriting a follow-up thank-you card to let them know you enjoyed meeting them and enclose your business card. Almost no one does this. When somebody gets something handwritten, it says you are considerate and know their time was valuable.

Here's a challenge I just did with some of my team. Physically talk (in person, by phone, or on a live video chat) to three new people every day for the next five days using these stay connected techniques. Then, report back and watch how your business grows. Little things amount to a lot. Three people a day for five days a week over the span of fifty-two weeks a year means an additional 260 connections you will make over the next year. If you made 260 additional connections, would you be doing more business?

When someone on my team objected by saying, "Yet a lot of the connections I've made aren't doing anything for me; in fact, it's a waste of time," my response was, "I want to challenge your thinking. It's not just about the connections you make today, it's about the people they know. Now that you've made a connection, you've opened yourself up to being referred by them."

There's real value in staying connected. I heard that one of the top salespeople in the nation challenges himself to have forty conversations a day. Some are new contacts, some are old contacts. The important part is that he stays connected on a large scale.

All this connecting and reconnecting can wear on people; this is not for the faint of heart. It takes real intention and dedication to make a go of it. It's also hard when you don't feel like going to that next event or connecting with people, but make yourself do it anyway.

Think of some unique ways to stay connected with a great next step. Now challenge yourself and introduce yourself to three new people every day for the next five days. Staying connected might be just what your business needs.

Activities Build Relationships

People regularly come by and discuss ways to increase their sphere of influence with me. The sphere of influence is the number of people they have relationships with who know them, like them, and trust them. I usually hear a version of this: "I handed out a bunch of cards and did not end up with very many people who were interested," "I sent out a postcard to a whole group of people, and not one responded," or "I showed up at one meeting and said hello but didn't end up with any business."

For some reason, people think one simple step in a good direction equals reaching the destination. The thing that's missing in all these scenarios is the personal factor. People don't know who you are just because you say hello one time or shake their hand one time or send them a postcard in the mail. How do you build more relationships to expand the number of people you can influence? You do this through activities. It sounds simple, but most people overlook the fact that you need to do something together to build a relationship. Why do a lot of businesspeople play golf? Golfing takes an awful lot of time and is a maddening sport. A lot of people do it simply to build relationships with other individuals. The golf pros reading this will probably call me, asking how I can think it is mainly about building relationships, yet that's been my personal experience. I'm still a horrible golfer, even after investing in some great clubs.

The point is it doesn't matter what the activity is. When you're doing an activity, the focus is on the activity instead of one another. This enables you to get to know people a little more naturally. Think about all your great friends; how did you become good friends with them? You probably shared an interest; maybe you volunteered at a food bank, or perhaps you went to the same church. I don't know, but I'm willing to bet you shared some kind of mutual activity that enabled you to become better and better friends over time.

There's one exception to this. Some people will naturally trust you based on the recommendation of someone they trust. You get relationship equity when you are referred by someone or simply when you are highly recommended. All this does, though, is speed up the process of building the relationship. The other person has fewer questions about whether you're good and more expectations and belief that you will do something good for them.

Someone once said, "If you want to have a lot of friends, be a good friend, and you will meet a lot of great friends. If you want to have a lot of connections, take time to share activities with the people you want to get to know and build the relationships you've wanted all along." Don't believe me? Give it a test run: Volunteer alongside the same person at an event for the entire day. See if you build any kind of relationship. If you're struggling to connect with someone, do a task or activity together. You may end up with a friend for life or one of your biggest fans.

Consistency

It seems like things in this world are moving faster and faster. This leaves little time to be present and intentionally consistent. People's attention spans are getting shorter and shorter. According to Discovery Therapy, the average adult's attention span is 8.25 seconds.[19] It may sound short, but think about your own attention span.

What does attention span have to do with being consistent? Being consistent requires doing the same thing over and over, regardless of whether it's boring and you don't feel like it. You need a strong *why* here. Why am I doing this? Think about growing a plant from seed. What if you bought a pot, filled it with dirt, and planted a seed? You give it a thorough watering, and then you leave and never do anything again. Is the plant going to grow and become a strong plant that will produce lots of fruit? Probably not; why? Because you failed to water it regularly; you didn't add fertilizer. These are two crucial factors if you want to grow a strong plant. It's not a situation where you can water the plant once, leave, and then start picking fruit.

Unfortunately, this is how most people consider their businesses. They go to one individual networking event and think they should be getting business. They write one thank-you card and think that person will be so enamored with them that they'll send them all their business. They make one phone call and expect the

---

19 Elias, M. (October 31, 2023). Human attention span by age (11 statistics). Discover ABA Therapy. https://www.discoveryaba.com/statistics/average-human-attention-span

person will be mesmerized by their superior action. Plants can't grow unless they're surrounded by dirt. Your business isn't going to grow unless you get dirty and be consistent. Getting dirty is the hard stuff. Making phone calls, following up, answering the phone at the first ring, being available when it's inconvenient—that's getting dirty. Being consistent means doing all of that on a regular basis. This is when you get the results. When you do the hard things day after day, and you do them consistently.

Picture this. Every time you do the hard things—whatever those are—you're watering your plant. And that plant is going to grow into a beautiful fruit tree. You have to know and believe your tree will bear fruit ten, twenty, one hundred times. When you see the big picture, and you take steps toward it consistently, that's where you'll see results.

But our attention span, you argue. The rate at which things move is so fast. Those things are distractions. Naysayers will tell you that you don't want to take the time, you should do something quicker and easier.

I often tell people it takes ten years to become an overnight success.[20] Achieving anything of value requires dedication and consistency. Do you need to be smart with what you are consistent about? Yes, you do. Look around at the people who are most successful and see what they did consistently to build their businesses. That's a window into the future. Most people will say, "Well, it's too difficult to do the hard work consistently." My answer is that when something is difficult, you have an opportunity because there's a good reason why not everyone is doing it. Take the opportunity. Don't waste it—be consistent!

Appreciation

When people say something nice to me, I always say flattery will get you everywhere in life. Flattery and appreciation are very

---

20 The origin of this saying has been attributed to many people, from novelist Tom Clancy to Amazon's Jeff Bezos.

different, though. I think of flattery as saying something over the top, like "You are the most handsome man in the entire universe." Don't get me wrong; I like hearing that stuff. I'll tell people to lay it on thick. But at the heart of it, I don't necessarily feel like the flattery is sincere. Sincerity is the key to appreciation. I also think flattery can easily roll off the tip of the tongue. But appreciation is heartfelt and thought through.

I first learned about the need for appreciation while owning my first company. One of my employees worked very hard, and I thought I only needed to show appreciation by paying her a good wage. I was naïve and foolish. Just an ounce of sincere appreciation can inspire people to new levels. As I continued with my lack of apparent appreciation, her morale continued to fade. Looking back at it now, I'm surprised it lasted as long as it did. I don't know that I could have put up with my boss having such a lack of appreciation as she did at the time.

It's so simple. Look around at what people are doing for you and simply say something about it. "I see that you went out of your way today to make sure this was taken care of. I appreciate you and your hard work." Something as simple as that can make a ton of difference.

People often work because they have to. Because they need a job, they need an income, they show up to work every day and go through the motions. Imagine if you inspired people; would they do better work for you? I do better work when I'm passionate and inspired. So how do you get that passion and inspiration? By showing people they're valued and appreciated.

Appreciation can also come in a different package; sometimes just listening to someone and letting them feel their ideas matter and will be considered makes them feel appreciated. Now, I'm not saying you have to do the things they suggest. I'm saying you need to listen to what they request or are thinking about. Even if you never do anything they request or suggest, simply listening to them and considering their ideas without criticism can show a ton of appreciation. Appreciation says I see you, I'm thinking about you, and I value you. In my book, appreciation isn't necessarily adhering to someone's specific request. It's simply acknowledging how much you value that person and their thoughts.

My biggest struggle, though, is taking the time for appreciation. When I get a handwritten note card in the mail, I feel blown away—wow, a simple thank-you card. What a way to show appreciation. Showing appreciation requires we slow down through our hectic, fast-paced days. But when we do, we keep people onboard with us. We keep them inspired. Because they know they are appreciated where they are. They don't have to go looking for appreciation somewhere else.

Watch the impact for yourself. Pick three people and show them sincere appreciation. Stop in the middle of a conversation and specifically address something you appreciate about that person or something they did. Watch the change in their facial expression. It will be so meaningful to you, and you may think to yourself, "Why didn't I show them this appreciation before?" Write a thank-you card to someone who did something nice for you. It could be somebody who sits right next to you every day; it doesn't matter. A handwritten note card in today's world is priceless and shows a ton of appreciation. Watch how the recipient interacts with you the next time you see them. Vendors, friends, strangers—lather on your appreciation (not flattery), and watch how it changes the conversations and the relationships you have. Appreciation will become completely irreplaceable.

Building Trust and Rapport

Have you ever been to a sports game where two opposing teams' fans sit beside each other? In almost every other scenario, these people could be best friends. I don't know if you've seen videos of shouting matches, drinks being poured on people, full-on fist-fights, full-out brawls—people get very passionate about their sports teams. Now, imagine you're talking to someone who has a strong opinion about something. If you say something against that opinion, it's like you are trashing their sports team. Most everyone has an opinion, but that doesn't mean it is a good one.

How do you deal with someone who has a terrible opinion that you know is incorrect? How do you get them to see a different angle? Most people just tell someone they're wrong and hope for the best. You might as well dump a beer on that person. My point is it's not going to end well. So what do you do instead? You acknowledge their opinion and validate them. Validation does not mean agreement. It means you understand and are sharing that you understand why they have their opinion and that their opinion is valuable even if you disagree with it or know it is wrong. When someone feels like their opinion is validated, they feel like you're on their sports team. Now, you can have an open conversation because you stand for the same team.

Validation sounds something like this: "I can totally see why you would think that. I would probably think something similar had that happened to me." In this case, I don't agree that the answer is correct, only that it is valid, and I understand why they would think what they do. The second I argue against them or their opinion, they shut down and act like I'm on the opposite team. If I can validate someone, they feel I'm on their side. I can keep the conversation going and am open to being led in the right direction because I don't oppose them. Salespeople often invalidate people by telling them why they shouldn't think the way they do and then hoping for a good reaction. I see this time and time again. Your conversations are one of the easiest things you can fix to gain more ground. When you are on the same team, you can lock arms and start cheering on the same side. And guess what? When the team wins, everyone wins.

Chameleons Blend In

People are always trying to fit in. Why? We inherently know we like people or things that seem familiar to us. We like people who talk, act, and look like us.[21] Sometimes, however, a group of peo-

---

21 Seidman, G. (December 18, 2018). Why do we like people who are similar to us? *Psychology Today*. https://www.psychologytoday.com/us/blog/close-encounters/201812/why-do-we-people-who-are-similar-us

ple don't want to appear to be someone different than who they are. You hear these people say, "I am who I am, and people can accept me or not. I'm not going to be fake." When I hear this, I cringe. I get the heart of it: They want to be accepted for who they are. This is, however, a self-centered approach.

When we are in the sales business, it's not about us; it's all about (or should be all about) our customers. The people we serve. It seems to me that the best way to grow a business is to have a lot of people who are very happy with your services. So let's get back to why it is a good thing for people to feel a sense of familiarity with you.

I went to Mexico and was coaxed into attending a timeshare presentation. The first guy we met with was a local, and though we liked him and he spoke English well, I didn't feel like he understood what I needed at a deeper level. Then, in comes an American from the same state I am from. We started talking, and he was able to build a sense of trust with me quickly, simply because we shared a bunch of the same experiences, or so I thought. He seemed familiar, even though my situation did not seem familiar. Did I buy the timeshare? I'll let you decide.

So how can someone be a chameleon, staying true to themselves and not becoming a sellout? If you visit Disneyland, they will tell you that every worker is an actor, and their work is a stage. Are they all sellouts? Are they not true to themselves? Do they suddenly become everything they portray at work, even when they are off the clock and at home? I think the answer is simple: When they clock out and take off their costumes and uniforms, they go home as the same person they showed up as. When we are comfortable with ourselves and who we are, we realize that playing a part for our business so our customers have the best experience takes skill. It takes real effort and skill to provide a level of service that seems familiar and reliable. The littlest things can make a big difference in making people feel comfortable. Here's what I mean.

If you read about matching and mirroring, you will be told to sit like your customer. If their legs are crossed, cross your legs in the same manner. If they have their head tilted, you also should tilt yours. If they use the phrase *Cool, man,* you use the same phrase. Sales trainers tell you this helps put the person at ease because they find themselves in a familiar situation with like company. Excellent sales professionals know how to lead and put people at ease by providing a familiar environment for their customers. They don't view the situation as being a sellout or as losing their freedom to be who they are. Being able to fit in anywhere and with anyone can only be mastered with real practice and skill.

I'll leave you with this. When I was growing up, my father told me, "I want you to be able to dine with the president and eat with the homeless." I didn't understand the magnitude of what he was telling me in my early years. But now, I know that to do this, you must be a chameleon. You must be able to meet each person right where they are if you want to fit in. Be yourself, but take cues from the people around you. It takes real self-control not to talk about politics or other topics you feel passionate about. Remember, it's not about you, and a business relationship can quickly sour because of a few poorly spoken words. If the customer is talking about family, talk about family. If they are talking about finances, talk about finances. Avoid sensitive subjects while you are onstage (meaning talking to customers). This approach will help others identify you as a safe and familiar person. Be wise with what you say and to whom; words have a strange way of coming back to haunt us. But also have fun; you don't need to be a strait-laced robot. Read the room and add a sense of belonging. People will be more comfortable, and your conversations will be more meaningful and go deeper. Don't believe me? Try it yourself. Go somewhere you don't fit in and see what happens, then go somewhere you don't fit in but adapt to your surroundings. Watch the difference; it may surprise you. Good luck and have fun with it. You are, after all, onstage, so give a performance to remember.

Everyone Wants to Win

Do you know how the lottery works? States sell a ridiculous number of tickets for a small amount of money, and the only thing you get in return is the slightest of odds that you could win. Now, the winnings you *could* take home would be astronomical. You have this tiny glimmer of hope that you might win something by putting just a little bit into it. A recent national jackpot was more than a billion dollars. People bought tickets in droves for the opportunity to possibly win one billion dollars. (The odds of winning the larger jackpots are approximately 1 in 300 million.[22]) As you can see, the chances of winning the lottery are so slim that you're more likely to be eaten by a crocodile, get struck by lightning, or travel to the moon. If you think none of those things are likely, you are right. So why is the lottery successful? It's because everyone wants to win.

I'm talking about the lottery, but this transcends every part of people's lives. How often do you hear a friend say, "You know what? I'm really looking forward to losing today"? Or one of your friends sits down at the blackjack table in Las Vegas and says, "Can't wait to leave all my money"? No. People think they have a chance to win, and even if it's the slightest chance, they still believe and have hope that it could happen to them.

Why is this important when dealing with sales? It's because you already know what the person you're trying to sell to wants. If we use the analogy of the blackjack table, you're the dealer, and you already know what cards the player has in their hands. You may not win every single hand, but you already know what's in their hands. This gives you a major advantage. You might say, "Yet I don't know what winning looks like in every situation." And I would say, "Neither do I." I will say, though, if you don't know what a win looks like and you're in sales, you need to do some research. Here's my guess: If you put yourself in the other person's shoes and ask yourself, "What would I want in this scenario?" you will come up with what the win is. Then it comes down to helping them believe that by working with you, they will win.

22 Doyon, J., & O'Donnell, N. (March 3, 2024). What to know about playing the lottery (from a math professor who won). NBC Bay Area. https://www.nbcbayarea.com/news/national-international/what-increases-chance-lottery-win/3408041/

We can do this in a bunch of different ways. I like the idea of walking people through the process and telling a story about how they will end up winning. It might go something like this. "One thing I know that's important to all my clients is that they're more successful utilizing my services than those of anyone else they could be working with. I want you to know I will help you save money in all these areas and pay special attention to the concerns you shared with me to make sure you end up in the best possible position. It's important you know that your success is my number one goal. Simply put, if you're successful, I'm successful."

I think there's a lot of room in that statement to add more specifics about whatever you're selling and the possible steps you can take to ensure the client's success. The important point here is that you are creating the possibility that they will win by working with you. If you can instill complete confidence in them by explaining how they're going to win, creating excitement, you will earn the sale. In these situations, people usually describe how they are successful, and they believe that somehow, this translates to the buyer's or client's future success. Instead, the client thinks the salesperson is out for themselves when they describe their own successes. Your past successes have little to do with this client who's sitting in front of you and whether they believe you can help them succeed. Find a way to communicate and create the possibility that by working with you, *they* will win and not fail.

Now that you know what people want, you hold the cards. No one wants to lose in any situation, so get excited and communicate how they will win. By communicating this simple message, you can inspire others to great action.

Create the Offer No One Can Refuse

Do you get offers in the mail almost every day like I do? Half or more are something like *Buy this expensive item and get 10 percent off the next one. Buy two screen doors and get your third screen door free. Ten percent off your next meal* at some meal prep place. I'm not trying to be hard on these places; I'm sure for their business, these are or could be costly offers to give people. We're always doing things to try to get attention and bring people to the front step of our business. But most of the time, businesses doing special offers say people don't show up. My answer is that it was an offer they could refuse. Your job is not just to give an offer; it's to give an offer in such a way that someone can't refuse.

Let me give you an example: If I offer free coffee for people who come and talk to me, I might get a couple of people, but then they realize they have to talk to me. Is this an offer they could refuse? In most cases, I would say it is. Let's restructure the offer. "Meet me for coffee, and one person will get an autographed football card of Tom Brady." Suddenly, people are coming out of the woodwork to get the offer they couldn't refuse. In the meantime, you're getting exactly what you want, which is getting in front of those people. I'm not telling you to run out and buy a whole bunch of autographed Tom Brady cards unless that will change the trajectory of your business. I'm telling you to find the offer that people can't refuse. Usually, you just need a little tweak to the offering, including something of value that will really excite people. You'll have people coming out of the woodwork.

Think about the last couple offerings you had. Did you have a client appreciation party? What did the value proposition or the invite look like? Did it do a good job of creating an offer that people couldn't refuse? What about with your employees? Are you hosting a happy hour? Are you selling it to them as an offer they can't refuse? No matter what you're doing, you have to frame things so people are excited to participate. This is usually just a small difference from our initial offering. No matter what you're offering, step back, take a closer look, and read it over. Would you want to go? Would you want to participate? Even better questions: Would you be excited to go? Would you be excited to participate?

Here's the challenge for you. Get a piece of paper and a pen, or grab your phone, right now and write an offer to entice someone to use your services. Now rewrite that offer after you've had a chance to review it and create an offer you couldn't refuse. Then try it. Sometimes the win isn't getting this long line of people that wraps around the block. Sometimes the win is just a couple of strong potential clients who are excited to talk with you. When people are excited to talk with you or spend time with you, they utilize your services. You're creating raving fans. Raving fans tell other people about you. When people are saying good things about you, good things happen. Now, go create an offer that no one can refuse.

Ask for Money, Get Advice, but Ask for Advice, Get Money

Have you ever noticed that when you need additional funds, and you go around asking for those funds, people, banks, and lenders all seem to give you advice? The advice is usually something like suggesting your expenses are too high, you need more income, or you don't meet the ratios, but here's what you could do to meet those ratios. I've found that when I need money, no one wants to give it to me, but when I don't, people beg to loan it to me. It seems counterintuitive, but it does make sense when you think about the logic behind it.

Years ago, when I worked with a tech startup, we were required to raise funds. At the time, tech startups were the hot commodity on the block. I read everywhere how people were throwing money at tech startups. I ended up paying an investment group to go on a tour, hoping to raise funds. What I found on that tour was enlightening. My team went to five locations, each representing a different area where investment in startups was heavy. We were all given fifteen minutes to pitch our idea. People would then write their comments and say if they were interested in investing.

Startups have a high failure rate, so it wasn't unusual that the group was skeptical and cautious with their money. I would be the same way if I were the investor instead of the one looking for investment. So I made the pitch several times and was able to watch the successful groups from other companies give their pitches. More often than not, several people would stop me after the pitch and begin grilling me on why I thought my idea had legs or could be successful. Most of the time, I think people were looking to make a minuscule investment for a substantial piece of the company and hoping they could win with that strategy.

You can imagine how difficult things get when you're seeking investment and all the people you go to ask for the moon. I would give it my best shot, telling them all the reasons why this was such a good investment and how they could make their money back, but nothing seemed to resonate. As I watched the successful companies, I saw them offer boilerplate facts, no selling at all, but one thing was evident. Most of the people who were successfully pitching had already had a successful exit or sold a previous company. It's no wonder people would be excited about an investment opportunity with someone who already turned a prior investment into much more money. It's like getting on a team with an all-star player. How do the rest of us make it out of the minor leagues?

I felt like I was a huge failure after going on that tour; I don't think I got even a dollar of investment money. It was brutal. I was beginning to think no one would invest in the company or me. Then, I started having one-on-one conversations. In one of those conversations, someone told me (and I don't even remember who it was) that if you ask for investment, you will get advice, but if you ask for advice, you will get investment. Well, I have a theory that if you're already at the bottom, it's really hard to go any lower, so you might as well try something different.

When I sat down in those one-on-one conversations, I simply asked, "What do you think about this opportunity, and how can we improve it? Ultimately, I'm looking for investment; do you know anyone?" It was amazing how this approach changed the conversations. People began to become interested in the opportunity; you could almost see the wheels turning in their brains. Most of them felt that with their expertise, our company could be successful. Many of the potential investors had good ideas; the issue with most investors was their available time. You want them to share their ideas because when they do, they are showing personal interest in your opportunity. Some people worry about soliciting ideas for fear they may need to implement them, but the truth is you need to have the time to execute and implement the ideas, or they just remain ideas. Most people will dream big and execute small.

After taking this theory of asking people for advice to heart, we ended up raising enough funds to get the company off the ground and develop our product. It was a painfully long road that was not for the faint of heart. But what I took away from it was invaluable. If you need money, if you need people to come alongside you, don't come with the need at the forefront. Come looking for advice. People will identify the need on their own. This is your best shot at receiving funding, a loan, or financial support in general. Even if you don't reach your financial goal immediately, if you're sincere in wanting advice, you will gain support from some of the best.

One of the best mentors in my life connected with me through this process. His name was Russell, and he gave all sorts of support. Quite frankly, without it, I don't know that we could have accomplished our goals. It's the difference between asking for a handout or giving something. When we go into the world with our hands out asking for something, we just want people to give to us. When we approach things with our hands down, we're asking to give something. We're asking to give our thoughts, our experience. When you have actual substance, and you're not just asking to take, take, take, people usually respond by giving. There is more to all of this, like the fact that you need to have your information dialed in before approaching people. But assuming you have everything you need to share the information properly, when you come with that approach, you will find a much different answer. Ask for money, get advice; ask for advice, get money.

The Ghost Message

In today's world, people have become increasingly more uncomfortable with valuable communication. They hide behind devices, technology, or other people so they don't need to communicate effectively. I'll give you an example. In my position, I reach out to people I do not know to make connections, and I do this with no expectations. Here's the thing most people should know. Making connections with people is great. You never know when that connection may be valuable. I've had people reach out nine years after meeting them, and it was a valuable connection. One of my rules is always to leave people with more respect than what they entered the conversation with. In other words, be friendly and respectful to people. You may not be interested at all in anything they have to offer today. But that doesn't mean you can't be nice about it.

Listen to them, thank them, and leave a good impression. Most likely, other people are not giving that kind of respect. Imagine if you were in their shoes. When I didn't realize the value of all relationships, I did not always treat these encounters in a delicate or respectful way. I think the realization of this comes with maturity. Okay, I get it. I'm not going to listen to every single multilevel marketing pitch out there just to be nice. I'm not saying you have to sit through that kind of pain. You might need to, but most likely, you can let them know through positive communication that if you become interested in something like their product, you will let them know, but you're happy to meet for coffee or connect on other things.

But here's one of my pet peeves: People who are friendly and agree to the meeting and then cancel at the last second and will not return a single text or call. This is ghosting, and it just means the person on the other end is too afraid or not mature enough to talk with you about their level of interest. By not responding, they think they are sending a clear message that they're not interested. While this is true, acting this way is a very unkind and disrespectful way to maintain any future relationship. The saying I love about this one is, "The adversaries you create today might be the allies you need tomorrow." This has held true in my life for sure.

Responding to Ghosting

So, what do you do when someone ghosts you? What most of us want to do is insult them. We lash out in some way and tell them how they need to grow up. While this might feel good in the moment, the same holds true in the reverse. What do I mean by that? Don't step on their toes, either. When you're on the receiving end of ghosting, treat others how you would want to be treated. Maybe follow up a bit later with something like, "Hey, maybe you missed my message, but I would still love to connect." You never know what's going on in a person's life. You don't know the circumstances that surround why they've ghosted you. Chances are it's not something big in their life, but it could be. We all have a lot going on these days, and sometimes things fall through the cracks. If you reach out to someone a second time and they still ghost you, perhaps reaching out to them in a different form of communication may be helpful. If you are calling or texting, and they prefer email, this could be the answer. And if they do not want to connect with you, I wouldn't push it. Most people will make it clear in some way if they do not want to be contacted.

Check in every so often and make yourself available, respecting that they may not be ready to meet. This is a hard thing because it can feel like you've been rejected, and if we're being honest, I have definitely felt rejected when things like this happen. I try to remember that "It takes a top-performing sales rep five touches and an average sales rep eight touches to generate a meeting or other conversion."[23] It's important to know that you can't let one person determine who you become. You have value, and for whatever reason, this person is not meant to be a part of your life. Move on; there are plenty of other opportunities and plenty of other people who are willing and able to connect.

My biggest takeaway is to make sure you don't ghost people. You can be clear and concise, letting them know you're not interested in their product while leaving their integrity and ego in place. Always let people leave the conversation with more respect than what they entered with, and try your best not to take being ghosted personally. And last but not least, if you see this person out and about or hear from them later, don't hold a grudge; respond with kindness.

---

23 Pipedrive. (n.d.). 74 essential sales statistics for 2024. Pipedrive. Retrieved March 16, 2024, from https://www.pipedrive.com/en/blog/sales-statistics

8. Managing Challenging Conversations

Discusses how to balance honesty with tactfulness in sales and leadership roles, the dangers of being overly honest, and the exploration of your tactics and the effects of your words.

WARNING—Challenging conversations ahead

IT'S NOT JUST WHAT YOU SAY BUT HOW YOU SAY IT. What if I told you that no matter what you said or did, you would still have plenty of challenging conversations? I can't promise they wouldn't be painful, too. The truth is no matter what anyone tells you, you will need to have uncomfortable or even downright terrible conversations at times. Why? Because when you're speaking with a customer or a team member, you need to say difficult things or take difficult actions if you want to lead others successfully. It can be detrimental to the goal if no one is willing to take the difficult steps or have the difficult conversations.

Now that we have established that you will need to lead if you want to set yourself up for success, I want to give you the good news. Although the conversations and situations may not be comfortable and may not go according to plan, there are ways to navigate difficult conversations to end up with the best possible result. Notice I didn't say a good result, just the best one possible. You need to mentally prepare yourself for the stress that may come with anticipating and having challenging conversations. But rest assured, once you've had these conversations and they are in your past, you won't look back and regret them as long as you navigate them in the best way possible.

After these inevitable conversations, I often feel like a fifty-ton weight has been lifted off my chest. The tricky part is to stay the course during a stressful conversation. Remember, say what you need to say, and don't be afraid. Enough about having tough conversations already; let's jump into this one.

Be Kind; Be Bold

Being kind doesn't mean tiptoeing around difficult issues. It doesn't mean you can't speak your mind. It means you are thoughtful with your approach and bold with your words.

It would often be more convenient to say something that someone wants to hear rather than what they need to hear. Being bold with your feedback often means leaving your comfort zone. This is a necessity if you want to maintain a level of authenticity. One thing I'm known for saying is, "You may like what I have to say, or you may not like what I have to say, but one thing is for sure. You will know the truth." In our society, it's often taboo to hurt someone's feelings or to say something that might be off-putting. I think many people don't even know how to take critical feedback. But when you tell people the truth, you can couple it with kindness, and that's when you earn people's respect. People know when it's difficult to tell the truth.

When you tell the truth, there's often this fear of loss. You tell yourself, "If I tell them the truth, what I'm actually thinking, they may run the other way, and I'll lose a customer or an opportunity." That may be true. I don't want to sugarcoat things. But let's look at the alternative. If you know the truth and don't share it, and they find out later that you know the truth, do you lose their respect? Will they think you didn't share it because you were being selfish? Will they think you didn't share the truth because you wanted to protect your own interests? Those are all things I might think if I found out they knew the truth and didn't share it with me.

I'm not telling anyone to be flippant or rude in their approach to telling the truth. It's my opinion that anything, no matter how hard it is, can be said in a kind way. Often, putting yourself in their shoes can help you understand how they might receive what you're about to say. When we put ourselves in other people's shoes, it's amazing how our perspective changes. I ask myself if I would want to know the truth. I love the saying, "If you always tell the truth, you never have to remember what you said." The other saying I keep in mind is, "One lie is told and a thousand others after to protect it." How exhausting.

Have you ever caught someone in a lie? What did you think of them and their motives? We all have lied before; this is a human trait. This includes me. I've lied and had to pay the price for it, and let me tell you, if I could go back in time, I would have told the truth right from the start. I would have been bold and done my best to be kind. Being forthright is a sacrificial kind of action. The weird thing is that when you take this action, you actually gain quite a bit. People begin to respect that you will tell them the truth even if it costs you to do so. Earning the respect of others is no easy task, and keeping it is equally difficult. We live in a time when people often don't want to hear the truth. They'd rather be fed something that feels good. This kind of approach will come back to haunt you, though. The truth usually comes out anyway, so why not let it come out of your mouth first? This isn't a one-size-fits-all answer to everything. All kinds of dynamics and situational differences will be present in each opportunity. Read what I wrote about the importance of timing. You never have a second chance to make a first impression. Once you take an action, you can't take it back.

What conversations are you dreading or preparing for? Do you want to earn the listener's respect, or do you want to tell them what they want to hear? Be kind but bold, and tell them what they need to hear because though they might not like hearing it initially, if done correctly, they may appreciate it in the end. I've often been surprised when I speak boldly and become more comfortable with being bold and explaining the truth right up front.

Because I know when I do so, I don't need to remember what I said, and my truthfulness better prepares the person on the other end of the conversation for what's in store. And if I do it in a kind way, I just may earn their respect.

Do you have opportunities for this? Role-play it a few times. Talk to others the way you would want to be talked to. Unless, of course, you like yelling at yourself, then don't talk to people that way. When talking to someone, use a calm, cool, collected, yet straightforward demeanor. My guess is you will end up winning a lot of people over in the long run and will become a respected individual in many other people's lives. You will become more appreciative when others are kind and bold with you, and as you make this a habit, it will get easier to perform each time. Why? Because we become better at the things we practice.

Being Too Honest

Being too honest with your customers is like having a poorly brewed cup of coffee. It's black, murky, and full of grounds. If you're going to brew a good cup of coffee, you need to use a filter. You need to remove all the grounds so you can leave that little bit of goodness. It's still coffee; in fact, I would say it's a better cup of coffee because it's filtered. So how do we filter the information so we're still being honest but not giving people something they don't really want?

I didn't like coffee, but then I moved to Seattle and lived there for about eight years. Everything they say about Seattle and drinking coffee is probably true. I never really liked the taste of coffee. Then, one time, I met this barista who made me this coffee drink that was amazing. I realized that if the coffee was done right, I loved it. Fast-forward all those years, and now I pretty much love coffee. But not just any coffee. For coffee to be good, it has to brew at the right temperature for the right amount of time using a good bean that is ground to perfection. I also like white chocolate in my coffee, but we'll leave that alone for now.

By the way, people will tell you they want the darkest,

murkiest cup of coffee until they taste it. Then, all of a sudden, they want that delicious white mocha instead. What do I mean by this? One of the most common things I hear is that you need to tell your customers everything! You can't even leave out the smallest details because you aren't being honest if you do.

I worked on a transaction where the buyer and seller were at complete odds with each other, and they were at their wit's end. You could say they were almost to the point of hate but not quite there. Things were so tense that you could cut the tension in the room with a knife. I had the fortunate opportunity to be the go-between for the parties. It almost felt like there was no possible win between the two of them.

I got on the phone with the seller and made a request for the buyers. They wanted to take possession early, and that seller flew off the handle. "You know what?" he said. "I don't ever want to see them again. I'm never going to agree to that. They can take their offer and shove it." I asked, "If they're okay with taking possession a few days later, is that acceptable to you?" He reluctantly agreed.

I immediately got on the phone with the buyers. Now, a rookie move would be to tell them I just got off the phone and that the seller told them to shove it. That's the black, murky coffee I'm talking about. Instead, what did I tell them? I brewed them a nice little white mocha. I simply said, "I spoke with the seller, and he does not feel like he can give possession early, but he's still interested in making sure the deal happens, so he offered to give possession a few days later." Ultimately, the buyers agreed to this. Was I being dishonest with them? I fed them the information they needed to make a good choice. I did not feed them more than that.

When emotions are high or could get high, look at what people are ultimately saying and not the words that come out of their mouths. In this particular case, I tried to figure out what the seller was trying to say and what he probably would have said had he not been frustrated. In the end, it all worked out, and everyone was happy. Now, imagine if a different approach had been taken. You go to your client with that nasty, dirty coffee, spill it all over everyone, and then say, "Well, that's what they gave me. You told me you wanted the truth." If God has been gracious enough to give you wisdom, honor that wisdom and use it. Just because someone says something doesn't mean people are ready to accept what has just been communicated. It's your job to be the filter and to serve up the information in a clear and understandable manner tailored to their needs.

Do not leave out the essential facts, but filter out a lot of the garbage that does not need to be included. This will help keep your customers focused on the goal. So whether you like coffee or not, try a good cup. It may change your life. And if you filter your words, oh, how sweet your life can be.

Right-Right and Right-Wrong

Have you ever been conversing with someone who always needs to be right at any cost? They explain to you how you are wrong and their point of view is correct. Even though they are correct and you acknowledge that they are correct, you are frustrated because they left you feeling belittled. So, in this situation, I would say they were right-wrong. They were correct about what they were saying or arguing, but they left you alienated and feeling put out. The idea here is to speak the truth in a loving or caring way. Sometimes, this is not possible because the person needs a reality check, but in most situations, it is. I leave you to decide which it is. Remember, words can have a lasting effect, good or bad, so speak wisely.

What does it mean to be right-right? If you can correct someone and give them the right information, and they do not feel like you are against them, demeaning them, or being careless with their position, you have it right-right. Let's look at an example. You overhear a coworker giving wrong information about a product to their client. You quickly interject the correct information, and you provide all the stats. You were 100 percent correct, but you just alienated your coworker by correcting them in front of their client. Your information was correct, but you approached the problem in a way that was not building a relationship. Now, take that same situation, but instead of correcting your coworker in front of their client, you simply ask them if they have a second, pull them aside, and remind or inform them of some amazing upgrades to the product they can share with their client. "Just thought it could be helpful," you can add. This would be an example of right-right.

Ultimately, we want to give the right information and build people up (right-right) rather than give the information and tear people down (right-wrong). When we can correct people in a way that empowers them and builds them up, they are more apt to stay positive with us. In other words, be kind and thoughtful with how you treat people today because you may need them to help you with something in the future.

Don't overlook the cost of always needing to be right. It's okay to let something go that is not important. Keep in mind that timing is key in almost every situation. Understanding when it is the right time to address something is even more important. Start looking for opportunities to be right-right. Correct people or give the right information in a positive way that builds people up. After all, being right-right just might be the direction that will get you where you want to go.

Be Prepared and Make Good Decisions

In my midtwenties, I was deathly afraid of flying in airplanes. I was worried the aircraft would fall out of the sky and crash at any moment. I remember sitting on a plane, feeling the engines dialing back before landing, and experiencing high anxiety, thinking we'd lost power. The other thing I worried about was falling out of the sky or breaking into pieces when we hit turbulence. So I decided to do what any sane human would do. I decided to tackle my fear by becoming a pilot.

This may not seem like a big deal, but inside, I was freaked out every time I would go up in the air. I would often call my family and say, "It was nice knowing you. I love you, Mama. I'm going to some pilot training today." After I started training, I realized many of the things I was scared of were not really that bad. In fact, it's a lot riskier to drive in a car than it is to fly in an airplane. According to the National Safety Council, the risk of dying in a motor vehicle crash in 2021 was about 1 in 93; there were too few airplane deaths in 2021 to calculate the odds of dying as a passenger on an airplane.[24]

Are there real things to be scared of? Sure there are, but if you're prepared and understand them, will you be scared? Probably not. I began to look into the dynamics of flying. My brother actually worked for a small airplane manufacturing company named Boeing. He explained to me how they stress test the airplanes. They take the wings of a 747 and bend them to the point where the tips touch each other without breaking. After he told me that, I thought back to all the times I looked out the window of the airplane on some long trip and saw the wings bouncing up and down a little bit. I remember feeling anxious that the wings might fall off.

Another thing someone told me in in-flight training is that air is like water. If you're in the middle of the lake, and you hit a wave, do you think the boat will sink? Hopefully not, unless you're in an old, nasty boat that isn't waterworthy anyway. The idea is that the boat is designed to ride the waves like airplanes are designed to ride on air, so when you hit a bump in the air, the airplane is not going to fall in a tailspin to the earth. In fact, planes are designed to withstand turbulence. So, if I know the aircraft is designed to withstand hairy situations, then I know it will be okay. That only leaves two other issues: the pilot flying the plane and me, the concerned passenger.

I actually crashed an airplane at one point in my life. Fortunately, the two passengers and I all walked away unhurt. All the years of pilot training culminated in one moment when I needed to make good, solid decisions, and those good, solid decisions saved lives.

---

24 National Safety Council. (n.d.). Preventable deaths: Odds of dying. Injury Facts National Safety Council. Retrieved on May 7, 2024, from https://injuryfacts.nsc.org/all-injuries/preventable-death-overview/odds-of-dying/

Here's what I learned in pilot training, and it's applicable in sales and leadership.

One poor decision doesn't cause a disaster in most cases. A wreck is usually caused by a series of poor decisions that build on one another. Example: I'm in a rush to leave, so I don't fill up the airplane with gas; this is the first poor decision. Then, I don't check the winds for my destination as thoroughly as I need to. This causes me to fly into a headwind and burn more gas—the second poor decision. Then I'm in a hurry, so I don't want to stop at one of the airports to get gas along the way—the third poor decision. This ultimately results in me running out of gas and crashing the airplane. This is called the chain of events. If you want to avoid a plane crash, you must break the chain of events as they happen. This means being able to identify poor decisions and change course quickly.

Just because someone asks you to do something does not mean you need to do it. We all make mistakes when we're scared or frantic. However, remaining calm and steadfast is our best opportunity for survival. Going back to my plane wreck, the tower called me in on a straight approach rather than going through my standard approach. I complied when I wasn't prepared. Rather than setting yourself up for failure, find a different way.

Stay calm in difficult situations. The goal is to win, and your best chance of winning is to avoid failure. So when you feel yourself getting tense, scared, and worried, take a deep breath, look at the chain of events, remain calm, and make the best decisions to land the plane. Your plane may be a stressful situation at work or dealing with a strong-minded individual. Remember, you are the pilot, and you have been trained to land that plane.

Dominating a Situation

Some time ago, I was talking to someone at a horse racetrack about how horses are intelligent and intuitive animals with large personalities. He mentioned how horses figure out who the dominant horse will be. Intrigued by this, I asked him to explain. I imagined they might have a race, and the fastest horse is the dominant horse. Maybe it's the horse with the most mares. My friend explained. Two horses will walk up to each other, lock chests, and push back and forth. The dominant horse is the one who can push the other one the farthest. After this process, the horses know who the dominant horse is.

I pondered this for some time. And then it struck me: This is how humans also show dominance. Let me explain.

People don't lock chests and push each other back and forth, but it is a metaphor for determining dominance in a conversation. Have you ever had someone keep pushing the limits? You stay humble and kind, and they keep pushing. Inwardly, you're so frustrated because you've allowed them to be the dominant horse. The answer is to push back. This doesn't have to be an aggressive action, by the way. Some people just push to see how far they can push you. They want to know what they can get away with. Pushing back could simply be saying no. Wow, what a revelation. Just by simply saying no and not allowing them to push you, you've shown them where the limit is. Now, if you want to push back, you say no and let them understand what they need to understand. "No, we're not going to do that," you say. "In fact, going forward, we're going to do this." I push back on them, and I set the tone for going forward.

Will the pushing stop if I push back? Not necessarily. This could repeat several times, and the idea is that each time someone pushes you, they understand they won't get past a certain point. In fact, they might actually lose ground because they pushed you. That's letting them know you're the dominant horse. Again, I want to reiterate that this doesn't have to be an angry or aggressive action. It can be very calm and peaceful but matter-of-fact and unwavering.

Most people try to avoid conflict. I would argue that by avoiding conflict, you are aiding someone's bad behavior. So the next time someone keeps pushing limits, telling you that you need to do this, that, and the other, explain to them in a kind way that actually, that is not the plan going forward, and present your plan.

Watch as their expression fills with confusion. As with anything, use your best judgment. If this is your boss, and you're refusing to do your job, it's probably not a good move to try to lock chests with them. But if you feel like someone is out of control and is pushing, pushing, and pushing, push back, then push back a little farther. They'll get the picture, and it'll change the way your interactions take place. Going forward, they may not try to push you anymore when they know what they'll be met with. So be smart, and don't be afraid to push when and if you need to.

Drop the Bomb, Then Clean Up the Mess

Have you ever been in this situation? You have to say something difficult, and you struggle to find the perfect words, stumbling over them and giving excuses for things you haven't even said yet. Then, finally, you slowly say that hard thing you've been wanting to say all along.

This is how many people deal with needing to express something difficult. No, it won't be looked at favorably, so they try to clean up the mess before anything happens. Then they drop the bomb; they say the hard thing. And once that thing is said, they have no choice but to clean up after it. They have to explain what they meant and why they said it.

I liken this to cleaning your carpets just before you trample through the house with the muddiest shoes possible. You will have to clean the carpets again. So here's a suggestion to consider. When you have something difficult to say, drop the proverbial bomb right up front. Smack the person right between the eyes with whatever you have to say. Then soften it, if needed. You can always clean up the mess after you say the difficult things. For goodness' sake, don't skirt around the issue, building up a whole bunch of needless anticipation and anxiety. You can say anything you need to, and it doesn't have to be mean or rude. It does not matter how difficult the topic is. Most likely, a situation caused you to get where you're at; just accept it for what it is and deal with it head-on first. Then, take the time to explain or share your feelings.

I found this to be the least painful process for delivering difficult news to someone you don't think will be receptive. Think about it like you are going to the dentist and may need a root canal. The dentist talks to you about everything: You may need the tooth replaced, or you may need a filling. They ask about your regular care, like brushing and flossing. You sit there, confused, wondering if this dentist will ever get to the point. Finally, the dentist says it looks like you will need a root canal. This is what you needed to know all along, only now, you are already exhausted from all the talk about everything you didn't need to know about.

Don't be that person. Give it to people straight right off the bat so they can ask questions and you can address concerns. This is the proverbial bomb I am talking about. Think about dropping it right up front and leave yourself plenty of time to clean up the mess.

Firing People

No one likes firing people. While I suppose there are those occasional situations where the person you are firing really deserves it, and you're happy to see them go, can we all agree this is one of the toughest conversations to have?

Back when I was single, there were two conversations I hated having: breaking up with a girlfriend and firing someone. Essentially, it is the same conversation. You're saying you can find somebody who can do that job better and that they are no longer needed. I struggled with this for the longest time and thought there was no good way to do it. However, I found the best decision anyone can ever make is their own. So my goal with firing people is to help them realize it's their decision and in their best interest. When I ask others how they fire people, most say they have an awkward conversation that usually goes badly, and they're on pins and needles the whole time.

When you manage people, firing someone is an inevitable part of your job. How wonderful would it be if people who left didn't hate your guts and actually appreciated you for letting them go? This isn't always possible, but I found that it is possible a good part of the time. So, without further ado, here are some additional thoughts that may work for you.

+ Give people the benefit of the doubt and try to work with them first by mentoring or offering assistance. You never know what battles people are fighting at home or in life. So you may want to try to give them as much grace as possible.

+ Make your expectations known for what is needed in this job or position. You could say something like, "If you want this job, we need you to complete these tasks in this time period, and if you can't do that, then you're showing us you are no longer interested in holding this position." The expectation is always reasonable and obtainable. What you're doing is trying to determine whether they have any desire to keep the job and invest in making the situation successful.

+ If all else fails, the next step is to ask them to step into your office. I look them straight in the eye and say, "This job isn't working for you, is it?" and shake my head no. You may be surprised that 90 percent of the time, the person will look back at you, shake their head no, and say, "You're right, it's not."

+ Now that we've acknowledged that this job isn't right for them, I give them an opportunity to be successful somewhere else. I'll usually say something like, "Since we know this job isn't working, we can't keep you here in a place where we know you won't be successful. So what I'm going to do is free you to be successful somewhere else because keeping you here would be doing you the biggest disservice. This will give you an opportunity to thrive going forward."

+ Then, I let them know I will give them a transition period over the next two weeks so they can start looking for a new job and this makes the transition more seamless. As a side note, if the person you're dealing with is toxic, you may want to cut ties that day and let them know that today is the first day of their freedom. Sometimes, employers will give a little bit of paid time as goodwill, and other times, everything stops, and a check is handed to the fired person right then.

+ Let people leave with the same or more dignity than they had when they first met with you. When you take an approach like this, though it sounds funny, you're giving people the opportunity to save their dignity. They feel you are being considerate of them and their future. Their only successful option is to transition to a different role somewhere that is a better fit for them. Rather than letting them feel rejected and telling them they're fired, you've encouraged them to take better steps to a more successful future. You're also doing your job as a people manager by moving unsuccessful people out of positions they cannot handle and putting successful people into those roles.

+ My goal is not to have people walk into a room, and I look at them and say, "You're fired!" Personally, I don't have the heart for that, and I just don't see that situation going well in most cases.

If you're willing to try the approach I outlined, I think you will find a much softer landing when you do have to fire people. You can all win if you help put people in a situation where they are better positioned to win. By helping the employees move on, you are also opening up more possibilities for your team to find a key player who can excel in your newly opened position.

The Conversation Ender

We've all been stuck in uncomfortable conversations that seem to go on and on with no end in sight. You're sweating bullets waiting for a moment to end the conversation gracefully, but it just never happens. I've had people tell me they like to say, "Oh look, I've got another call coming in," or "I've got an appointment." This usually does the trick, but some people will persist and ask you to get back to them when you finish that conversation or appointment.

I have tried almost everything I could think of to end conversations by gracefully getting the other party to stop talking, feel content, and walk away. I've done crazy things like talking riddles. Although I found this hilarious, it didn't actually stop people from talking. Instead, people became more confused but then became more talkative because they thought I didn't understand. That kind of backfired on me. I've tried not saying anything at all; I've tried talking a ton. For the conversations where the person persists, I've found only one trick to be effective: giving a pep talk.

If you're playing for a sports team, and you're about ready to go out on the field to challenge one of the most difficult teams of the year, what does the coach do? He gives you the pep talk. It usually goes something like this: "There could be a thousand games, and you might lose 999 of them, but today is your day. Today is the day you are going to prevail. Why? Because you are the victor! Anyone who comes against you will not succeed today. Now go out there and get them." The team members, feeling empowered, rise up and take on that competition. Now, they may still end up getting their butts kicked, but at least they had the courage to face the situation.

What's the correlation? When I'm talking to someone on my team who wants to keep talking for whatever reason, they probably need support of some sort. Maybe they don't feel understood; maybe they're scared. I don't know, but they keep talking. So I go right into a pep talk, and when I'm ready, I end the conversation. Here's an example: "If there's one thing I know, it's that you're a victor. Now, this situation might be difficult for most people, but it's you who will prevail here. Why? Because you're John Doe, and John Doe doesn't back down from situations like this. In fact, situations are afraid of John Doe. And when you look at this situation later, you'll realize how easy it was. Because you're John Freaking Doe! Now go out there and get it!" After getting hyped up, most people do not stand around and continue to talk. Instead, they take that little bit of the courage you bestowed upon them and run with it. When they run with it, they're running away from you and toward the situation.

Remember, although the conversation ender may be a valuable tool, it will become ineffective if overused. You'll know when to use it. It may feel a little scary to hype someone up in the middle of a conversation that doesn't want to end. But if you're restless enough, and you've tried everything else, you'll be excited to see how this works. Now that you've heard this tip, it's on you to practice it. Go hype up someone and end that conversation to free up more of your time for other valuable things you could be doing.

Sometimes the Best Answer Is Silence

Just because someone asks you a question doesn't mean you need to answer. In fact, that is why, in the United States, you have the right to remain silent. Personally, I think if more people utilized this right, there would be far fewer issues to resolve.

Have you been in those conversations where you have lots of random filler conversations going on? People keep saying random things just to keep the conversation going—most of which is not meaningful. But people are so afraid of awkward silence that they keep talking. The awkward silence never comes, but instead, a lot of things are said that maybe you wish would not have been. You can have a better conversation if you say less. How can this be? If you slow the conversation and allow moments of silence, it won't kill you. Silence doesn't need to be considered awkward or stressful.

Have you been in a situation where people get heated and demand you answer them? They have the questions all outlined: Answer this and this, and while you are at it, answer this. You feel overwhelmed because they have painted you into a corner. You feel like you are out of options, and you have no good answers. All the questions they have asked put you in a bad position no matter how you answer. What can you do? Just take a deep breath and remain silent. Wait for them to take the next step in the conversation.

Once you stop engaging, the other person becomes frantic because they can no longer control the conversation. This gives them few options.

In response, they usually try to force the situation by saying something like, "If you don't say something, I will do this," and "this" is usually a painful option you will not like. Or they hurl insults as a way to get to you. Don't fall for these tactics. Remain cool, calm, collected, and silent until you think it is wise to speak. Once the other person realizes they are no longer making headway, they usually give up and stop the threats and insults. Once they become reasonable, it may be time to speak again. You will know when the timing is correct.

This simple act of remaining silent and not engaging the other party can sometimes give you tremendous control in the conversation. Conversations and communication are difficult when only one of the two parties is engaged. Remember, the person with the most power in any negotiation is the one who can walk away.

9. Personal Growth and Persistence in Sales

Highlights the pitfalls of expecting instant success, the importance of understanding one's strengths and motivations, the power of resilience, and the value of maintaining focus and managing one's time effectively.

FEELING DISCOURAGED IS NORMAL and can be part of the growth process. If I had a penny for every time someone came to me feeling discouraged, I would have a mountain of pennies. Know you are not alone, and a lot of people feel this way. Have you ever explored the process of how paper is made? Tree pulp is beaten until it is so refined that it can be rolled into a piece of paper. The fibers break down a little more each time the pulp is beaten, and eventually, the fibers have been broken down just enough to bind together and form a nice piece of paper. That seems like a grueling process. I can only imagine how hard it must have been to make one piece of paper before modern-day machinery. I'm sure there must have been many times when two people would be beating pulp and would look over at each other and say something like "This sucks." The moral of the story is that the refinement process for our lives can be difficult, tiresome, and downright discouraging, but if you persist, you will end up with something you can be proud of. We can all feel beaten down at times, but the sign of persistence is that you keep getting back up. Personal growth comes when we are so dedicated to our success that nothing can hold us back. This next section will cover how to persist through difficult challenges while setting yourself up for success. It's what I've learned the hard way, so you don't have to. Enjoy.

Getting Started

The best way to get where you want to go is to get started. Be fearless, have faith, and move forward. You wake up, open your eyes, and it's go time. You think to yourself, "I'm so cozy; do I really need to get up?" The weight of your day starts to become a reality. The anxiety begins to overwhelm you. Sometimes, just the act of getting out of bed in the morning feels like an enormous task. But remember, every journey starts with the first step, even if that step is simply getting out of bed. When we realize someone out there has it worse than we do, it makes getting up a little easier. And you know what? After you take that first step, every step after that is easier. Motion decreases anxiety and worries and distracts us from our desire to be comforted.

How do you motivate yourself to take the first step? I think it's by being present. That means not focusing on everything you have to do that day or that week or that month or that year but realizing you only have control over this moment. What's happening in this moment? If you want to be successful, you'll consciously take steps toward success. Have a daily plan you can work toward, and it should be more than just staying alive that day. There should be something you're looking forward to, something that encourages you. Before you go to bed tonight, find something that motivates you, something to look forward to. Write it down, take a screenshot, and post it as your cell phone wallpaper. It doesn't matter what it is as long as you're excited or happy about it. Then, in the morning, when that first step comes, and it seems extremely difficult to think about facing the day, read what you wrote and look at the picture that represents it. They will remind you how happy and excited you are about your goal. Then take that first step.

Another step that is difficult sometimes is the one that takes faith because it's a step into unknown territory. In many conversations I've had with salespeople, we've discussed how even though a step toward success is exciting, and they know it is the right one, change can be scary because it's not what they're used to. It's unfamiliar territory, and when we step into something that we're not familiar with, it can cause us to pause. This is where we have to rely on our determination, which points to the fact that it's the right direction, the one we chose.

Think about the trust fall. Do you trust the person standing behind you to catch you if you were to fall backward? This is daunting for most people; it's human nature to want to be in control. When we have to trust a situation or others, we get this feeling of lacking control. When we lack control, we try to regain it and usually flub things up while trying to control the situation and make things better. Once we have vetted something for potential danger and know we have made the right decision (or mostly know it was the right decision), we've done our part; now it's time to let the situation play out.

What does taking the first step have to do with letting go of control? When we take a first step into an unknown territory, we have faith that things will turn out okay. We trust the process will be successful. We believe there's opportunity. The good thing is that even if the first step isn't perfect, you can correct it with all the steps that follow. But until you take a first step, you can't move forward.

I want to encourage you right now to take the first step toward your goals, toward the things you've been thinking about. It's not about the first step being perfect, and I'm not guaranteeing your situation will end well. You've got one chance at life, so take the first step toward your best life. And if you stumble on the way, get back up and keep on going; most of us do stumble. But we learn from our mistakes, and before we know it, we're running along the path of life. And it was all because we took the first step.

If You Think You're Right, You're Right; If You Think You're Wrong, You're Right

What if I told you that you have the power to predict the future? What would you do? Would you walk into every appointment with a kind of assurance that you already know what's going to happen? Would it change the way you had conversations?

I tell people all the time to imagine you're the number one expert in your field. People from all around the world call you up and ask you for advice on how to make magic happen. You're in such high demand that you barely have enough time to eat during the day. Success is not a question; it's the norm. Whatever you touch turns to gold. If you have that attitude, and you're walking into appointments, or you're talking on the phone with people, or you're texting or emailing people—however you're communicating—would it change the way you communicate?

I think it's pretty safe to say it would for most of us. You would be so self-assured that you would have success, you wouldn't even question it. You wouldn't be worried about losing deals or people deciding to go with someone else. Why? Because there's plenty of other business out there. After all, you're the number one expert in your field in the entire world.

Now, let's look at how most people feel and think about themselves. "I'm good, well, most of the time." "There's always somebody better somewhere." "I don't know if I'll have another customer." "I need to pay my rent, so I don't want to lose this person."

It's easy to get caught up in life; life is stressful and complicated. When you have little or no self-assurance, how does that affect your conversations? Are you making statements or begging for business? Do you exude confidence or reflect self-doubt? If you don't believe in yourself, no one around you will believe in you.

Imagine you go to the doctor, who says you need open-heart surgery. You ask the doctor if he thinks everything will be okay and if he feels confident in his skills. He sits there looking at you. After an awkward silence, he reluctantly says, "Yeah, I feel good about it, I think." Alarms go off in your head, and you can't get out of the doctor's office fast enough. There is no way you're going to let this guy do open-heart surgery on you after that kind of answer.

Now, imagine you visit a second doctor's office, and she exudes confidence. She's won awards; she's quick-witted. You ask her if she feels confident about performing your open-heart surgery, and she doesn't hesitate at all; she says, "Of course. I did five last week, and all five had great outcomes." She has so much confidence and belief in her ability that now you believe in her ability. Both doctors had the same opportunity and quite possibly have the same skill set.

If you think you're right, you're right, but if you think you're wrong, you're also right. Sometimes it's not about what's going on in the situation. It's what's going on inside you. I'm not saying you should fake being able to do open-heart surgery if you lack the ability. I would never want to see you take someone's life into your own hands. If you have the ability but are telling yourself things that are paralyzing you and keeping you from believing you have the ability, stop!

Most of us are more capable of doing something than we ever give ourselves credit for. But here's the thing: Most of us will never get a chance to achieve full success if we don't think we can. The simple belief that you have an opportunity and an actual chance to achieve something is powerful. When you do that, other people believe in you, too. It's a self-fulfilling prophecy. It's almost like you can predict the future.

There's also a saying that goes, "Show me your top three friends, and I'll show you your future." You become like those you hang around. If you want to level up, hang out with people who have the skills and attributes you want. They will rub off on you.

The Superfan

What's something you can believe in for yourself? I get it; you're your biggest critic. What if you suddenly became your biggest fan? I'm talking about a superfan. One who's got a front-row seat to your life, who's yelling and screaming and crying when you walk into the room because they know you can do no wrong. You're their superhero. Wow, wouldn't that change the way you talk to others? Do you think that could change the trajectory of your life? Having a solid belief in your abilities can take you to new heights.

Don't listen to the critic in your head. No one ever gets very far when listening to naysayers all day. For the next week, I want you to pretend you are your biggest superfan. Do everything the superfan believes you can do. Take on challenges the superfan thinks you can win. When self-doubt comes in, sic your superfan on them for a talking-to. We'll call it the week of the superfan. During that week, write down everything the superfan said you could accomplish. Then recap and see everything you did accomplish. Was the superfan right? My guess is that your superfan predicted the future.

What's Your Superpower?

X-ray vision, bulletproof skin, or being able to fly would all be super cool superpowers. Everyone has something they're so good at that it could be considered a superpower. You know what I'm talking about. You walk into a room, and someone there is so charismatic that you're drawn to them. You want to talk to them; you want to engage. I would say charisma is their superpower. Perhaps you know someone you can throw a couple of numbers to, and before you know it, they've calculated everything three or four different ways, and every calculation is exact. Some people are amazing at writing, baking, dancing, singing—the list goes on and on. The point is that we are all talented at something. Have you explored what you're talented at, what your superpower is?

A superpower can be anything you are exceptional at. What most people don't do is incorporate their superpower into their daily lives, thereby helping their businesses thrive. If something is your superpower, it's something you're passionate about and love to do. Another applicable saying is, "Do what you love, and you'll never work another day in your life." How amazing would it be if you could incorporate something you love that you're amazingly good at into your business and actually give yourself an edge over everyone else? But how does baking have anything to do with sales? How can charisma help with statistics? These things don't inherently go together, so we don't typically put them together.

What if you could be creative and find a way to tie your work and talents together? Whether you're a salesperson who loves baking or a charismatic accountant who tinkers with old cars, you should feel confident about whatever your superpower is. Maybe you're still building the skill, but when you possess talent or ability in that skill, and you're actively working to improve it, the other skills you're developing tend to be enhanced. This can instill great confidence in anything you do.

Not every superpower will mix with every task or duty, but surprisingly, the majority of them will. Using your talents at work is a way to make you shine. Many of us know what our superpower is because we love using it, or maybe we're just a little further along in life. If you're someone who has not yet explored what their superpower is, that's okay because once you figure it out, you won't want to leave it behind. When you go through the list at the end of this section to identify your superpower, you may not be surprised, but you should be reassured about what you're good at.

Your superpower doesn't require you to be perfect at something, but it does require a degree of mastery above the norm. Just because it's your superpower doesn't mean you can't grow in that area. You can always be better at something; you can always be honing your craft. And along the way, you may develop other superpowers—you don't need to stop at one thing. If you're fortunate to have multiple superpowers, congratulations! You can have a superpower and waste it, but if you're reading this book, I doubt you want to do that. Perhaps you're hesitant to utilize it. I encourage you not only to utilize your superpower but to make it part of what you do and who you are. When you start utilizing your gift, others will take notice, and you'll start getting comments like, "Wow, you're really good at this." When you start hearing those things, you know you're on the right track.

Take a moment to reflect on these questions and see if any particular themes or consistent strengths emerge. Your superpower often lies at the intersection of what you love, what you excel at, and what brings you fulfillment and impact.

SUPERPOWER DISCOVERY QUESTIONS

Passions and Hobbies

What activities make you lose track of time?

What did you love doing as a child?

Natural Abilities

What do people often seek your help or advice for?

What tasks do you excel at effortlessly?

Personal Traits

What qualities do others admire in you?

How do you handle challenges?

Dreams and Impact

What positive change do you wish to bring to the world?

What future aspirations excite you most?

Instincts and Confidence

When have your instincts guided you successfully?

In what situations do you feel most confident?

Feedback and Recognition

What compliments or recognition do you frequently receive?

Have you received awards for something you did exceptionally well?

Reflection

Are there recurring themes or patterns in your answers?

Which activities or traits bring you the most joy and satisfaction?

In the end, you don't need to have X-ray vision, you don't need to be bulletproof, and you don't need to fly on your own. Just identify and use your God-given talents, and watch how your superpowers transform your daily life.

If You Want to Be Great, You Have to Do Great Things

Albert Einstein, Mother Teresa, and Dr. Martin Luther King Jr. are a few examples of people who went above the ordinary and did extraordinary things to become great. Most people don't think they have the same opportunities as people who become great, as though, somehow, those who did extraordinary things had a glowing sign that read, COME OVER HERE AND DO THIS, AND EVERYONE WILL THINK YOU'RE GREAT. Instead, I would say they all dealt with extreme hardship but had perseverance. Mother Teresa became great by thinking less about herself and more about others. There is a story about how her feet were deformed from wearing shoes that were too small. When asked about it, she talked about how she gave the shoes that were better to the people who needed them.[25] And Martin Luther King Jr. sacrificed his entire life for unity. I think they all had something in common: extreme sacrifice.

The good news for you? You can do great things, and they don't have to be at that scale to be great. But good things really are an enemy of great things. Because the second you say good is good enough, you never quite reach great. If you go to a restaurant and the service is good, you're happy. You have no negative thoughts about the experience or the restaurant. But what if the restaurant went over, above, and beyond, and it was such a great experience that you told all your friends? Now, because the business did a little extra to be great, they are thriving. People are storming the doors to experience greatness. I'd be willing to bet

---

25 Lambert, A. (September 3, 2021). How Mother Teresa's shoes reveal her spirit. Denver Catholic. https://www.denvercatholic.org/how-mother-teresa-s -shoes-reveal-her-spirit

you could list examples of when you had such an amazing experience, you couldn't wait for it to happen again.

What's the difference between good and great? Usually, it's something very small and simple. For a server, it could be a bit more conversation, asking about the people's experience, and refilling their drinks more often. For a salesperson, it could be simply stopping by the client's house and making sure they're enjoying their purchase after everything's done. It could be sending a simple thank-you note of appreciation for something others may not have noticed. It doesn't have to be a parade, an all-you-can-eat buffet, and front-row seats to watch your favorite NFL team.

Using the first three famous people as examples, we start to see a pattern. It's a pattern of sacrifice. It's a pattern of giving more than expected. The next time work is due, put a little more effort into it. A manager would ask his staff, "If you were being considered for employee of the year, would you be winning that award with the work you did today?" If the answer is no, then go back and put out great work. When you do great things consistently, people think great things about you, and that's how you become great.

Good Intentions Aren't Good Enough

Have you ever heard someone say, "Well, it was the thought that counted"? I say that's completely wrong. It's the action that counts.

Most good intentions die from inaction. We set out to do something good, but it just never quite comes together. A lot of times, the opposite of that happens. It doesn't matter how good your intentions are to start with; how you finish the race is what matters.

If you told me you were going to give me $100,000 cash, I would think, "That's a great intention. You set the stage; now let's see what happens." Then you bring me a McDonald's sausage biscuit instead. You explain to me how you intended to give me the $100,000 cash, but for one reason or another, the only thing you can give me is this McDonald's sausage biscuit. Do you think I'm disappointed? Do you think I'm sitting here thinking, "Wow, what great intentions you had?" No, I'm not happy about it at all because you set an improper expectation. But at least I like sausage biscuits.

Why does any of this matter? When you tell people—including yourself—that you will reach a goal or accomplish a certain task in a specific amount of time and you haven't completed it, you failed with your actions. You don't deserve anything for good intentions. We live in a time when everyone who shows up gets a trophy. You shouldn't get a trophy unless you accomplish something. Participation awards are not handed out in the real world.

Don't be tricked into thinking for one second that starting with good intentions means you are owed something. In the business world, we are rewarded for results, not intentions. Let me give you another example. If I have an employee, and my intention is to pay them their hourly wage, but I don't, should I explain to them that they should be thankful for my intention to pay them even though I was not able to? No, these people will be very angry, and rightfully so. They gave their time and effort and planned to be reimbursed for their time and effort.

Here's an important point. We're not just talking about having good intentions with other people. Those good intentions could be for you. You start off in a new job and tell yourself, "I'm going to really excel here. This will be good, and the first thing I'm going to do is dominate this list." And when you don't, you let yourself down. Good intentions need to be followed up with **intentional action.** When you say you're going to do something and you have the intention of doing something good, write it down, treat it with respect, make sure you make good on your statement, or at least do everything you can to make that happen. Then you won't end up with a participation award; you'll end up with a real-life trophy. People will know they can trust you and that you are dependable. Let your yes mean yes and your no mean no. This is important because your coworkers are depending on you in most cases. Don't be the weak link; be the strong link in the team and help everyone excel.

Understanding Your Motivations

I once hit rock bottom. After riding high for years, the market completely collapsed. I couldn't sell anything to save my life. I thought, "What the heck is wrong with me? Where did all my success go? Have I suddenly become completely inept in my ability to sell?" I tried very hard in every direction and kept hitting dead end after dead end.

When something like this happens, after a while, you start believing something is wrong with you. And the things inside you that keep you going, like your dreams and aspirations, fade with all your repeated negative experiences. The reality sets in that you are now a failure. You start to think about the days when things came easy, you said the right things, and money came effortlessly.

At this point in my life, I looked around and saw that all the things I'd worked so hard for were now being snatched away from me. I built this giant home and could no longer afford it. I'd wanted a Porsche Turbo, but I had to sell that, too. I'd worked superhard to get an airplane; who even owns an airplane? It all quickly evaporated. I had to make a decision. "Do I have what it takes to be strong and move forward? I have the rest of my life; what will I do with it?"

Everything that motivated me before was no longer motivating me at all. I realized houses, cars, and airplanes are just things. Here's the crazy part about things: Once you have them, they become insignificant and completely unfulfilling. So what is it that's worth anything? I found the people I cared for and the relationships closest to me motivated me. I decided I didn't like what I had been doing for the last twenty-five years. I declared total burnout and decided I wanted to become a plane salesperson. Luxury jets, to be specific. I didn't anticipate what a highly coveted sales position it was. After dashing all my hopes, I decided to move to a completely new area and start back in the sales position I had been in all this time.

One thing was lacking, though. I needed to know what motivated me. Just like motivational speaker Zig Ziglar said, "People often say motivation doesn't last. Neither does bathing—that's why we recommend it daily."[26] I had a picture of my daughter; I kept it with me. Anytime I didn't want to do something, anytime I didn't want to take a step forward, I looked at that picture. I knew I couldn't let her down. I needed to be strong for her so she had a father she could be proud of. This was more motivating than anything else I could find. When I completely ran out of steam, this simple picture would push me to take one more step. I used this picture for a few years and still find it to be motivating to this day.

When life gives you lemons, you must have something that will push you to make lemonade. What motivates you? Without this simple motivation, you could miss the key ingredient that will help propel you to greatness. Don't just write it down—have a picture of it and look at it ten times, a hundred times, a thousand times each day if you need to. Because, just like bathing, it doesn't last. Have it right there when you need it, reminding you why you're doing what you are doing. This small, simple action of reminding you of the why may be the thing that helps you take the next step to success.

Don't Reinvent the Wheel, Make a Better Wheel

When I'm faced with complex situations at work, I'm often tempted to come up with something completely new that's never been done. Most times, I've found that's not what's required. What's required is for me to take a deeper look at the situation and simply improve it. I think a lot of people get mixed up and think they have to be original and come up with something completely different or something that's never been done before. You can do that, and it can turn out okay if you do, but it just may take a lot more time and energy.

I'm not sure who invented the wheel in ancient times, but they

---

26 Kruse, K. (July 8, 2013). Zig Ziglar: 10 quotes that can change your life. https://www.forbes.com/sites/kevinkruse/2012/11/28/zig-ziglar-10-quotes-that -can-change-your-life/?sh=938d87e26a0e

were really onto something. They created something that has withstood the test of time. And even though their invention was great at the time, it looks nothing like some of the car wheels today. I imagine when that ancient dude hammered a wheel onto his chariot, he took it around the neighborhood, and everybody was like, "Wow, look at the wheels on that chariot." Fast-forward a few thousand years, and now we've got these high-tech tires made of rubber that can run without air and won't fall apart. I'd say this is a great example of someone not reinventing the wheel but making a better one. People could argue that the tire was a completely different invention. I would say that's true, but at the core of it all, it was somebody making a better wheel. They looked at what someone else had already accomplished, and using different materials, different dynamics, and all these different things, in the end, they just made a better wheel.

When I build off someone else's wheel, I take all their time and energy and then add to it. I would like to believe that anyone who's created a successful process has probably put a lot of time and effort into making it so. Does that mean it's the best possible process it could be? Maybe it was at the time. But times change, dynamics change, and ideas can be improved.

I love the saying that you're either growing or dying.[27] Nothing stays the same; everything is always moving in a direction. I prefer to be on the growing side rather than the dying side.

What are some steps you can take to create a better wheel or a better process that someone's already invented? It's actually simpler than you think. All you need to do is ask the successful people what they do. And second, watch the successful people and their process to see how it's done. Then, you can simply map it out and make a few changes, and a better process emerges.

You may need to be kind to yourself because you may not get the process right the first time as you try to make a better wheel. When things do not go well, I often tell people, "I didn't fail; I

27 E3 Strength. *Lou Holtz: Growing or dying* [Video]. https://www.youtube.com/watch?v=hnHki6AW0qY

learned how not to do something." If you think about it, everyone needs to learn how not to do something to learn how to do it right. Because, believe it or not, you learn a lot from your failures. I think one of the biggest mistakes people make is being afraid to fail. If you want to succeed big, you need to go out and try to fail huge. Lots of little failures can amount to a large amount of success. I don't know anyone who's achieved great success without failure.

Here's the point. If you want to do something fantastic that will revolutionize your business or life, don't try to reinvent the wheel. Simply take something someone's already made successful and make it better. Just make a better wheel. Learning from the people who came before you will save you an incredible amount of time and energy.

Don't Focus on Everyone Else

When you look around in today's world, success seems to appear at every corner. But what you don't see is the reality. People in all relationships typically put their best foot forward. On social media, people don't post reality. Maybe you've seen someone out in the world taking picture after picture in front of a building or a sunset. They probably take fifty photos so one of them can be edited to look amazing.

Another example I love is when people take pictures of a fantastic party. The food, the music, the setting. And if you were to zoom out, you'd see maybe three people showed up at the party. But looking at the pictures, you would think they had a turnout of hundreds.

It's crucial to notice that people don't highlight their failures, their mistakes, and the difficulties they endured to get where they are today. It's important to keep a grounded point of view. When we start comparing ourselves to others, there's always someone doing better, which means we don't measure up. If you want to fail, compare yourself to everyone else constantly, and you will be on a fast track.

Focusing on everyone else takes away your ability to do what's most important, which is to work on what you're working on. To paraphrase novelist Paulo Coelho, no two people are the same, and no two journeys are the same. You'll go through different things than somebody else will, and vice versa.

If we want to achieve a goal, we can't concentrate on what everyone else is doing. That will only take us farther from our goal, and we risk losing the very thing we're running toward at full speed. I love the analogy of a runner. Imagine you're watching the hundred-yard dash at a major track-and-field event. All the runners line up, kneel down, and get into starting position. The starting gun goes off, and they start running as fast as they can. One of the runners in the front wants to know if they are actually in first place. While running as fast as they possibly can, they snap their head quickly to the right and then forward. It is the most awkward-looking thing. By trying to see where they were to make sure they were winning, they took their eyes off the goal, and at that split second when they turned their head, they slowed down. By taking your eyes off the goal and concentrating on others, you risk losing the race.

There are constant distractions all around us. When we notice and give those distractions time in our thought process, we have to make up for it because we lose valuable time and effort that should be used toward our goal. Don't get distracted or focus on what anyone else is doing. This is you against yourself. Realize what you're risking when you want to take your eyes off the prize. Concentrate on being better, not what others are doing. Everyone runs a race; run yours in such a way that you will win.

Practice the Basics to Become Great

If you want to be great at anything, you have to start with the fundamentals. You have to master the basics and memorize them. It should be something you can do blindfolded. Let's use the example of building a house. The most critical part is preparing the foundation. You map out where you want the foundation poured, you reinforce it with steel rebar, and then you finally pour the concrete. After it's completely set up, that's when you build the house. This is the same process we use for business.

I read a story about John Wooden, one of the most successful basketball coaches of all time. He would often have his team practice putting on socks and shoes and then tying the shoes correctly. What a mundane task. What Wooden understood, though, was that if someone didn't put on their shoes correctly, they might get a blister. If they get a blister, then they can't play their game right, and if they can't play their game right, they may not win. So, while putting your shoes on seems like such a mundane task, know that every little piece of your foundation contributes to the success of your future.

What are the mundane tasks in your current job? Do you just brush them off because, of course, you know how to do them, or have you mastered them, practiced them, and can you do them without thinking because you know them inside and out? Success isn't something that just happens at the top. Success is a bunch of little wins, little bits of progress that stack on top of one another to get you ultimately where you need to go. If you don't build that foundation correctly or stack up the successes correctly, then your whole world can come crumbling down.

There have been many times in my life when I've tried to take a shortcut. Maybe it was not buying the nicer product because I thought I could save a few dollars. Maybe it was not having something done thoroughly when I could do half of it at half the cost. But time and time again, I've found that if I do it right, I do it once. If I don't give it my best and go the extra mile at the outset, I typically have to revisit the same issue multiple times. As a result, I don't save anything; in fact, it takes me twice as long or costs twice as much. That's what I would call a loss.

While you're thinking about all these grand ideas and where you want to go, I suggest concentrating on the small things and taking the extra time to learn them thoroughly. Be a master of the basics, so if anyone asks you any questions about those things, you know them inside and out. People tend to trust us more when we know things and are confident about them. When everything underneath us is solid, it's much harder to shake us.

I've read many, many stories about businesses or individuals who got too big too fast, only to fail as quickly as they succeeded. Things that start slowly usually end slowly, and things that start fast usually end fast. If you don't take the time to build something lasting, you aren't putting time into your foundation.

Examine where you want to go. Make a list of all the basics that can get you there and become a master of them. Then each day, add something else to your mastery list. There is no such thing as instant success but if you build a foundation correctly and thoroughly, day after day, you will end up building a strong business and a firm foundation. This will help you reach greatness.

Expecting Motivation to Last

It's a common misconception that if you're excited about something initially and really dedicated to it, then the excitement and motivation will last and will take you through the entire long journey. I think of motivation like the battery strength in your cell phone. You get it all charged up, and you think you're ready to go. Then, before you know it, you've used up all your battery life—time to put it back on the charger.

Another way to look at it is as if you're going to go on a journey through the desert. If you start on this thousand-mile journey with a large amount of water, you should be able to make it just fine. The problem is that you haven't been on a journey like this before and don't realize how much water you actually need. So, halfway through the trip, you're completely out of water and struggling hard. You should have planned to stop at a few watering holes on your trip through the desert so you could make it to your final destination. To put it another way, the journey you are on will take more preparation and motivation along the way to keep yourself on track than you probably planned for.

I think everyone starts strong and determined. They think they're invincible when they start. But little by little, they get worn down and brought back to reality. Now, reality doesn't equal failure. Reality is just realizing the enormity of the task you're undertaking. When your initial expectations are overly optimistic, you really suffer when your motivation starts to wane.

So how do you get motivation to boost you up along the way? First of all, you'll encounter a lot of de-motivation from all sorts of factors. When something doesn't go right in the process, de-motivation happens. You lose the deal you thought you had locked up. De-motivation happens. Your car breaks down; de-motivation happens. One way to stay motivated is to realize that de-motivation will happen. The other way is simply to add additional motivation into the mix.

Where can you find motivation? This is different for each of us. List three places you go to become more motivated, places that recharge your soul. Any place can serve this purpose and refresh your mindset as long as it does not cause harm to you or others. Then, put these places on the schedule. I like going to YouTube and listening to motivational speakers. Surrounding myself with successful, motivated people is another way to motivate myself. Sometimes, if I really want to motivate myself, I give myself permission for an easy win. I set up something I know I will win at, and I allow myself to go through that process. Because if it's been too long since I had a win, I want to experience the feeling of a win—even if it's a small one.

You become like those you hang around. If you hang out with a bunch of winners, guess who you will become? Dan Peña, the Trillion Dollar Man, says, "Show me your top three friends, and I'll show you your future."[28] This is why, as people enter different parts of their lives, sometimes they surround themselves with different people. The old friend group no longer fits with their future. This is a hard thing to do. No one likes leaving longtime friendships or relationships. But some people are so motivated to make a difference in their lives that they're willing to take the necessary steps.

---

28 Wings Like Eagles. (2019). *Show me your friends, I'll show you your future* [Video]. YouTube. https://www.youtube.com/watch?v=nBEM_7oZsgI

Motivation won't last. And you can't expect it to last without effort. You have to be intentional about refilling that battery, making sure you regularly get refreshed at the watering hole. You've surrounded yourself with great people, and little by little, if you could see a video of yourself, you'd be winning. I've seen people with no hope and no skill transform their lives by knocking on doors and asking for business. I'm at a place in my life where I believe anything is possible. In fact, the word *impossible* says I'm possible. It's not about if something is, it's how it is possible. So, if you're going through something right now, be encouraged. Stay encouraged and add motivation so you can last.

Now, take that fully charged cell phone and use it as a tool to find some motivation. It's all there waiting for you to come and get it regularly.

Stage Fright: Get Comfortable Speaking in Front of Others

You're standing in front of a large crowd. Your palms begin to sweat, and you feel extremely nervous, thinking that everyone is looking at you. Then you realize they **are** all looking at you. In fact, as you stand there, stumbling over your words, you notice people start to tune you out. Internally, you begin to panic. You feel like this is a complete failure.

"They're not interested in what I have to say. What can I do?"

I haven't seen this exact scenario play out, but I know that I— and many others I've spoken to—have feared this very thing when speaking in front of a group.

Early on, I decided I wanted to be a strong public speaker. I realized that if I was going to be successful, I would need to stand in front of people, engage them, and feel confident while doing it.

Can I be honest? I didn't start out being able to speak in front of groups without a lot of ummms, uhhhhs, and other verbal fillers. I also got a ton of butterflies before stepping up to speak. That nervousness didn't go away overnight. I started small—speaking to small groups—and eventually worked my way up to hosting events with thousands of people.

Was I nervous speaking in front of thousands? No. But it was a journey to get there.

By now, you're probably asking, "How do I get comfortable speaking in front of people?"

The answer is simple: **practice.**

I can already hear the objections—*"But I'm terrified of speaking in front of people! How am I supposed to practice?"*

One of the best things I did to practice public speaking in a safe environment was join **Toastmasters.** It's a great organization where people—just like you and me—go to sharpen their public speaking skills. You'll find people at all skill levels, and in my experience, it was always a supportive environment. No one was there to judge me negatively. Instead, I had opportunities to learn, refine, and build confidence.

Another benefit? You get to hear how other people speak and, even better, hear *behind-the-scenes* how nervous they are.

Of course, there are those rare individuals who seem like natural-born speakers—people who walk onstage for the first time and *own* the room. That's great for them, but it's not the norm. For most of us, nerves and fear of judgment are completely normal when speaking in public.

Here's something else I've learned: **public speaking isn't that difficult if you're a master of your topic.**

If I were asked to speak about rare cars, and I knew everything about them—the parts, the history, the years they were made—I wouldn't worry about what people thought. I'd be confident because I know my stuff.

Watch other speakers you enjoy speak to a group while you take notes. Chances are you will get some great tips from just observing how someone you respect or enjoy presents.

Another tip? Video yourself speaking.

Watch the video and ask yourself: *"Would I enjoy listening to this?"*

"How should I change what I'm saying?"

Most of us are our own biggest critics, so chances are you'll catch things you want to improve. If you need a second opinion, show it to a trusted friend or mentor and get their feedback.

What we rehearse and know well is easier to deliver confidently.

Keeping the right mindset is also important. You've probably heard the classic advice: *Imagine everyone in the audience is naked.* Supposedly, this thought helps calm your nerves. In your mind, this takes the focus off you as the speaker. However, the best strategy is whatever puts you at ease. I don't personally use the classic advice, but if it works for you, use it.

Instead, I've had success with speaking as if I'm talking to just one person, not an entire crowd. This makes the whole experience feel more natural and far less intimidating for me.

Be easy on yourself. Know that most people are nervous about public speaking. Some would rather face death than speak in front of a large group!

I hope you're not one of those people. But if you are, there's hope.

Practice what you preach. Become an expert on your subject. That way, when you deliver your message, people will be getting real value.

And remember: The more you do it, the easier it gets. Even if you don't love public speaking, when you listen to feedback, make adjustments, and push yourself to improve, you *will* get better.

Start small. Give a toast in front of friends. Once you feel comfortable with that, speak to a small group. You'll start to realize that it's not as scary as you once thought. And when you do, that stage fright will slowly fade away.

Artificial Intelligence: Don't Forget to Think for Yourself

I'm reminded of some of the old-school CEOs of iconic companies, including Lee Iacocca, the CEO of Chrysler for many years, and Dave Cole, the CEO of OuterWall (Coinstar and Redbox), a personal mentor of mine. Some of them started in the lowest positions possible. They learned to sweep the floors, then they learned the next position, and so on, and eventually, they knew everything that had to do with running the company successfully. They could go into every aspect of it, and they would know whether it was being done correctly or not. Having that knowledge was invaluable when it came to running the company. So much so that the investors and everyone else knew that this particular person who had all that knowledge was most qualified to run the company.

What does this have to do with AI? Artificial intelligence has taken the world by storm. Pretty soon, we'll be at a place where people no longer have to think for themselves. You hear songs that appear to be written and sung by famous people, only to learn they were sung by artificial intelligence.[29] Drive-thrus are taking orders through artificial intelligence. Almost every aspect of our lives will be affected in some way by artificial intelligence. Maybe you're reading this book right now and it's already happened because I wrote this book five to ten years earlier.

What we don't know makes us dependent on others. If I'm lost in the woods, and I don't know how to use GPS or a compass, I'm going to look to the person that knows how to use it, and I'll listen to them to be sure I get back home. No matter what the topic is, we are dependent on knowledge. Just because information is readily available does not excuse you from the need to learn it for yourself.

If we blindly follow artificial intelligence suggestions for life and decisions, we will become so reliant on it that we will be unable to sustain ourselves without assistance. It's my opinion that the people who will have the most value in the future will be the ones who learn most aspects of their job without solely relying on machines. How could this be possible if most of the world is run by machines?

You don't have to obstruct the process to understand it. You will be able to identify when something is going wrong if you

29 Smith, N., Lippiello, E., & Pereira, I. (November 3, 2023). AI songs that mimic popular artists raising alarms in the music industry. ABC News. https://abcnews.go.com/US/ai-songs-mimic-popular-artists-raising-alarms-music/story?id=104569841

understand how each part of the process works. If you are a good writer, and AI writes an acceptance speech for you, and you can realize it did not do so in the desired format, you can save yourself a lot of embarrassment. Also, if you understand processes and don't rely on only machines to complete the tasks or processes, you can identify areas for improvement. Artificial intelligence is just a tool. You were born with natural intelligence, and if you use it correctly, you will shine.

The problem with real intelligence is that it goes away if you don't use it. Just like the muscles in your arms or legs, if you simply sit on a couch and never use them, they will atrophy. You can dumb down your brain if you do not use it regularly. Stay sharp, stay alert, and learn everything around you, even if something is doing the work for you. Your abilities and knowledge will directly affect your earning potential.

Please understand that I do think artificial intelligence will play an even stronger role in the future, and that it can help with many tasks to make things more efficient. Where we get into trouble is when we rely on it solely. Remember, think for yourself, learn the tasks and the deeper reasons why things are happening around you, and earn the position of leadership; reach your full potential! Hopefully, you don't ever get to a point where you are just blindly led without any thought of your own. Build up your brainpower and use it regularly. The people who have the most opportunities are the ones who use AI and their own intelligence in conjunction. In my opinion, they will have a strong advantage over people who do not use both together.

10. Maintaining Balance and Avoiding Burnout

Explores the fallacy of overnight success, the dangers of social overload, the value of self-care, avoiding burnout, why failing is a gift, and the importance of maintaining balance between work and personal life.

• •

MAINTAINING BALANCE TO AVOID BURNOUT IN ONE'S LIFE is tough to do. Most of us fail miserably at it. Many books will talk about the importance of a healthy body and mind. But what we are focusing on in this book are strategies for the mind to help give you some guiding principles for success.

Here is what I find: We push ourselves and push ourselves, thinking we need to make one more call or appointment, write one more email, but that last email, call, or appointment never comes. It's always just out of reach, and getting to the goal can become overwhelming.

Many people start strong and later find themselves struggling to continue. In the sections that follow, we will talk about how to move toward your goals confidently, and I'll share some helpful tips for avoiding burnout. When you don't take time to recharge and plan, you find yourself running on empty, which makes everything harder. I don't know about you, but I don't want life to be hard; I want it to go as smoothly as possible. Keep reading if you do, too.

Small Steps Toward a Big Goal

Don't you love it when you can take a giant leap forward, when you can make a large amount of progress in just one simple step? I know I do, and there's probably nothing more grueling for me than when I have to be patient and do a lot of little things to make progress.

I experienced this recently. I have a vintage car that I'm completely restoring. If you know anything about vintage cars, you know the metal can become swiss cheese when it rots away, and you have to cut it out and weld in new metal. You've taken a giant leap forward once that metal has been replaced. Then comes the hard part.

When you weld a new metal piece into place, it leaves a big bead where it was stitched together. Have you ever heard the term *grinding*? As in, I've been grinding all day long on this project, or I'm grinding away. The term should have been derived from metal workers. To make the seam look flawless, you must grind it slowly, carefully, and thoughtfully until the seam is gone. If you think this process must take a long time, yes, it does. Patiently and methodically grinding the seam is definitely one of those challenges where it's me against myself because I want to take giant leaps forward and finish quickly, but to get it right, I have to take small steps in small increments, which take time and patience. While small steps forward are challenging for people, especially in today's world, where we lack a lot of patience, taking small steps is a must if you want to get to your goal productively. This process is the same whether your goal is with your business, your job, or your family.

What small steps do you take every day toward your goal? At work, do you focus on some of your projects a little longer to be sure they are completed sooner? Do you take a little more time to make sure your customers are completely satisfied? With your family, do you take some extra time to converse with your kids or your spouse? When you take the extra time, the result is a byproduct of the small steps you take every day. Even though the steps may feel laborious, bypassing them will actually set you back. Don't overlook the small steps. Even when they don't feel significant, and you don't feel like you're making progress, those small steps are a necessary ingredient for your success.

I remember watching a funny video about this old guy who was taking baby steps forward but moving his feet rapidly. A woman sitting in her car watched him in the crosswalk, thinking, "Hurry up," because even though this guy's feet were moving quickly, he just wasn't making much progress. That's how I feel a lot of the time. I'm just moving my feet back and forth as fast as I can, but I'm not making a lot of forward progress.

I think it helps to understand how part of the process is feeling like you are not making progress. Also important to remember is that you shouldn't compare your successful journey to someone else's. It's easy to view their wins and feel they were able to reach their goals quickly. But I'm willing to bet if you ask them, they took a million small steps forward to get there.

The Overnight Success

There was a time when people thought I was an overnight success. When they asked me how I quickly became successful, I would tell them it takes ten years to become an overnight success. Most people don't see everything you do on the back end to win on the front end. Especially in the world of social media, people fast-forward through the hard part, or what some would say is the boring part, and only show the highlight reel. Most of us don't go over all the grueling details, even when sharing with friends. When people ask how your day was, you probably don't say, "Well, I designed a new marketing piece and ran through the verbiage about twenty times, then reviewed my process for getting it out, which took about a third of my day. Then I dealt with all the issues from the day before." Most of us don't share details about all the small steps and probably only talk about the giant leaps.

It's okay, you don't have to talk about them. Just know those small steps are a crucial part of reaching your goal. So grind away, little by little, and watch everything come together. When you take those small steps and maintain a positive outlook, the end product can turn out much better.

Social Overload

In today's world, we have so many social networks and social interaction opportunities to choose from. Social networking of all types has been a very useful tool for many people when building their businesses. You can get out in front of a lot of people, interact with quite a few of them, and bingo bango, you build your business. But everything comes with a cost.

Social overload happens when we cannot mentally handle the volume of interactions. Some of us get there quickly, and others can handle more before they feel overwhelmed. I get overloaded when I regularly push myself past my threshold. What's my threshold? Because I am a very social person, I can handle a lot of social interaction. Other people are not as comfortable with engaging socially, and they have to force themselves to have social interactions.

It's been my experience that people either take energy from us or give energy to us when we interact with them. My threshold is based on how much energy I have left in the tank. If my social tank is running low, I won't be able to give that much without pushing past my threshold, but if I feel refreshed and my tank is full, I can give a lot before feeling overloaded.

Social media is one of those things that's never-ending. Here's what I mean. You go to a party or a networking group. Events will have a specific start time and end time, so you can mentally prepare yourself for that. Once the event is finished, it's over: You completed your mission. The problem with social media is how it's ongoing. People can message you about anything at any time, and if you don't get back to them, they can comment on how you didn't get back to them.

I hope this never happens to you, but in the world of now, things seem to go faster and faster. People's expectations grow, and their threshold for patience becomes almost nonexistent. My threshold is reached when I can't turn off the need to accomplish social tasks, and it becomes a vacuum sucking the life right out of me.

Most people don't know how to guide their social interactions; they let themselves be guided by them. They put no parameters around anything and let social interactions run rampant in their lives. They answer messages at all hours and don't take time to recharge and fill their tank. If you're an introvert, I would venture to say you probably feel this almost every day when forced to interact beyond your comfort level. As you pile more and more into your life, things can more easily fall out of balance.

Here's an example of a situation that may lead to social overload. You're at dinner with family, and instead of enjoying the time and being present, you're on social media and ignoring everyone sitting right in front of you. This could cause stress in your personal relationships, which in turn will contribute to burnout. What's the answer? Today's phones can tell you screen-time usage. Smartphones are one of the most significant accountability devices ever created. Now, I'm not telling you how much time you need to spend on the phone or with your loved ones. That's more of a personal decision you need to make for yourself. I will say this, though: If you want something to be sustainable, you have to leave room for other things to be inserted. You can't be on your phone all day ignoring all the people and activity around you without sacrificing something. And you'll find that if you have too much of anything, it's not good for you. That doesn't mean there can't be times when things take a bigger chunk of your time. Just understand that a life without downtime is usually not sustainable.

How to Avoid Social Overload

It is possible to be socially engaged without being socially overloaded. First, acknowledge it can happen. Then, set the stage:

how much time are you actually spending on something? What does your daily life look like when utilizing it? How is it affecting your life? Make room for social interaction, and give yourself permission to have time and a place to use this tool. The key is to utilize it; it's not something that utilizes you or controls you. Finally, give yourself permission to say no. It's empowering to be able to say, "I'm not getting back to these messages until this time tomorrow," "I'm only going to do one post here," or "Once this social engagement is over, I'm taking some time for myself." Just because something is dinging at you, the phone is ringing, or people are asking for something doesn't mean you have to act right at that moment, especially if your overall well-being is at risk.

I once worked three months straight without taking off one single day. That's what I call an unsustainable situation. Did I need to do that to get started? I think I did. Did I get a benefit from doing that? Heck, yes, I did. Could I do it today? Only if I had to. I know myself a lot better today than I did back then. Excitement and joy can overshadow a lot of stress. We don't even see or feel it because we're too excited. It's like when we meet a significant other; at first, we are enamored and would do anything for that person. But after the honeymoon phase, reality sets in. This is how it is with a new job or opportunity. The intensity isn't sustainable.

Don't avoid social interactions altogether. We need them. Everything in sales and marketing is about trying to get in front of people. If we can be social, it's like free marketing. But when we become overloaded, it takes the wind out of our sail and the skip out of our step, and begins to load on extra weight. If you set some good habits now, you are less likely to suffer from social overload. It's easier to add things to your plate than it is to take them away once you've already had them playing a part in your life. And look, when you're not overloaded and you're firing on all cylinders, things are happening, life is good, and more importantly, you're making good progress. Now, get out there in a mindful way and get socially active.

A QUICK GUIDE TO HEALTHY SOCIAL MEDIA USE

Set Boundaries: Allocate specific times for social media use and stick to them. Consider using apps or phone settings that limit usage or set reminders for breaks to avoid excessive screen time.

Curate Your Feed: Regularly review and curate your social media feed by unfollowing accounts that don't add value or contribute to your well-being. Follow accounts that inspire, educate, or entertain in positive ways.

Practice Mindful Engagement: Be conscious of your interactions. Engage meaningfully by commenting thoughtfully, sharing responsibly, and avoiding impulsive reactions to posts or comments that may provoke negative emotions.

Take Breaks and Unplug: Schedule regular breaks from social media to focus on real-life activities, hobbies, or spending time with friends and family. Consider occasional social media detoxes to reset and reduce dependency.

Prioritize Mental Health: Be aware of how social media affects your mental health. If you feel overwhelmed, anxious, or inadequate due to social media use, seek support or consider professional help. Prioritize your mental well-being over your online presence.

Hard Times Now, Good Times Later

We live in a world where everything is immediate. If you don't have "it" now, you lose. Remember, the person with the most strength in any negotiation is the one who can walk away. You can't walk away from the debt you already owe. But you can walk away from the debt you're thinking about creating. This doesn't have to be monetary debt. It could be related to time, relation-ships, or other things. You see, we take care of the things that are most important to us. First, though, we must determine what is most important to us.

A friend in my past shared a saying that was profound at the time and highlighted the need for hard work and how it pays off in the end. The saying was "Hard times now, good times later."

I can almost hear someone asking, "Isn't it just to keep grind-ing and grinding and grinding, and it's going to be hard, and then one day it's over?" I don't believe that's what our futures hold.

Because we live in a world of now, people have little patience for anything. I was recently talking to someone who said back in the '60s, she didn't even have a credit card. If your washing machine broke, and you didn't have the money to repair it, you had to save money to fix or replace it. Nowadays, all of us are stricken by debt. According to *Business Insider*, the average Amer-ican adult holds about $104,215 in debt across mortgage loans, home equity lines of credit, auto loans, credit card debt, student loan debt, and other debts like personal loans.[30] The quest to have everything now has backfired on us. Many of us have fallen into this mentality. What if there was a different way of thinking about it that actually kept you in control?

I use *hard times now and good times later* as an analogy to remind me that with everything, there's a reason, a season, or a lifetime.[31] When I'm going into a new business endeavor, project, or time-related commitment, and I know there will be a lot of hard work, I want to know that it will pay off in the end. I'm creating patience within myself, not expecting an immediate result.

When we slow ourselves down and exhibit patience, we can have a greater reward. Let me explain. Things that start fast gen-erally end fast. Things that start slowly generally end slowly. I say

---

30 Streaks, J. (May 29, 2024). Average American debt in 2024: Household debt statistic. *Business Insider*. https://www.businessinsider.com/personal-finance/average-american-debt?op=1

31 The poem, "A Reason, a Season or a Lifetime," by Brian A. "Drew" Chalker.

this because when we build a strong foundation for something, it is typically built to last. If we really care about something, we will slow ourselves down and take extra time and attention because we care so much about it. Going fast is when I buy a cabinet from IKEA and try to put it together without reading the instructions. I often tell my wife, "No, I've got it." Then, after struggling and struggling and putting together a Frankenstein cabinet, I finally break down, do the hard thing of reading all the instructions, and painstakingly put it together piece by piece. It's amazing how the cabinet actually works after that, and it's pretty nice because I followed the steps I needed to take to create the best cabinet.

What do you want in your life that you don't have patience for? Do you need a new car, or, better yet, do you want a new car? You just need to save up your money. Do you need a new job? You just need to build up your skills. Whatever you desire, do the hard things first by preparing yourself before you seize it. It will be worth it.

I know what I'm saying is completely counterintuitive to how we live today. Do these questions sound like you?

+ "You mean you want me to hold off and have patience rather than taking something now and paying for it later?"

+ "You mean you want me to invest in those skills before I try to take on a job? Can't I just learn it as I go and wing it?"

+ "You want me to invest in my relationships, but won't they just take care of themselves?"

Some of you may find it exciting to restrict yourself and hold back your temptation to move forward on something prematurely. I think wisdom is knowing when you're ready. Having self-control is a virtue, no matter how tempting self-indulgence is.

I'm not saying you shouldn't reward yourself with something you enjoy, and I'm not saying there aren't times when you need to put yourself into situations and grow. What I am saying is that for a long-term goal, you need to look at everything from start to finish and plot a successful path—not just *a* path but *the most successful* one. And when you step back and look at that road map, don't take the shortcuts that will put you back in the end. Do it right; do it once. Set yourself up for long-term success. Sometimes, a little bit of patience can create a lot of reward. Don't be afraid of hard times now; look forward to the good times later.

Life Is Like an All-You-Can-Eat Buffet

Have you ever been to Las Vegas and seen the amazing buffets at restaurants and casinos? You walk into this beautifully decorated spot, and there is every kind of food you can imagine. There's steak, lobster, crab, waffles, pancakes, vegetables, fish—every food your heart could desire. When you get there, you look around and start to strategize. "I know I only have so much room," you say to yourself. "How am I going to get the steak, the lobster, and three pancakes plus dessert?"

The answer for me, at least, is that I can't fit all that in. So I walk the whole buffet, looking at each item and deciding whether it is worth it. If it is, I'll take a little piece because I only have so much room on my plate. I usually get about halfway through the buffet before my plate is so full that I need to sit down, eat, find out what I like, and take a second run at it. After all, I have to get my money's worth, right? It's not an inexpensive experience.

What does this have to do with life? Imagine your life as an all-you-can-eat buffet with all sorts of amazing and wonderful things to experience. The problem is that you can't load up on every single dish. You can't take on every single project that your heart desires. What ends up happening is your plate overflows and becomes completely unmanageable. You become completely gorged on life, and you no longer have time to sit down and enjoy the fruits of your labor. When someone asks me, "How's it going?" I will often say, "Life is like an all-you-can-eat buffet; sometimes you like what you get, and sometimes you don't, but you keep going back for more because it's an all-you-can-eat buffet." People usually laugh and agree.

How do you decide what you want to do when there are so many good things to take hold of? If you took on every single project that came your way, you would be so busy, you would almost freeze because you couldn't make progress on anything. This is where you need a strategy. You need to know where you want to end up. You need to look at every single thing that you're doing and decide if it gets you closer to your end goal. If it does not, you can make a very powerful statement: "No."

Just Say No

Some of us are people-pleasers and have a really hard time saying no. This one statement can actually be a big blessing to the people you say no to. What do I mean? If you say yes to something and you're not fully engaged, or you can't participate in a helpful way, you're not doing them any favors. You're setting yourself up for failure. And when you set yourself up for failure, you fail the people around you as well. I joined a certain organization as a volunteer, but I had little time to give. As a result, people asked if I really wanted to be involved because they weren't seeing the effort. If I'm being honest, I had a sincere desire to give the effort, but I had no bandwidth. I had too many things on my plate.

When everything is important, nothing is important. When I realized that I was not a benefit, I made the hard decision to step away from the organization. One benefit for them was finding somebody who was able to contribute more than I had, and the benefit to me was a reduced level of stress because I didn't have that on my plate anymore. Sometimes, when you remove something from your life, the initial letdown is worth it because the result will be much better. I often tell people they either have to deal with the tough part of a problem at the beginning or the end of the situation. If you deal with it in the beginning, you get it over with, and the remaining part of the process is usually much easier.

I love the saying that you can have anything you want. You can have it all? What they don't tell you is that you can't have it all at once. We couldn't handle that much on one plate at one time. A little bit of reflection time and planning can go a long way with this. When I know what I want to do and be a part of, when I know clearly what my goal is, I can pass on all the things that don't line up. That way, I'm making room for the things that do. You can't be fully committed to multiple things at one time.

You only have so much time in your life before you can't take on anything else. Ask yourself what you have on your buffet right now. What's your goal? Where are you going? Does it make sense to participate in those things, or are they taking away from the room you need for something more important? If I could go back in time to my younger self, I would warn myself about this very issue.

FOMO

At some point, I was worried that maybe I wouldn't have other opportunities and someone would pull something off the buffet, so I wouldn't be able to try it. This is the fear of missing out (FOMO). I've learned over time that if you're alive and breathing, other opportunities will present themselves in your life. Will you have the time and ability to take that opportunity? Or will you be so filled up with all the things you put on your plate that you have no room to add an amazing dish?

I also want to leave open the possibility that you will grab a new plate at some point. Maybe you realize the things you've been filling up on aren't what you want. You can put that plate down, go back to the front of the line, grab a new plate, and take another run at it. You are not stuck. You have your plate, and you have the buffet in front of you; only you can decide what you want to put on your plate. If the food's bad, don't eat it. Don't just leave it on there because you don't want to waste it. You only have so much room. Grab the things you like and that are good for you. Put it on your plate and enjoy. Why? Because life is like an all-you-can-eat buffet: sometimes you like what you get, and sometimes you don't, but you keep returning for more because it's an all-you-can-eat buffet.

Don't Expect Perfection, Only Excellence

Expectations can be a killer, both for us and for others. The problem with expectations is that no two situations are ever the same. At least not entirely.

When I hire new employees, I tell them I don't expect perfection. In fact, no one's perfect. I usually pause then and wait for them to respond. Next, I'll say something like, "Do you know anyone who's perfect? I know I'm not perfect." They usually laugh and agree.

I'll then ask them, "Since I don't expect perfection, do you know what my expectation is?" I'll pause again to give them a chance to answer. They usually struggle for a second, look around the room, make a few guesses. Eventually, they ask, "What do you expect?" And I tell them, "I only expect excellence." They laugh.

I ask what the difference is between perfection and excellence. They come up with some pretty good answers about what the difference may be. That's when I step in and say, "This is my simplified version. Perfection is not obtainable; it means you never screw up. Since we are imperfect humans, that's not obtainable. Excellence says you can screw up one way, one time. Then you never screw up that way again. That's excellence. You learn from your mistakes, and you don't make the same mistake twice." I laugh and tell them I'll help them bury a body one time, but after that, they'll have to drag it out on their own. (I did clarify that I was joking. I wouldn't help someone bury a body.)

The goal here is to set excellence—not perfection—as the goal. Why is it important to clarify this? If you're someone who strives to be a high achiever, you may be striving for something unrealistic, which is perfection. Sometimes, people are not just hard on those around them but even much harder on themselves. I used to look at being hard on myself as a way to push myself further. And that worked to an extent. But I wasn't aware of the costs. I wasn't aware that I wasn't giving myself room to be my best version because I was constantly shooting for something that wasn't possible. But how wonderful would it be to be okay with excellence? You know, I've never heard two people walking down the street saying, "You know, the experience with the barista was excellent, but it wasn't perfect. Probably won't go back there again," or "The way that instructor guided us through that process was excellent, but it wasn't perfect. We can never go to one of those classes again."

It's my personal opinion that we need to give people (including ourselves) the room to be okay with failure as long as we learn from it and don't duplicate the failure in the same way. If you're a high achiever or strive to be one, you already don't want to fail. You're running scared that things won't go exactly how you want them to. That fear often will keep you from learning the best way to do something because it's in our failures that we learn how not to do things. I've even heard people say, "If you want to succeed, go out and fail. It's the quickest way to success. Then you'll learn how not to do something the wrong way, and you can master it by doing it the right way."

You aren't perfect, and you never will be, so stop trying to be. Instead, realize the brilliance of being excellent! Then, without fear of failure, go learn from your mistakes and become excellent at everything!

Ignoring Is Ignorance

It's ignorant to think a problem will just go away if you ignore it, yet this is how most people think. The only way I know of how to deal with problems and make them go away is to acknowledge them, process them in my head, make a plan, accept the problem, and send it on its way.

Have you ever been hit with enormous issues or stressful situations that paralyze you or cause so much anxiety that you almost end up in a panic attack? How do you handle that? Most people say they just ignore the issues and put them off to deal with later. But the only way to make stress, anxiety, and unpleasant issues truly disappear is to deal with them.

The Nightmare of Stress

I wake up in a room where all four walls are covered from floor to ceiling with clocks, the old analog clocks that have a big hand and a little hand. I notice the clocks on one wall stop working. This cascading effect acts as a wave around the room. I immediately take action and start fixing clocks, but as soon as I work my way around all four walls, it begins again—all the clocks start breaking again. That is my recurring nightmare. It didn't take much to figure out the meaning behind my nightmare. I didn't feel like I had enough time to do everything I needed to do. As soon as I would start to get to a place where things were almost manageable, the process would start all over again. The feeling of despair and stress radiating through my soul was unmanageable. I was so stressed out that my stress came through in my dreams.

My dreams are usually a happy place. Maybe I show up in Fiji one day, hanging out at the beach, or I'm sitting at my favorite restaurant with my friends and having a good time. But this nightmare proves I'm dealing with stress in my life even when I'm supposed to be enjoying my time of rest. We all manage our stress differently, but one thing I have found to be true with many people is that we try to ignore the stress and hope it goes away.

Here is the reality: When you're stressed, something is going on that you have real feelings about. Ignoring it doesn't make it go away; it just makes it worse. The sooner we can acknowledge whatever is going on and process it, the sooner the stress will walk away from us.

Most people don't acknowledge stress and deal with the issue at all, but if they do, it's usually in private, at night in their sleep, but in the meantime, stress has been brushing up against them the whole day (or however long they've been carrying stress with them. What if you could short-circuit the entire process? Imagine that you look at stress and ask it why it's there, and then you acknowledge it, telling it, "Oh, you're here because I feel overwhelmed with too many things to do, and I feel like there's not enough time to do it. Well, stress, thank you for bringing that to my attention. What you're telling me is very real. You know what I'm going to do? I'll take the next thing I can do and make sure I do that well so I can mark it off my list. And by the way, stress, while you are real, I'm doing the best I can, which is how I'm dealing with it."

The next time you're stressed or bothered about something, treat whatever it is like it's another person standing next to you. If you ignore that person, they may throw a hissy fit because you didn't at least acknowledge them.

I find it's a lot less painful to acknowledge things and address them head-on so I can move on and work past them. Even as I'm writing this, it sounds easy. But when you're in that moment of deep stress or an intense emotional state, it's not exactly easy to chill out and act like everything's good. The nightmare is real for most of us.

As I get older, my tolerance is less and less. When I used to see an old man walking down the street with a luggage roller, I thought to myself, "I would have just picked that thing up; I wouldn't use a roller." And that's what I did when I was younger. Then one day, I realized it would be way more convenient and a lot easier if I used a luggage roller. I think we get wiser as we get older, and hopefully, we learn from our experiences. Work smarter, not harder. What we lose in enthusiasm, we gain in wisdom.

One thing I realize is that high stress is not sustainable. Stress will literally kill you. I've had friends get sick with odd diseases or have a nervous breakdown; all sorts of bad things happen when uncontrolled stress takes over. No, not all stress is bad, and sometimes, stress can catapult us forward and get us to where we need to be. Where's the balance, and how do you know the difference? If you are unable to be present and enjoy your life—you can't just stop for a second and look around and appreciate where you are at the moment—you probably need to manage your stress. If it's just a matter of being stressed because you have an appointment or a deadline, and the stress subsides when it's over, I consider that temporary stress. It's the prolonged stress that can take over your life and make your life unenjoyable. When you feel so out of control that you don't even feel like you're running your life anymore, when you look around the room and the clocks keep breaking and there's nothing you can do, your stress is unmanageable. That's when you need to send your stress and your problems on their way.

Here are a couple of things that helped me manage this kind of stress:

- **Write down what's on my mind.** The other day, I wrote down thirty things that were on the top of my mind. Wow, how stressful is it for my brain to be able to continually remember and worry about all thirty things? There's something about writing it down that takes it off my mind. I don't have to worry about forgetting something or dropping something if I don't keep it on the top of my mind. Writing it down gives me a little bit of space so I can breathe. It usually takes me until the next day to start feeling relief.

- **Feel in control.** When I feel out of control, and things are spiraling, how can I feel peace? I can't unless I organize things. And ultimately, I must believe I am in control of the decisions I make. You may feel like the bills are too much, so you have to work. You might think you'll let somebody down by not completing something. Those may be real situations, but what they don't do is take away your control. You have one of the most significant gifts of all, and that's choice. A life well-lived is a tremendous gift. Don't get me wrong, I'm not saying don't ever do anything difficult. Some of the most rewarding things in life are the hardest to accomplish, and rightfully so. The difference is in choosing to go after those goals. It's when we don't feel like we have the choice that we become spectators of our own lives.

The next time you find yourself in a room full of clocks and feeling completely out of control, step back for a second; step out of the room. Take a deep breath, look at the situation, and ask yourself where you want to go. Take back control with these two simple suggestions because a constant nightmare is not a place to live.

Sending your stress and your problems on their way is liberating. You'll get a ton of things that you've been carrying right off your back. This will enable you to move faster, jump higher, be happier, and, ultimately, perform better. By the way, sometimes stress comes to visit several times in a day, and it needs the same process every time. It's okay if you have to do it more than once. Eventually, you'll get faster and better at acknowledging your stress, letting it flow through you, and concentrating on the things that are most important. But whatever you do, don't just ignore it. Why? Because that is . . . well, you understand. Good luck!

Work Hard, Play Hard

I remember the day I got my first official sales job. I was so excited to get licensed and be able to set up my business. So excited that I sat down at my desk, looked at my brand-new business cards, took a deep breath, and then had this aha moment. Who are my customers? Where will I find them? And that's when the real work began.

I went on a ninety-day work spree without taking one single day off. I was a machine. Working days and nights, I handed out a thousand business cards in those ninety days. If I knew one thing, it was that I was determined to succeed. The only thing I knew how to do for sure was work. No one would outwork me. I remember my boss talking to me and praising me for all my hard work and dedication. I had no thought about even stopping to take a break. I was what was called a freight train.

Being young, I hadn't really experienced the need for rest. At the end of ninety days, I was so exhausted I had to take off two days. For many years after that, I wore those ninety days as a badge of honor. Look at how hard I worked when I got started. Many people struggle to work one full day, let alone ninety in a row. I'd look around and judge people based on how I perceived their level of laziness. What I didn't realize at the time was that my work ethic, though strong, was not sustainable. Which brings me to work hard and play hard.

I think working hard is self-explanatory. Whatever job you take on, dedicate yourself to that goal and craft while intensely concentrating on the goal. Playing hard; what does that mean? Does it mean going to the bar on weekends, getting trashed out of your mind, and forgetting what happened? Some people would say that's playing hard. What I'm talking about, though, is doing things that bring you rest and joy. We aren't computers, and we're not machines. We glorify people who seem to have those capabilities. Look at him, he's a machine; look at her, she doesn't stop. To be the most productive version of yourself, you need to take time for rest. We were not meant to be machines.

It's also very helpful to have goals and things to look forward to. A way to treat yourself. When people don't have anything to look forward to, they bury themselves in work. Which leads me to the next question: Why are you working so hard? I tell people all the time that I work for my family. Work is not my reward; being able to take care of my family is. Perhaps you have a different reason for working hard, but whatever it is, you probably aren't working just to work. Work is not the reward.

People often say, "Do something you love, and you'll never work another day in your life." I understand this theory, and I commend the few people who find immense joy in their work; for the rest of us, it's a means to an end. We may find a lot of satisfaction in our work, and that's commendable. But there has to be a deeper reason for why we're working. So work hard, play hard. You have to find a balance in life.

I often think that when people say, "Find a balance at work," they mean don't work very much and spend most of your time relaxing or doing something fun. But that saying doesn't mean you should work less; it just means you should reward yourself for your hard work. Balance doesn't mean equality; it just means there is some effort on both sides.

To summarize: Work hard, be dedicated to the work you're doing, don't give up, and concentrate on the goal. It's okay to work long hours, but don't forget why you're working, and remember to do things sustainably. Take a break here and there, and maybe schedule a few days off to do something fun. You'll come back refreshed, with a clear mind, and you'll be able to go the distance.

Nothing New Under the Sun

As I get older, I realize that the same situations happen over and over again, even though they may have different variations. That's the basis for the saying "Those who do not study history are doomed to repeat it." We can learn a lot from those who have come before us. But here's how it typically plays out. People think their situation is unique. I hate to tell you this, but your situation is not unique.

"But it has this variation; there's this new technology involved; there's some kind of random factor that has never been dealt with before," I hear you say. Please understand that people are people. And there are only so many reactions and so many situations that can play out in various ways. While most situations are not identical, there are definitely pieces we can learn from to glean the results. Let me give you a couple of examples.

If you think your customer may get upset if you tell them something, you can look at other situations where people have told customers things that upset them and see how past customers reacted. Then you're not going in blindly, and you have a point of reference. If you're dealing with relational issues between you and a peer or an employee, the situation doesn't have to be exactly the same for you to glean wisdom from people who have been in a similar situation.

Some people don't value the wisdom of those with years of experience because they think those older folks are . . . dare I say it . . . old and outdated. I remember when I first moved out of the house where I lived with my parents. I literally thought there was nothing I couldn't figure out. I thought my parents didn't know all that much. After all, they weren't up to speed on how things worked in the current world. Yet, two years after I moved out on my own, I was amazed by how much my parents knew. I say this jokingly. It took me two years to realize everything they had been telling me all along was accurate.

Most people dismiss the advice or the experience of people who are closer to them. But for some reason, their minds are more open to taking feedback, or the possibility of something being revolutionary, from someone outside their circle. Sometimes, I tell people that others seem to learn only from a prophet. I'll ask people if they know what a prophet was in biblical days. Most people say, "Yeah, I understand what that was." Then I ask if they know what a modern-day prophet is. They say, "No what is it?" I say that it's anyone that comes from fifteen miles or more away.

There is nothing new under the sun. The sun rises in the morning, and it sets in the evening. Situations might have different complexities, but the outcome will be similar to previous ones. If we know that, we can learn from all the people who did the hard work before us. Don't be above learning from someone you think learned at a different time with different technology. Respect the people who came before you and do yourself a favor: Listen to them. Everyone has something to teach us, but not everyone has the ability to learn. Are you willing to listen? Wisdom is all around us, so take hold of it, and don't be above learning from anyone.

Turn Off Interruptions

We're absolutely bombarded with all sorts of interruptions: friends, family, text messages, music, honking horns, chirping birds—

COMMON EFFECTS OF INFORMATION OVERLOAD

Increased Stress and Anxiety

The persistent need to stay informed can lead to heightened stress levels. Struggling to process and prioritize information often causes emotional strain, mood swings, and even depression.

Sleep Disruption

Constant screen use and exposure to blue light affect sleep patterns, leaving us tired and mentally drained. Poor sleep further intensifies stress and hinders emotional regulation.

Reduced Focus and Productivity

A flood of information fragments our attention, making it harder to concentrate on tasks. This scattered focus decreases efficiency and leaves us feeling overwhelmed.

Negative Self-Image

Social media intensifies comparison as we are exposed to curated highlights of others' lives. This often weakens self-esteem and raises feelings of lack.

Strategies to Manage Information Overload

- **Practice Digital Detox.** Regularly disconnect from devices to reduce mental clutter and distraction. Simple habits, like setting screen time limits or taking device-free breaks, can restore balance.

- **Implement Mindfulness and Meditation.** Mindfulness practices help calm the mind and improve focus. Meditation encourages us to observe thoughts without judgment, fostering mental clarity and resilience.

- **Manage Information Strategically.** Organize how often you consume information. For instance, designate specific times for checking emails or social media, and avoid multitasking whenever possible.

- **Maintain a Healthy Lifestyle.** A balanced routine that includes exercise, proper nutrition, and adequate sleep strengthens mental resilience. Building supportive relationships also provides emotional grounding.

the list goes on. Never before in history have people been interrupted as often as we are today. Because of these interruptions, most of us have a hard time concentrating on things for longer durations. Even as I'm writing this right now, I'm being interrupted.

As the world around us gets louder and louder, we need to strive harder and harder to find places of peace and quiet. Anxiety and depression levels are at an all-time high. Why is this? While I'm not a psychologist, I think it's safe to think part of the issue is that we are constantly bombarded with information and interruptions. This does not allow for our brains, our psyches, and everything else to reset, and we need time to process things. Remember, we make time for the things that are most important to us. If reading this is more important than the ten text messages you get while reading it, you will avoid and ignore those distractions. I suppose the interruptions are not the issue; the real issue is our inability to focus on what is important and give ourselves permission to ignore everything else.

Have you ever caught yourself not silencing your phone because someone might try to call you or something may be taking place that you don't want to miss out on? Maybe you go on vacation, and instead of ignoring your email, phone, and voicemail, you're constantly aware of it because you can't turn it off.

Grab a piece of paper or something you can write on. Count the number of times you get interrupted while you're trying to read this short bit.

How are you able to keep your focus on a daily basis? How do you focus on things long enough to take in the information and accomplish your goals? We have to be willing to turn off the interruptions and ignore what's going on around us. We can do that for a short period of time. Maybe you take fifteen minutes, put in the earplugs, go into a quiet room, and you stay there. Having what I will call "quiet time" is vital.

Imagine you're a microprocessor that can process ten things at a time when, all of a sudden, you're flooded with a hundred things at once. At first, you think, "Wow, that's a lot more than average, but I think I'll try to handle it." But it doesn't take you long to realize you cannot handle that much constant processing.

Prior to the introduction of digital technology, most humans only needed to process one or two things at a time. That's not our lives today. But there's something sweet about the way things used to be when the pace of life was slower. Today, everybody expects everything immediately, and they have little patience because ten other things are waiting for them. I don't think we will change society as a whole, but we can change how we process the things around us. We can all control who we are and what we do for the health of our minds and the achievement of our goals.

Okay, how many interruptions did you have while you were reading this short bit? My guess is a case in point. We're so used to being interrupted that we don't even notice it anymore. Make a plan and create some quiet time in your life, even if it's only five or ten minutes—however much you can afford. This practice will become invaluable. This little bit of time is probably when you will be making the greatest planning progress. And if you're not good at quiet time at first, that's okay; you will get better at it as you do it more often. Good luck; your sanity and life depend on you.

11. Empowering Others for Success

Highlights the value of choosing your team, building up others, sharing success, knowing your audience, and being an invaluable resource. This chapter also emphasizes the importance of consistency, teaching others, setting time frames, and creating a duplicable process.

● ●

CAN YOU CREATE AN UNSTOPPABLE TEAM? If you do, what might be possible? My guess is almost anything would be possible. You see, when we surround ourselves with great people, great things happen. But that's not the only piece of the puzzle. We need to inspire and lead the people around us. If they have no leadership or guidance, they may not be with us for the long run. Usually, when people lack direction and encouragement, they find a place to get them.

The issue most leaders have as they lead a team is identifying what is most important or mission critical. Most leaders ask themselves the same questions you do: "Where should I spend my time, and what should I be doing daily?" If they are a strong leader, my guess is they ask themselves these questions often. Not only do they ask these questions, but they adapt and often take action to course correct, which keeps their team engaged.

The Power Player

When you become a good leader, you also inspire others to lead.

This is how power players are born. However, some key ingredients should be present to aid in team development. Are you inspiring and encouraging? Are you creating goals and executing them? Are you modeling successful behaviors that will drive the team toward success? If leading and inspiring your team is where you want to go with your business, then you will find this next section inspiring. Don't wait to act; there is no better time than now! Keep in mind that if the goal is success, you must take steps every day to get there. Once you do, it's much easier to get there again and again. Let's quit wasting time, and let's get rolling!

Choose Your Team

Choosing your team is an important task. How do you pick the right people who will become key players and stay for the duration? Here are a few things I found about choosing the right team members.

Should you only pick all-stars? The problem you have with all-star players, in general, is they may not allow the other players to shine. They are the ball hog, and everyone passes the ball to them so they can have their glory moment. It's the selflessness of the team that can make magic happen. You see this in pro sports all the time. A sports team will hire an all-star player with the hope that the player will take them to the championship. More often than not, that player gets hurt or doesn't have a great season, and the rest of the team suffers.

One of the most inspirational movies I've ever seen is *Miracle on Ice*. It's based on the true story of the 1980 Olympic US hockey team that, against all odds, beats the reigning champions from the Soviet Union. That movie had me sitting on the edge of my seat pretty much the whole time. I bring up that movie simply because it's a great example of the ability of an incredible team. I don't know if there was an all-star there; each player did their part and executed perfectly. From the outside, it looked like there wasn't a single weak link. I wonder, though, did the coach who put that team together look for an all-star cast, or was he just looking for the best possible team players? Perhaps he was looking for both.

Another great movie, *Moneyball*, highlights the power of having players who are specifically good at one piece of the game. Ultimately, this gives their team a statistical and practical edge over the competition.

Why do I bring up teams, and why are they important? I don't know many people who have achieved a high level of success and done it alone. There are usually people supporting majorly successful individuals. You hear this at almost every acceptance speech: "I would like to thank this person, this person, this person." The list goes on and on because those individuals know they could not have achieved what they did without the team.

How do you select a good team? Different people will give you all sorts of secret ingredients and suggestions, but here are mine.

Potential

I will take potential over performance most of the time. It's great to find an all-star, selfless player. Most of the time, that's not a possibility because those people are few and far between. If you want to have amazing people around you, you have to look for people with the ability to be great. Most likely, you have specific needs. And anyone you bring on to support your business and your efforts needs to learn those specific needs.

Teachability

When someone has been in a business for a long time, they have developed a routine and their own way of doing things. If their way of doing things is exactly how you do them, then you may have that rare opportunity with an all-star. What I have found is people have a lot of habits if they've been in a business for a long time, and most of those habits are things I usually need to change in order to have them do things my way.

Are they teachable? If you take a high-potential individual who isn't teachable, all you have is a high-potential individual with no way to reach their full potential.

What do I mean by teachable? Can they take feedback and adapt quickly without taking offense? The last thing you need is a severe amount of pain and drama when you are in desperate need of help.

Care for Others

Do the people you consider hiring care about other people more than themselves? Are they people-pleasers? When I sit down to interview someone for a job, I see a red flag if their first question is, "How much do I get paid?" In the past, those words have been a clue that they are more interested in what they will get from the job than what they can give to it. I don't fault people for wanting to know how much money they're going to make. I just think there are more important factors that should come up first if someone cares more about the work they will do. A much better question is, "What are your needs for this role, and how could I contribute to the success of the team?" That shows me they might care about the job and how they could contribute to the success of the team.

Help Others Help You

Most people don't realize this, but they make money and find success if they help the people around them make money and find success. People might say, "But what if the boss is stingy and doesn't share in the wealth of their success?" My answer to that is simple. When you become invaluable as a team member, other people see that. Even if that leader or boss does not pay them fairly, the team member's track record of success will open doors in the future. This is the meaning of "Give, and you will receive" (Luke 6:38 NIV).

It's also important when you're choosing your team members to set the pace on day one. As I mentioned in chapter 10, I tell people who work for me that I don't expect perfection from anyone because perfection is impossible. The only thing I expect is excellence. I found setting that tone has helped create a place for my team to discuss our failures openly while setting the expectation that we will not repeat our mistakes.

Once you have an amazing team in place, you will not have to worry about parts of the process getting dropped, and you can concentrate on developing more business and opportunities. You will revolutionize your life when you surround yourself with excellent people.

A final thought: If you realize you've hired the wrong person, let them go quickly, and hire a better person for the job. One bad apple can spoil the bunch. Be thoughtful when hiring; if someone's not working out, be quick to identify that and let them go. The sooner you find the right mix, the sooner you'll be cooking. There is no substitute for an amazing team of people, so start building that team today.

Setting Proper Expectations

Have you ever been offered something only to find out it came with strings attached? You get a phone call; someone offers you a free trip or stay somewhere. Then, when you get there, you find out there are added fees; you get one free lunch instead of a meal for two; you have to pay for transportation when you thought that was included. And the list goes on and on. In this situation, you aren't told these things up front because most people wouldn't make the trip if they had all the information.

This is an example of intentionally not setting proper expectations. How often do we unintentionally set improper expectations? Let me explain. Have you ever accidentally left out a detail when inviting someone to your house? Maybe you didn't tell the invitee that someone they didn't get along with would be there? While this oversight could be completely innocent, you didn't set the proper expectations.

Most people do not realize half of what you do as a master at your job. This is where you have to set proper expectations. When you set the proper expectations for your clients, they understand what they will be dealing with and are prepared and thankful, and have a greater chance of succeeding. When you're going into an unknown situation, it's unnerving. You don't know where things start; you don't know where things end; you don't even know where things are. You're just blindly walking around, hoping things end well. At least, that's how it feels when you haven't set the proper expectations.

Imagine a kid on the first day of school. If you walk around with them, showing them where their locker is and where their classroom is, telling them how long class is and showing them where lunches are served, it may be a little unnerving, but you set that kid up for success. Compare this to the kid who was not given any of that information, has a serious struggle, and almost gives up after the first day of school. School itself wasn't the problem. The problem was not preparing them by setting the proper expectations.

Whatever task you perform to help your clients, most likely, it's not the task that is a problem. It's how you prepare your clients. Do you initially sit down with your clients before everything takes place and go over all the possibilities for what could happen and what to expect? Better yet, do you have a document outlining all the possibilities? This can help set proper expectations. When you take that extra time in the beginning, you're building a strong foundation and setting proper expectations.

Some salespeople find this approach scary because they fear the client may not want to proceed once they know all the ins and outs. I have found the opposite. When I can talk about the issues that may arise and prepare my clients for how to handle them, I create a smoother, better experience that is far more likely to succeed. If your clients are not prepared and something happens, they want to blame someone for the uncomfortable situation they're in, and most likely, that will be you. In that case, expect a barrage of questions like, "Why didn't you tell us? Were you trying to hide something? Are you not experienced enough that you didn't truly know?"

Trust me when I say this is not where you want to be. When you can address concerns before they happen, you can keep people calm if they do happen. This shows your clients you are a professional and gives them peace that they're in good hands.

In my experience, very few people follow this process. You have one chance to create an unforgettable first impression. Do that by spending the time and setting proper expectations right off the bat. Your people will thank you; you will thank you. And you will find that far fewer issues arise because you've already addressed them before they had a chance to take place.

Build Up Others Around You

Words have power. I often underestimate the power of encouraging words. Think about that guy who's crawling through the desert and sees an oasis in the distance but can't quite muster the strength to crawl any farther. So he lies there, having almost made it, until one of his friends starts yelling in the distance, "Hey, you're almost there. You can do it!" He musters a little more strength. He crawls a little bit forward. But his friend persists. "You can do it! You're almost there! Get up, don't lie there. You're going to get there, and it's going to be amazing. Now get your butt up and start walking; you're almost there." Somehow, the strength this guy didn't have fills his body, and he makes it to the oasis.

This is an example of what encouragement can do. I do a group exercise at my office, where we display the power of encouragement. I give someone a marker and tell them to jump as high as possible and mark the wall. I usually place some paper just out of reach on the wall. I put it much higher than I think these people can actually jump. I have the person jump several times and place a mark as high as they possibly can. I ask them repeatedly, "Are you sure that is as high as you can jump?" They always respond, "Yes, I can't jump any higher." Then I ask the room full of people to say encouraging things like, "You can do it! You can get higher!" Then I have the people cheer for the jumper.

Every single time, people jump six to twelve inches higher. I don't know why encouragement is so dang powerful . . . but it is.

When your team wins, you win. How much more powerful could it be if you were to build your team members up with daily words of encouragement? Plants need sunshine each day to survive; your team needs your encouragement in the same way.

Here's a challenge for you. Start encouraging the people around you in small ways. Things we think are trivial are not. Make your encouragement sincere and thoughtful. If you notice someone did something great, tell them. If they're struggling to get something done, encourage them. Tell them how they're going to get there and how it's going to be great. Take mental notes and watch the people around you blossom. And when the people around you are succeeding, you will, too. It's funny how we become encouraged ourselves when we start encouraging others. Try it.

Choose Your Words Carefully

Equally as powerful as encouragement is discouragement. Like money, words, when spoken, are spent and cannot be taken back. Words matter.

How many times has somebody said something and then said, "Wait! That's not what I meant"? Remember the saying, "You have one chance to make a first impression"? Verbal communication is a big part of your first impression. People are often in a rush to communicate, and they don't choose their words carefully or thoughtfully. Throwing words out frivolously is like being a waitperson holding a giant tray of food packed to the hilt and running through the restaurant, hoping you won't spill everywhere. If you do spill food all over everyone, you can say you're sorry and didn't mean to do that, but the person who's covered with food is probably less than happy, no matter how graciously they respond. That's the same type of reaction created by carelessly spoken words.

How do we avoid this kind of situation? Take a deep breath

and think about what you are trying to communicate. Think about what your goal is before you speak. Don't spill words all over someone. Most of the time, when people choose the wrong words, it's because they just blurted out the first thing that came to their mind. While this may work some of the time, this could be the one straw that breaks the camel's back, the one thing that makes the other party decide they don't want to use your services.

I remember one negotiation clearly. I was offering another person the opportunity to work with me. They were doing their best to negotiate. I became frustrated that the process was taking longer than I thought it should. I spoke up and said, "You don't have to be this difficult, you know." Well, let's just say that did not go over well. I ended up with an earful about how I lacked understanding, and I had the proverbial door slammed in my face. While this whole situation was very uncomfortable, I did learn a valuable lesson: Be like water, not a rock. Water is free-flowing and, with persistence, can break through anything, including the hardest of rocks. You would think rock is the stronger of the two, but its greatest strength is also its greatest weakness: its inability to move.

We can maintain our composure by thinking clearly and choosing our words wisely. We can often take glum situations and turn them around at the last minute. Sometimes, that feels like a miracle; you think there's no way it will turn around, and then suddenly, because of your carefully selected words and calm demeanor, everything turns in the right direction.

While I can't offer a list of words you shouldn't use, I can offer the following points:

+ Don't use words frivolously. Use words that accurately reflect what you're trying to communicate.

+ Don't say things you don't mean.

+ Don't take shortcuts because you feel rushed.

+ Don't be impatient when someone doesn't understand what you're trying to describe.

✦ It's much easier to choose your words carefully than to try to recover after saying the wrong thing.

Here's the challenge for you. Recall a situation where you said the wrong thing; write down what you said. Look at it and replay it like it's a movie and you are the spectator. What could you have said differently that could have changed the whole trajectory for the better? Often, we use similar methods to communicate with people. If we can sharpen our skills, we can begin to change the whole direction of our conversations. When we find the right words, we find significant opportunities to win. Words have power, and if you use them wisely, you can put yourself in the best possible position.

Make Yourself Invaluable

Employees often ask how to get a good pay raise. This brings forward a few thoughts. I appreciate that they are strong enough to ask the question. Most people don't realize that asking how to get a raise is often the wrong question. So the question becomes, what is the correct question? I tell my employees the question they should ask is how to become invaluable—because invaluable people are indispensable. And when you are indispensable, the company will want to pay you more.

The next question they ask is, "How do I become invaluable?" Now, that is something to explore. If you're working and doing the bare minimum, then you don't stand out from anyone else. The people who go above and beyond are the ones who are noticed. What does going above and beyond really mean? Most of the time, it's doing small things. It's underpromising and over-providing. When it's Monday, and something needs to be done by Friday, people will be pleasantly surprised if you have it done by Wednesday. When you anticipate people's needs and are proactive about them, the whole dynamic of the team can change for the better.

At one point, I was building my own house. I wanted to help construct some of the landscaping, so I showed up early in the morning with a shovel, ready to get my hands dirty and eager to do even the most minuscule jobs. When the day started, several other gentlemen were shoveling dirt next to me. These guys were being paid by the hour, so they weren't especially eager to get the job done. On the other hand, being the homeowner, I wanted to get through the project as quickly as possible. I began shoveling quickly, and I moved fast throughout the process. At first, the guys worked at their own pace, but once they saw me moving quickly, they didn't want to seem like they were lazy, so they also picked up the pace. We must have blown through the project in half the time—not because I had any more skill but because I set a good pace.

Imagine a job foreman looking over their crews and deciding who gets to lead, who gets to stay, and who has to go. Imagine that foreman is instructed to give someone a raise. If you're the pacesetter, and you're consistent about it, who do you think they will pick, and who do you think will get the raise? Too often, we get comfortable doing the bare minimum, hoping and hoping we will get a big break one day. In reality, the big break is waiting for us. We can show up every day, become invaluable, and watch success happen.

Somebody once said, "I'm not very lucky, but the harder I work, the luckier I get." Some might say, "But if I work hard every day, I'm afraid I'll be taken advantage of. I'll be doing more than what I'm being paid for." Yes, that's true; you may be doing more than you're being paid for. The question is, what kind of example do you want to create, and where do you want to go in life? Because if you want to stay in the same spot doing the same thing and getting paid the same amount, don't change a thing. Think about your current job; list two or three things you can do that would make a significant impact on the people around you without the expectation of being recognized or reimbursed at this time. Tackle those items, and do it willfully and joyfully. You'll start to notice people thanking you. You'll probably start to get praise from your leaders. When they start to notice you and use you as an example of superior work, don't ask for a raise yet; ask them if there's anything else you can do to contribute to the team's success. If they have some ideas, listen to them.

They are telling you how to become invaluable.

Once you've mastered that list, ask them if you're invaluable. If they say yes, let them know you work hard to become so and would like them to acknowledge your hard work by considering a raise. The amount you ask for will depend on the job and how valuable you have become. Try not to be greedy; ask for a reasonable raise. They will notice when you're fair and considerate. They may get the wrong impression if you ask for too much money. Look at this as an opportunity to build from, not a one-and-done.

Also, invaluable people know their surroundings. If the company is suffering and doesn't have enough money to maintain operations, they won't be able to give you a raise no matter what you do, even if they want to. Use your common sense (which is something that doesn't appear to be very common at all these days). Once you become invaluable, you can smile at yourself in the mirror every morning and say, "Mission accomplished."

Teaching Others

The original *Karate Kid* is one of the best movies I can remember on mentorship. This kid who's getting beat up and having a really tough time in life meets his mentor, Mr. Miyagi. Throughout the movie, you see Mr. Miyagi mentoring him, and the kid learns some valuable lessons and is able to win in life. It wasn't just the kid who won, though. If you watch that movie, you'll see Mr. Miyagi looks on with pride at the kid's accomplishments. Who got more out of that situation of teaching in the *Karate Kid*? Was it Mr. Miyagi or the kid? I'd say both.

When we mentor others, we gain satisfaction from witnessing their progress and achievements. The joy we get from helping other people comes from sharing our knowledge and enabling others to reach levels they might not have attained without our guidance. One of the greatest rewards is providing others with opportunities they might not have had otherwise. The Karate Kid can be successful in his life because of what someone poured into him. The bullies in his life no longer have power over him.

Also, when we teach other people how to be great, we sharpen our own skills. If you want to be good, master a skill; if you want to be a great master of a skill, get good enough to teach it. It's through teaching that we hone skills and bring them to refinement. Teaching other people is a way of giving a part of ourselves. When we give of ourselves, we see the goodwill multiply in our own lives and in others.

What skills have you mastered enough to teach? Is there a Karate Kid in your life? Are you a Mr. Miyagi? Or are you the Karate Kid and need a Mr. Miyagi? We can start as one and end up as the other. Most likely, you will have an opportunity to be both. Remember, you learn by teaching. And by learning, you can become great. Becoming great means you have something to give. One of the biggest gifts is being able to give. And when we give, we get. Maybe you think you don't have the time or the energy. You don't need to have time or energy. You just need to be open to possibilities. We always make time for the things that are most important to us. Changing someone's life can be pretty important. All of us have the ability to do that. Every person has something they can give. The big question is, are you willing? Give, teach, and watch your life transform.

Whose life can you impact today?

Easy, Duplicable Processes

A duplicable process is something like making phone calls. You'll have a list ready, the time blocked off on your calendar, and the phone headset fully charged. An easy duplicable process done daily will yield so much progress over a year that you won't even recognize where you started.

Step back and look at your business, and ask yourself what you can do every day that will have the greatest impact. Start by writing down as many things as you can think of, then narrow your list to the top three things that, if you did them every day, no matter what, they would move the ball forward. This will be your target list—your simple road map toward success.

Most people are scattered when it comes to work or business. The target moves every day, you don't know what you'll end up doing, and the process is not duplicable. For those of us who are trying to find new business, make things more successful, and find new ways to do things, the secret is in focusing and executing.

+ Think back to your list of three duplicable daily tasks. Is there a way to make them easier to do? A better way of asking this is, can you streamline the process?

+ Why should you make your tasks easy? Because if they're too difficult, you won't do all three every day.

+ Why should the process be duplicable? Because you need to get into a groove if you want to make something second nature so you'll do it every day.

Not Every Task Is Fun

Sometimes, things aren't easy simply because we don't want to do them, not because they're hard to accomplish. What's amazing is that we become good at anything we practice. I say this because if there's something you hate doing, you can practice it, and you will get better at it. Will you love doing it? Maybe later. When people become experts at things, those things suddenly become more enjoyable for them.

When I look at all the successful people in business, I find one common denominator: They all have processes, and they follow those processes daily. We do what we don't enjoy so we can do what we do enjoy. But what if you have to do a task you absolutely despise? While you despise the actual task, you probably don't despise the results.

Remember the first thing I said in this section? "An easy duplicable process done daily will yield so much progress over a year, you won't even recognize where you started." You must be consistent if you want to win consistently. Go back to the list of three things that, if done consistently, will move your goals forward, and commit to doing them every day for the next three months. Spend at least thirty minutes on each one. Mark your starting date on your calendar. Write down what you want your results to be. Now go!

Watch how much progress you make in that time using your easy, duplicable process. It is like riding a bike. At first, you don't think you will be able to ride the bike successfully, but through repeated attempts, it becomes easier and easier, and before you know it, you're zooming around town with ease.

Give a Time Frame

I find it interesting how people prioritize things by the time frame they're given. Have you ever heard yourself say something like, "Whenever you get to it is fine. No rush; just let me know if you have time to do that little extra for me."

I was always afraid to ask people to make something a priority. I worried that if I asked them for priority, they might charge extra, or it might infringe on their free time. At the heart of it, I never wanted to inconvenience someone. Here's how I learned my lesson.

I found a 1964 pinball machine. It was in pretty good condition except for the fact that it didn't work. Come to find out, it needed a complete rebuild. There was one guy in the area who worked on pinball machines. I contacted him, and he was happy to work on it for me, and he asked me when I needed it back. At that point, I wasn't in a rush, so I told him just to get to it when he had time. Six months went by, and I reached out to him. He said he hadn't had a chance to work on it. A year went by. He still hadn't had a chance to work on it. Eight years went by, and I finally picked it up from him. He hadn't done one thing to that pinball machine in eight years.

Had I known this would be the outcome, I would have rephrased what I said initially. I could have said something like,

"When's the soonest you can get it done?" Who knows, maybe it would have been done in two years. What could I take from this situation, and what should I have learned? 1. Give a time frame every single time. 2. Set the expectation. Never leave it open to interpretation without guidance. When I picked up the pinball machine eight years after dropping it off, he was still like, "What? You said you weren't in a rush."

If I had said I needed it in a week, even if he was a procrastinator, he would probably get it back to me in two weeks. If I don't give a time frame, I'm still waiting for it. When I'm negotiating deals, I always give a response time frame. I never leave that open for interpretation. If there's no time frame, then in business situations, people will use the extra time to their advantage. If you're offering to buy their product, they may just look for another person who will pay more for the items they are selling. Or if they contacted you to hire you for services, they will often look for someone who will offer their services for less. They know if they want to use your services or accept your offer, you'll be waiting on the sidelines, offering them the same deal at a later date. If you write an estimate for something, make it good for only the next two weeks or thirty days. If you're making an offer to purchase something, let them know you need to buy something within the next twenty-four to forty-eight hours. Put some kind of time pressure on whatever you're doing. It's less about the amount of time you give and more about responding to you within a specific time frame to complete their end of the deal.

A time frame forces people who do not want to make a decision to have one in a certain amount of time. No answer is an answer. That usually means no. If you're worried that someone won't respond, tell them that if you don't hear back from them by such and such a time, you will understand that to mean the answer is no. Sometimes, the simple fear of loss is enough to make something happen.

I have numerous examples of times I told people just to get back to me whenever they think they have time. So far, that approach has not worked well for me, which is why I always offer a time frame now. When you do, make sure both parties agree on the time frame given unless you are in an intense negotiation. Then you may need to give a date that they must comply with or else you will take action of some sort. I should have said something to the pinball machine guy like, "Can you have it completely refurbished in six months? And if he said yes, six months was a perfect time frame, we both agreed, and the time frame is set. The pressure is from the expectation for the work being done within a clearly set time frame. If there's one thing I can make clear here, it's never to leave time frames up to chance or when people "feel like it." More often than not, they're never going to feel like it. There will always be something more pressing and more important that will get in the way.

If you don't want to push people too hard on time frames, don't dig in on the exact time frame, but tell them how you need it by a specific date and ask them if that is possible. If they offer a time frame that's a week longer than you want, take another run at it and ask them if they can complete the work by the date you requested. Restate how it's important, that you really need it; can they help you out? If they still say it's not possible, offer a time frame that's a little closer to theirs and ask them if they can make that work. Nothing's finished until both parties agree to it. And without setting time frames, who knows when that will happen.

It's my understanding that you need key elements for a contract to be legally binding. According to Cornell Law School, those are "mutual assent, expressed by a valid offer and acceptance; adequate consideration; capacity; and legality."[32] While a specific time frame is not legally required, most contracts do include one.

Start paying attention to all your time frames. Time is money, so why not frame a little extra?

---

32 Legal Information Institute. (n.d). *Contract*. Cornell Law School. https://www.law.cornell.edu/wex/contract

12. Taking Control and Moving Forward

The final chapter focuses on leadership, overcoming adversity, and taking action. It discusses choosing your words wisely, taking responsibility for failure or success, the importance of small steps toward a big goal, and how to put your knowledge into practice.

LIFE IS SOMETHING YOU OBSERVE, PARTICIPATE IN, or make happen, but the key is that it's happening, no matter your level of involvement. If you are anything like me, and I'm guessing you are because you are reading this book, then you can't just stand by and be an observer. It's painful to watch life pass you by and lose the opportunities that could have been yours for the taking. Being a participant is okay, yet not completely satisfying. For most of us, it's a decent place to start, but you quickly realize that if you want to make the most out of life, you need to make things happen. I like the saying of taking the bull by the horns. Life is the bull, and the horns control the rest of that giant beast (your life). When you take it by the horns, you put that big beast where you want it. Do you want to leave your success or failure to chance, or do you want to take control and move your life toward success? I choose success, and to get that, I need wisdom. Where can I find wisdom? Well, I hope you have found this book packed with it. Like a toolbox, some tools you rarely use, but others are your favorites, which get used daily. Think of this book as your toolbox. Hopefully, you have equipped yourself with a bunch of new tools to use along your journey toward whatever goal you have set for yourself. Pull out your favorite tools and work away; it will be amazing to see what happens.

I hope you find this last section as inspiring as the eleven before it. Remember, you have one life to live. Learn from the mistakes and successes of others. Squeeze as much as you can out of this little thing called life. Hopefully, these last sections inspire you to take your bull by the horns and make your life everything you have dreamed of. This final section is all about ways to take control and move forward in life.

Maybe Good, Maybe Bad, God Knows

Have you ever spoken to someone who was completely down and out because something bad happened to them? If you have, you're not alone. If I had a nickel for every time someone came to my office feeling defeated, I would have a piggy bank's worth of nickels. Here is a story I like to tell them. It's called, "Maybe good, Maybe bad, God knows."

A man goes to the same restaurant at the same time every day and orders the same breakfast from the same waitress every day. And every day when he walks in, the waitress asks him the same question: "How are you today?" and he always gives the same response: "Maybe good, maybe bad, God knows."

Now, after you've heard this response a few times, it can get frustrating. The waitress knows he has good and bad days, but he always answers with the same response. One day, she hears he is having financial problems, so she thinks to herself, "Today's the day I'll get a different answer." When the man walks in that morning, sits down, and orders his same breakfast, the waitress asks in anticipation, "How are you today?" He answers, "Maybe good, maybe bad, God knows."

The waitress, visibly frustrated, says, "I know you're having financial problems. You can tell me. It's okay if you're having a bad day." The man looks her straight in the eyes and says, "Maybe good, maybe bad, God knows." The waitress storms off, then turns and hollers back at him, "One of these days, you'll tell me the truth."

The next day, something strange happens. The man doesn't come in for his breakfast. The waitress thinks, "If he doesn't come in for breakfast, something is very wrong." Since he's been coming in for years, they've become good friends. The waitress makes a few phone calls and finds out that the man and his entire family had been in a horrible car accident the night before. She decides to visit him in the hospital as soon as her shift ends.

When she gets to the hospital, she finds out the man is upside down in traction, wearing a full-body cast. It's safe to say the situation couldn't be much worse for the man, but he's alive, and he's going to make it. Seeing that she's a longtime friend, the doctors allow her to visit him. She walks into the room and whispers to him, "Hey, how are you doing today?" And the man whispers back, "Maybe good, maybe bad, God knows."

The waitress has had it. She screams at the top of her lungs, "You're having a bad day! You're upside down, in a full-body cast, in traction. You're having a bad day; just say it, you're having a bad day!" The man calmly and quietly responds, "Last night, I was in a horrible car accident with all of my family. The rest of my family in the car had some bruises and some minor injuries, but they're all okay, and I'm alive. Also last night, I found out that my house had a terrible wiring fire, and had we been home, all of us would have died. Maybe good, maybe bad, God knows."

The moral of the story is that sometimes, something we deem bad has to take place so a greater good can happen. This doesn't mean we will like it; it doesn't mean it will feel good; it just means it's the better option. So, if you're alive right now, you have another run at whatever is challenging you. Maybe good, maybe bad, God knows!

Talk Like Everyone Is Listening

If you ever visit a small town, you may go to lunch at a local restaurant. If you look closely, you'll notice some people quietly talking next to each other. That's because they know the waitstaff, they know the people sitting next to them at a different table, or they're saying something they don't want to share with the people around them. I grew up in a small town. Part of the charm of living in a small town is that everyone knows one another. Being someone who knew a lot of the people in the town, I had to be careful about what I said and where I said it.

I learned this was not the case when I went to a large city. People would speak freely without thinking about whether anyone who knew them would hear anything. I remember sitting at a table with a friend who looked at me in confusion and asked, "Why are you whispering?"

People often say things can come back to haunt them. Here was my rule. If you're going to say something, it should never be something you wouldn't say to the subject's face or post on the front page of a newspaper. The same applies to social media posts; this includes text messages, voice messages, and emails, no matter how private you think they are. In today's world, things we write or say are memorialized digitally, and they can come back to haunt us at the most inopportune times.

One of the controversial topics people need to consider not discussing openly is politics. There are always people on either side, and if you're a salesperson, you may alienate 50 percent of your sales base with your opinion. You can feel passionate about things, and you can go and volunteer. But the second you cross into telling people what they need to think, that's when you lose.

I often hear that I wouldn't be true to myself if I didn't openly share my feelings about my political stance. There is wisdom and stupidity in every situation. If it's wiser for you to earn a living and maintain respect, then you will be very careful with your words. Find a person or a close friend group and have open discussions with them; that's helpful. But I would warn against openly speaking about controversial topics that can alienate your sales base. Instead, welcome others' thoughts without judgment. It may help you see several other sides, even if you disagree. But above all else, watch what you say and to whom. Your words matter.

Think Before You Speak

You have heard the saying, out of the mouth of babes? I take it to mean kids will say whatever they think, good or bad, without a filter. Fortunately for kids, we give them more grace, maybe because we all know they don't have bad intentions but are just saying what they see or think without a filter. They haven't learned the proper manners associated with telling someone they are overweight or smell bad.

When I was a young man, I would say the first thing that came to mind at pretty much every chance. I was so much this way that my mother often said, "Think before you speak." I got my parents in hot water by repeating things they said to the people they said them about. Glad I'm still alive to talk about it.

I remember being angry hearing those words, but the phrase became a mantra for my life. I learned that words spoken cannot be taken back. We must think about the words we use because they have a lasting effect on those around us and ultimately can dictate how successful we can become.

A story about this stuck with me. A man—we'll call him John—heard that his dear friend—we'll call him Bill—had said something about him to a group of their friends. Bill spoke ill of John, and this hurt John deeply. Once Bill learned word had gotten back to John about the horrible things he had said, Bill went to John and asked for forgiveness. John thought about it and said, "If you truly want my forgiveness, take this bag of feathers, put some at the front of the post office, some at the grocery store, some at the park, some at the movie theater, and last, drop a few off at our friend's house. Then come back to me."

Wanting John's forgiveness, Bill did as suggested. He took the bag of feathers and dropped a few at the post office, some at the grocery store, some at the park, some at the movie theater, and last, he dropped some at their friend's house. The next day, Bill went back to John to report that he had delivered the feathers as requested and asked if everything was okay and their friendship was restored. John said, "I just need you to do one more thing."

Eager to fix the friendship, Bill said he'd do anything. John replied, "Can you go back to the post office, the grocery store, the park, the movie theater, and our friend's house and pick up all the feathers you left yesterday?" Bill said, "That's impossible. They have blown all around town by now. There is no way to pick up all the feathers." John looked at his friend and said, "Exactly. I may choose to forgive you, but there is no way you can ever take back the words you spoke."

It's easier to keep your mouth shut than it is to take back words spoken. Be slow to speak and quick to listen. If you can do that, you just might find more success and carry a ton less regret.

What Will You Apologize For?

I often tell myself, "You can do anything you want in life; it's just the price you need to pay for it." You always have a choice, even if you don't feel like you do. Make sure you are willing to pay the price if you are wrong. For example, if you want to jump off a roof right now, you can go outside and jump off a roof. The price you would have to pay might be some broken limbs, or you may not live through it. Still your choice.

We think we must obey every rule from A to Z. When we are hired to accomplish something, we're being asked to win. At the front of a battle, we see things others will not see. We must take action concisely and immediately. It's our job as leaders to make good decisions.

I worked at a place where I often would go against the grain, but in doing so, I would further the company's goals. Other leadership peers told me, "You shouldn't have done that, but look at your results! That's amazing!" In this scenario, I had to apologize for doing precisely what I was told not to do. Ultimately, I had a more remarkable result than my colleagues. As a side note, I ended up being recognized as the highest performer multiple years in a row. Let's look at the alternative. Had I done exactly what I was told, my results would have been dismal in this situation. I had decided I was willing to apologize for making good decisions that would further the company's success, but I was not willing to apologize for complete and utter failure.

If someone trusts you to drive a ship and tells you how they want it done, and you see that it will run aground by doing as instructed, you alter the course of your ship, bring it in safely, and apologize for being successful. If you win, it's all your fault; if you fail, it's all your fault. If it makes sense, lead in the best direction; if it doesn't, think about whether you should just do as you are told. Will you end up being successful, or are you writing your own resignation? You do have a choice about who and what you become, and if you choose wisely, you have an opportunity for even greater success. In the end, what will you apologize for, success or failure? You get to decide.

How to Deal with Problems

When I first started in sales, I thought there had to be some secret way of dealing with problems. I knew a couple of things for certain: Everyone has problems, and some people are better at dealing with them successfully than others. I thought, "They must know something I don't know. There must be some sort of process. Maybe talk to this person first, let them sit on it for a little bit, then ask again but in a stern way?" I felt like a mad scientist trying to figure out the concoction for successfully dealing with problems.

As life would have it, I lived next door to a multibillionaire. Now, before you think I lived in Beverly Hills or something, know that I lived in a small town in Oregon. The gentleman I'm talking about lived in a humble house that he and his wife bought in the '60s. From the outside, they looked like normal, everyday people. The amazing thing about him was that he took his father's mill and turned it into one of the largest building manufacturing companies in the world. One day, I thought, "If this guy can make a couple billion dollars out of nothing, he must know how to deal with problems."

I sat down with this multibillionaire and asked him how he

dealt with problems. "Do you have a certain process or way you deal with them?" He looked at me through his Coke-bottle glasses and said, "I deal with problems like a linebacker. I look for the very biggest one and tackle it; then I look up for the next biggest one and tackle that one. And before I know it, I look up, and they're all tackled."

I was astonished. That's it? After all, he was a multibillionaire, so I kind of figured he must know a thing or two. That's some advice that has stayed with me my entire life. You see, when you run from problems, they tackle you. But if you run toward the problem and tackle it, it doesn't have a chance to tackle you. When I look around, most of the problems people have become much bigger when they're not dealt with. We will always have problems, and more are sure to come. But I feel confident that if you run toward the problems and tackle them, you'll have a much higher success rate.

Don't Expect Instant Success

So many things in today's world are instant: instant pudding, instant coffee, instant service. Call someone on their phone, and you instantly reach them. People have little bandwidth for patience. A whole line of advertising says if you do whatever the ad advises, you will be instantly successful.

Many people have said the same thing I've realized in my work career: It takes years to become an overnight success.[33] Does it really take ten, fifteen, or even twenty years? I don't know if it actually takes that many—or it may take longer. The fact is, we can't expect instant success. I like to say, "Success comes in pinches and teaspoons, not cups and quarts." If you've ever baked something from scratch, you'll understand the metaphor.

We have to put our blinders on, stop looking at all the unrealistic, fake successes, and be present to be our best. Each step we

---

33 BrainyQuote. (n.d.). Overnight Success Quotes. Retrieved on June 17, 2024, from https://www.brainyquote.com/topics/overnight-success-quotes

take brings us closer to our goal. Someone explained it to me like this. If success is a staircase with many steps to the top, which step is the hardest to climb? The answer is the very last step. Each step up the Stairway to Success becomes successively more difficult. Most people make it about halfway up the staircase, realize that success is hard, and then fall back down to the bottom, only to start the process all over again, looking for some other new challenge and a new opportunity to be successful. They never make it to the top of any staircase.

So, what can you do? How can you make it to the top of a staircase? It's pretty simple: Keep climbing, no matter how hard it gets. I often tell people that when things get really tough, and you don't feel like you can make it any further, rejoice and get excited, knowing the final step is the last and hardest one. You must almost be there. This simple act of getting excited and shouting in triumph as an act of success can help us become internally encouraged. It can bring us to that last little bit in the climb to success.

Ignore the Pain

We live in a society where pain dictates what we do. If it's less painful to sit on the couch for the whole day than to do my work, I will. If it's more painful to sit on the couch all day, I won't. We judge how much pain taking an action will cause. When looking ahead, if we see a lot of pain, we often try to avoid it. What we need to be looking at is how to get to our goal. Ask any bodybuilder if they were able to get the body they have without any pain. I doubt you will find one who will say you can have a body like this without an ounce of sweat, determination, or pain.

I want to leave you with this bit of encouragement. If things are hard, it means you're doing something meaningful. If it were easy, everyone would do it. You are in this place in your life for a reason. If this is your goal, take it, put blinders on, don't pay attention to everyone around you, and work in such a way that you will win. Don't expect major breakthroughs right away;

expect small breakthroughs, and when you make it to the top of that mountain, you'll look back and realize it wasn't a mountain at all. You can do it!

Skill and Will

Every person needs two things to be successfully trained for any position: skill and will. Skill is the ability to successfully do the tasks in the intended way, even to be a master of those specific skills. If you were a blacksmith, it would be the ability to melt the metal, heat it, pour it, and form it by repeatedly hammering it into shape. For a computer programmer, it would be setting up the computer, learning the code language, understanding what language goes where, and finalizing the code or hosting it on a site. Skill is something that can be taught. People go to trade school or college to learn valuable skills for whatever occupation they plan to undertake.

Let's talk about will. I'm talking about the will that is your inner desire to succeed. Will is what divides most people in success and failure. This is something no one can teach. It's something you have to have all on your own. Imagine you're on a deserted island, and you have to survive. Do you have the will to do what you must to survive? Notice this isn't a question of skill. We'll assume you already have the skills in this scenario.

Have you ever seen the movie *Cast Away*? Tom Hanks's character survives a plane crash and ends up on a deserted island in the middle of the ocean. The movie is all about him being alone and trying to survive. He has many mental and medical challenges but also a strong will to survive. If he did not have the will, the movie would have just ended with him starving to death and dying.

What does will look like for you specifically? How badly do you want to succeed? Once you have developed the necessary skills, can you develop the will to succeed? I'm not just talking about willing things into existence. Some people say if you will something into existence, it will happen. I'm more of the opinion that if you have a strong enough will, you can overcome any obstacles. Many people have seemingly insurmountable challenges but a will that is bigger than their challenges. I recently read about Zion Clark, an MMA fighter who was born without legs.[34] If you want to talk about needing a lot of will, this guy takes the cake for me. He has half the tools other fighters have, and he's still moving forward. This is downright inspirational and heroic.

Almost everything inspirational happens for someone with a superstrong will. Our will usually starts strong, but as we move a little further from the starting point, our will gets tested. This is a key point. Are you going to give up just because your will is tested? Believe it or not, many people do because things aren't comfortable anymore. They are just not easy. News flash: nothing that's worth anything in life is easy.

Let's say you make it past the first test of your will. Good job. Can you duplicate that success when your will is challenged the next three, four, or five times? Each time your will is tested, it's that much more tempting to stop and give up. But do you know what the most satisfying event can be? It is looking back in triumph at how far you've come after your will has been tested over and over and you have refused to give up. You can be an example of what can be accomplished with a strong will. In my opinion, this is where real success happens.

Remember, we only need two things to be successful: skill and will. Learn all you can about the skills you need to achieve your goal and have an unbreakable will.

Are Leaders Born or Made?

I've been asked if leaders are born or made. This question made me think. I believe it's a little bit of both. Many of the strong leaders I know seem to have been born to lead. Does that mean they were born a leader? I think it means they were born with the

---

34 Miles, Will. (February 6, 2023). Zion Clark, MMA fighter with no legs, plans on being world champion. Sportskeeda. Retrieved on June 17, 2024, from https://www.sportskeeda.com/mma/news-zion-clark-mma-fighter-legs-plans -world-champion

qualities to lead. Are leaders made? I also think this answer is a little bit of both: natural talent as well as developed skill. Imagine a situation where you're on a deserted island with no leader. One guy emerges as the leader even though he is naturally an introvert with no prior leadership experience. Was he suddenly made a leader?

I'll answer that question with this example about precious metals. When dug out of the ground, it's precious metal. But it's not necessarily in the shape of a coin or a decorative ring you would wear. For that to happen, the metal needs to be heated, melted, and then formed into an object. It was precious metal all along and could become something great, but not until someone took the time to mold it through hard work did it reach its full potential. I view leaders this way. You're not born with all the answers and amazing leadership qualities. It's through tough situations and hard work, and probably lots of screwups, that you become something great. Just like precious metal, if you're never molded or pushed to be the best version of yourself, you will never become the showpiece you could have been.

Can people who show no actual leadership qualities lead effectively? I still say leadership is something you can learn. It may not come naturally to you, but if you're determined to do what it takes to become the leader you need to be, I believe it is possible. That said, not everyone is meant to be a leader. If leadership is not for you, that's okay.

Do you know what the hardest role is to fill? It's the second-chair violinist in an orchestra. The second chair needs to be every bit as good as the first chair but okay with the first chair getting all the credit. This takes a certain amount of humility and grace, which are difficult to find. I would consider someone with these attributes a strong leader in their own right.

Whether you're struggling to become the next president of the United States or to take on a strong second-chair position, take time to craft yourself into the best person you can be. Take the heat and let it mold you. Know that without it, you will never reach your full potential. And when things get too tough, remember the toughest step is the last step, which means you're almost there. True leaders are never done learning. If you're a leader, you're the first to take the heat. Be open because leaders aren't only born; they are made every day, just like you are being made right now.

Lead, Don't Follow

Did you ever play Follow the Leader when you were a kid? I did, and I always wanted to be the leader everyone would follow. I didn't want to be the person aimlessly following around the other kids. I didn't know where they were going or what they would do.

Who are the people you follow? You follow people on social media, around the cyber world, around the office, or wherever they might decide to go for the day. What if you were the person who people followed? What if you could become the authority so that no matter what you did, people would follow you?

There are many ways to lead. You can lead by example. You can lead conversations. You can lead small groups and large groups and customers.

What does it mean to lead? What does it take? Leadership takes the confidence to make the best choice based on the available information. One of the best movies I've seen about leadership was *U-571*. Matthew McConaughey plays a young officer who has his first assignment on a submarine. The American sub, which McConaughey's character helps to command, disables an enemy sub, and the crew boards and takes control of it. Once they've wrangled all the prisoners, the American crew goes to the top of the enemy sub, only to see their submarine being blown up by an enemy destroyer. They quickly rush into the sub and dive, dive, dive. Depth charges are all around them, and you don't know if they'll make it, but somehow, they do. The crew look at McConaughey's character, who is the highest-ranking officer still alive, and ask what they should do next. He tells them he has no idea what to do because he's never been in this situation before. An older crewmate asks him for permission to speak privately and tells him, "You're the captain now. Even when you don't know what to do, you're the one in charge."

This movie scene always hit me hard. The young officer had no idea what he should do, but because he was in a position of leadership, he was tasked with deciding how to move forward. His job was to lead that crew. I realized that I don't always have to have the perfect answer. If I'm in that leadership position, I don't need to be perfect; I just need to do my best to make the best decisions. If my decisions are poor, the leadership position will go to someone else. In the meantime, I will lead, and I won't be afraid of making a wrong choice. I'll make the best choice available.

One last thought to ponder. What example do you set when given a place of leadership? Do you instill confidence? I'm not talking about fake confidence; I'm talking about the faith of knowing you are making the best possible decision and that you would follow what you just said. Do your homework and convince yourself first; that way, you're a leader with conviction. You firmly believe what you're telling people. When you have a firm conviction, and you know you're doing your best, people are more apt to follow your lead.

Put It into Practice

As I get older, I realize my memory isn't what it used to be. I can't even remember what I ate for breakfast, let alone what happened yesterday or the day before. A strong memory is a gift, but there's no substitute for immediately putting something into practice. When something's fresh in your mind, you can retain the most, learn the most, and be the most creative with it.

Most of the time when I'm teaching people new concepts and ideas or skills, the person on the other end has a desire to master it before practicing it on others. Yet most people will never master something unless they use the skill they're trying to master. So what do you do when you don't want to screw up but you also need to practice this new skill?

I've learned how not to do a lot of things. I'll try something, but if it doesn't work out, I'll reassess and then try it a little differently. Someone once said the quickest way to succeed is to fail. In fact, if you really want to succeed, fail big. Thomas Edison said, "I have not failed. I have found 10,000 ways that don't work." In other words, allow yourself to learn how not to do something. Through this process, you learn exactly what works. You won't know what does work if you don't know what doesn't work. And you can't know any of that unless you try it. Information is best when it's fresh, just like food is better when it's hot off the griddle. Don't wait to implement something new.

Within the first hour after learning something new, people tend to forget about 50 percent of the information.

Within twenty-four hours, this loss can increase to about 70 percent.

Within a week, we tend to retain only about 25 percent of the information, and without reinforcement, we tend to forget up to 90 percent of what we learned.[35]

As you can see, there's no better time than now. Will it be perfect? No. Will it ever be perfect? I don't know. But I do know if you don't start trying today, you won't know very soon. Don't think about it, just do it. Take written notes or even mental notes. Improve your process each time you try your new skill. I always liked Wayne Gretzky's saying, "You miss 100 percent of the shots you don't take." Even if it's an ugly shot, it's still a shot, and if you're practicing, you'll get better. You also don't have to put yourself in a make-or-break situation; practice on somebody who's a little less critical. Maybe find a friend or a colleague. But don't wait until it is mission critical because that's when it's most important that you've practiced. And if you haven't practiced at all? What do you think your chances are? I often say to others, "You don't rise to the occasion like they do in movies, where some guy runs in and saves the damsel in distress. He had

---

35 Marousis, A. (March 30, 2023). What is the Ebbinghause forgetting curve? Examples and strategies for overcoming it. TalentCards. Retrieved February 3, 2024, from https://www.talentcards.com/blog/ebbinghaus-forgetting-curve/

never practiced any of the skills before, but all of a sudden, he was superhuman. Instead, you fall back to your lowest level of competence. Instead of saving the damsel in distress, you end up calling 911 and hoping for the best."

Put your newfound skill into practice now, today. Don't wait. You have your best opportunity to succeed while it's fresh in your mind. You simply need to go practice.

You Can Do Anything You Want in Life; It's Just the Price You Have to Pay for It

This saying is a way to empower others to take action on things that are worth the cost and to keep from actions that are not. One of my past employees asked me things like, "Do I need to come to work today?" I would respond with, you guessed it: "You can do anything you want in life; it's just the price you have to pay for it." She would get the hint that the price of not coming to work would be loss of pay and, if she didn't show up enough, the ultimate loss of her job. She never decided she wanted to pay that price. She didn't think it was worth it, I guess.

We can weigh the costs of many goals and dreams, and, low and behold, we are not willing to pay that price. When I was about ten years old, I remember my mom told me we needed to go to a friend's house. I didn't want to go. I asked her if I would still need to go if I had a broken arm. She looked at me, puzzled, and said, "Well, of course not. We would need to go to the hospital." I said okay and then went into the backyard, climbed up the tallest tree I could, and jumped out of the tree. I was attempting to break my arm. When I landed on the ground and knocked the wind out of myself, I quickly realized I was not willing to pay that price. I ended up going to our friend's house.

I find myself in conversations where people tell me I can't do something. The reality is you can do anything, including what they just said you could not do—as long as you are willing to pay the price. One of my first business experiences with this was when I was working with a planning department on some land that needed development. They told me I couldn't do that. I asked them why not, and they pointed to a regulation in a manual, then said, "Because it says this right here." When I asked if it could be changed, the response was "Only if you do x, y, and z." I told them to watch me change it. You see, I was willing to pay the price of time, effort, and resources.

When I was growing up, I had a limiting belief that I couldn't accomplish big things without someone else leading the charge or empowering me. It wasn't until I had a mentor named Steve who empowered me to take action on the goals and dreams that I had the strength to move forward. I would say I wanted to do something, and he would say, "Then do it." This seems like such a simple answer, yet it was profound advice for me at this point in my life.

An Outward Conversation with Your Inner Self

Another person who impacted my life once told me, "What your heart can believe and your mind can conceive, you can achieve." Wow . . . you mean I can do anything I want in life? How freeing to know the only limitation is me. Someone else asked me, "What would you do if you knew you wouldn't fail?" This is a good question to ask yourself. You are only defeated once you give up, meaning you don't fail until you stop trying. Most of us fail before we get started. We tell ourselves we could never do that thing. "I can't be successful; it's too risky, and I am doomed."

Do you hear yourself in those words? Have you ever had a conversation with yourself that sounded like that? Yes, I talk to myself; most people do. Call it your thought life, or if you are like me, call it an outward conversation with your inner self. I was never a person who liked hearing people saying self-affirmations. "You are a winner," "You can make it," or "You have what it takes" always sounded corny to me. Here's what I have found: Self-affirmation is way better than self-criticism, and most of us are really good at criticism. Why not throw some positive self-feedback into the mix?

Most great experiences and accomplishments are built over time because we make incremental steps forward. These small steps forward are easily derailed or abandoned when we get discouraged, so we must be vigilant about our goals. Don't let others' negative thoughts or opinions determine who you become. You determine what's worth working toward.

When was the last time someone empowered you to reach for a goal or dream? How did their empowerment impact you? What's holding you back today? You have what it takes and, in most cases, more than you need to reach your goal. Know you can do anything you want in life, it's just the price you have to pay for it. What do you want to do? Weigh the cost. Are you willing to pay those costs? Are you willing to put forth the effort needed to accomplish your goal? If you are, pay the price and get started. You have what it takes. You are destined for greatness if you are willing to pay for it. Now go get it!

Winners Don't Complain, They Make Things Happen

Think about the last few things that went wrong at work or home. Were they everyone else's fault? Were you a victim? Or could you have done better to avoid those kinds of issues? My guess is you can find an opportunity to make things happen in almost every situation rather than letting things happen to you.

Think about the game recap after any major league sport. While being interviewed, every single one of them keeps their composure as they're asked all the hard questions. "Why didn't your team play their best? Are you going to have a losing season? Do you consider the failure of this last game all your fault?" If you think it feels good, think again. What you don't typically hear the players do is complain. "Well, you know, my shoulder was a little sore; that's why I lost this game. Kind of had a little bit of upset stomach because I had a bowl of chili last night, made it so I wasn't able to win." You don't typically hear this type of excuse from star athletes. They take ownership of the situation, mention what they could have done better, and say they're going to win in the future.

Here's a secret: People don't want to align with losers; they simply want to align with winners. How do winners make things happen? They examine the situation and themselves, and they make changes. They own their success or their failure. What they don't do is blame everyone else when things don't go their way. An alarming trend among people today is their reluctance to take ownership of things within their control. This is a losing attitude. How many people love complainers? I don't know many people that do. But how many people love having someone on their team who gets things done, who somehow finds a way when there seems to be no way? They are creative and have a positive outlook because they know they are not stuck.

You are not stuck, either. If you feel like you are with something in your life, I have to tell you, where there's a will, there's a way. Even when it doesn't feel like there's any possible way, a way can be made. I hear some of you say, "But you don't understand my situation; it's more complicated, more difficult than any other situation." You're right. I don't know what situation you're in, and I don't know what the answers are for your specific situation. But I do know that no matter the situation, it can be made better and turned around. But you need to have the right attitude. You can't have an attitude of defeat or doom or failure. You need an attitude that says no matter the situation or how difficult things get, there is always a way, and you will find a way because you're a winner.

And winners engage; they don't disengage. They run to and at the problems; they don't let the problems chase them. And when you take a situation that looks bleak and completely turn it around, the amount of satisfaction you'll get from knowing you didn't complain but instead dug in and made it the best it possibly could be? Priceless.

Still not convinced? Go online and watch some of the winningest, most successful sports players in history. Then go to a game they lost. Watch the game recap where they're interviewed. Put yourself in their shoes. Pretend it's you sitting at your desk at work, and somebody's asking why the sale didn't happen, or why sales are down. What would you say? Would you blame everyone else, or would you find a way to take ownership and lead?

Here's the one thing I want to give you permission for. There are real-life obstacles put in our way. These are things that have to be acknowledged as part of the equation. If you are a roofer, and someone doesn't give you roofing nails to complete the job, you should speak up. If you are a salesperson, and you don't have the product you need to demonstrate, you're missing a vital tool, and you need to speak up and say what you need. Find a way to get roofing nails, or find a way to demonstrate a similar product, or find a way to get your product so you can do your job. Don't sit there and complain and hope things will change. Go out and get what you need. Don't complain about it; make it happen. Then one day, you'll wake up, and guess what? When you look in the mirror, you'll see a winner.

Your Next Move: Shut Up and Win

CONGRATULATIONS ON TAKING THE FIRST STEP toward mastering the art of sales and transforming your career. But reading this book is just the beginning—your journey to winning starts now.

Here's how you can take action today:

1. Implement What You've Learned

Don't let this book be another "good read" you leave on the shelf. Pick one strategy from the chapters and put it into practice right now. Whether it's perfecting your pitch, closing with confidence, or building genuine client relationships—action is where success lives.

2. Share Your Wins

Every victory, big or small, is worth celebrating. Share your progress and connect with a community of like-minded go-getters. Visit our YouTube.com channel @shutupandwin or tag me on social media by going to Instagram or X.com with the hashtag #ShutUpAndWinCo to share your story and inspire others to join the journey.

3. Keep the Momentum Going

Success isn't a destination; it's a way of life. Stay sharp by subscribing to my newsletter for exclusive tips, tools, and resources that will keep you ahead of the competition. Visit www.shut-upandwin.com and sign up today.

4. Help Others Win

Loved the book? Don't keep it to yourself. Share *Shut Up and Win* with your team, your colleagues, or that one friend who needs a little push to achieve greatness. Leave a review online and help others discover their winning edge.

You've got the tools. You've got the drive. Now it's time to shut up, take action, and win.

Let's win together,
Jed Etters

Index of Topics

Acknowledgments

Writing this book has been a journey of learning, perseverance, and growth, and it would not have been possible without the support, guidance, and encouragement of many individuals.

First and foremost, I would like to express my heartfelt gratitude to my family. A special thanks to my wife for her unwavering belief in me and her constant encouragement throughout this process. Your love and support kept me motivated and focused on the goal.

To my editor, Candace Johnson, thank you for your keen eye, thoughtful feedback, and tireless dedication to making this book the best it could be. Your thoughts and guidance have been invaluable.

To my friends and colleagues who offered their wisdom, insights, and sometimes simply a listening ear, I am extremely grateful. Your encouragement and feedback kept me focused during the most challenging moments.

A special thanks to Eric Gillman, who inspired me to embark on this journey and whose guidance was pivotal in making this book a reality.

To my readers, thank you for taking the time to explore this work. Your interest and engagement are what make this effort worthwhile.

Last, I am thankful for Joel and Sue Canfield. Your early direction and contributions played a pivotal role in shaping this project.

This book is a testament to the collective effort, inspiration, and kindness of everyone mentioned here. I am forever grateful.

About the Author

Jed Etters is a seasoned sales strategist, thought leader, and captivating speaker dedicated to empowering individuals and organizations to achieve unparalleled success in the ever-changing world of sales. With more than two decades of experience in the field, Jed brings a wealth of knowledge and a fresh perspective to the art of selling.

His journey into the realm of sales began early in life. Within a year of landing his first sales job, Jed transitioned to real estate, where he quickly distinguished himself through his ability to connect with clients, understand their needs, and deliver personalized solutions that exceeded expectations. Fueled by a passion for helping others succeed, Jed honed his skills across various industries, from technology and finance to real estate and beyond.

Jed is known for his innovative approaches and strategic insights that have transformed traditional sales methodologies. His practical advice and actionable strategies have empowered countless professionals to break through barriers, drive revenue growth, and cultivate lasting client relationships.

Jed's commitment to excellence extends beyond the boardroom as he is deeply invested in mentoring emerging talent and fostering a culture of continuous learning within the sales ecosystem. Through his engaging workshops, books, and influential presence on social media, Jed inspires individuals at every stage of their sales journey to embrace change, meet challenges, and move toward their potential for greatness.

When he's not strategizing his next sales conquest, Jed enjoys spending time with his family, flying small planes, driving classic cars, exploring the great outdoors, and seeking inspiration from the people and places around him. Jed is always happy to connect with like-minded individuals who are ready to take their businesses to the next level.

www.ingramcontent.com/pod-product-compliance
Lightning Source LLC
Chambersburg PA
CBHW071719120626
46550CB00001B/305